Confronting Poverty

Confronting Poverty

WEAK STATES AND U.S. NATIONAL SECURITY

SUSAN E. RICE

CORINNE GRAFF

CARLOS PASCUAL

editors

BROOKINGS INSTITUTION PRESS
Washington, D.C.

Library of Congress Cataloging-in-Publication data

Confronting poverty : weak states and U.S. national security / Susan E. Rice, Corinne Graff, and Carlos Pascual.
   p. cm.
Includes bibliographical references and index.
ISBN 978-0-8157-0390-7 (pbk. : alk. paper)
   1. Poverty—Developing countries. 2. Political stability—Developing countries. 3. Failed states—Developing countries. 4. National security—United States. I. Rice, Susan E. II. Graff, Corinne. III. Pascual, Carlos. IV. Title.

HC59.72.P6C66 2009
355'.03301724—dc22

2009039055

9 8 7 6 5 4 3 2 1

Printed on acid-free paper

Typeset in Sabon

Composition by Cynthia Stock
Silver Spring, Maryland

Printed by R. R. Donnelley
Harrisonburg, Virginia

Contents

Foreword   vii
Strobe Talbott

1   The National Security Implications of Global Poverty   1
Susan E. Rice

2   Poverty and State Weakness   23
Susan E. Rice

3   Poverty, Development, and Violent Extremism
in Weak States   42
Corinne Graff

4   Poverty, State Weakness, and Civil War   90
Andrew Loomis

5   Feeding Insecurity? Poverty, Weak States,
and Climate Change   125
Joshua Busby

6   State Weakness and Infectious Diseases   167
Miriam Estrin and Carl Malm

7   Conclusion and Policy Implications   202
Carlos Pascual and Corinne Graff

Contributors   231

Index   233

Foreword

Throughout history, conflict has arisen between and among major powers, often because a strong state tries to prove itself stronger than others. The good news about the current era is that the major powers are at peace; their going to war, while not unimaginable, is highly unlikely. That is largely because they have a stake—that is, a *national* interest—in the maintenance of a stable, prosperous and peaceful *international* system. One big piece of bad news is the subject of this timely and forward-looking book: the threat that weak and failed states pose to the welfare of people across the planet—a threat that is virtually certain to increase in the years to come unless strong states and the international community as a whole take concerted remedial action.

For states as for individual human beings, weakness and failure are often both a cause and a consequence of extreme poverty. Strong, prosperous countries have an ethical obligation to do all they can to end the poverty that degrades the lives of 3 billion people in the developing world. Yet poverty is also a national-security challenge for all, including the United States. Poverty increases the risk of civil war, facilitates the spread of many communicable diseases, exacerbates vulnerability to climate change, and creates conditions that violent forces can exploit. The global financial crisis has further destabilized the world's poorest countries, adding new urgency to the issue of weak and failed states.

This book, coedited by three former colleagues at Brookings—Susan E. Rice, Corinne Graff, and Carlos Pascual—serves as a timely reminder to U.S. policymakers that alleviating global poverty and shoring up weak states are not only humanitarian and economic imperatives, but key components of a more balanced and sustainable U.S. national security strategy.

Confronting Poverty: Weak States and U.S. National Security draws on examples from across the developing world, focuses on the effects of low income and bad governance in weak states, and explores the complex and often indirect dynamics that can lock countries—and entire regions—in a downward spiral of continued poverty and civil strife.

The book examines the phenomenon of weak and failed states in the context of four broad transnational challenges: (1) violent extremism, (2) conflict with spillover effects, (3) climate change, and (4) the spread of infectious diseases. The chapters that follow clarify the connections between these threats and poverty while correcting common misconceptions about what those connections are.

At Brookings, we put a premium on bringing hard-headed, high-quality, independent, fact-based research to bear on the twin tasks of analyzing the problem and proposing solutions. In that spirit, all the authors close ranks behind the need to prioritize economic development and poverty alleviation in weak states as a means of bolstering international and U.S. national security, and the concluding chapter elaborates on that overarching policy recommendation and highlights lessons learned about the effectiveness of aid in weak states.

Confronting Poverty grows out of a project on global poverty and U.S. national security that Susan E. Rice directed at Brookings from 2002 through January 2009, before she was appointed U.S. permanent representative to the United Nations. The book builds on the findings of the *Index of State Weakness in the Developing World,* an analytic tool that Rice published in 2008 in a Brookings report coauthored with Stewart Patrick, now at the Council on Foreign Relations. The index utilizes twenty indicators in four key areas of state function (economic performance, political governance, internal peace and security, and social welfare) to measure state performance and rank developing countries. The book also benefits from the expertise of then vice president and director of foreign policy Carlos Pascual, whose previous work at Brookings focused on conflict management and economic development.

Because two of the book's editors are now public servants, I want to stress that their chapters here reflect their personal views and research they conducted during their term at Brookings. Their work on this book was completed before taking up their current posts. The book does not represent the views of the U.S. Department of State or the U.S. government. In addition, since Brookings is committed to nonpartisanship in all it does, the editors invited authors with diverse perspectives to contribute chapters, so the volume also includes writings by Joshua Busby (LBJ School of Public Affairs at the University of Texas–Austin), Andrew Loomis (Department of State), Carl Malm (Georgetown University), and Miriam Estrin (Department of State). Loomis, Malm, and Estrin wrote their contributions while they were employed by Brookings, before taking up their current positions. Their views are solely their own and do not necessarily represent the views of the editors, Brookings, or any other organization represented by the writers.

Throughout the writing process, the authors benefited from the expertise of numerous colleagues. At Brookings, Michael O'Hanlon and Bruce Jones made important contributions to the book through feedback and other assistance with the project, and the authors would like to express their gratitude to each one of them. Brookings colleagues, and in some cases former colleagues, Daniel Byman, Justin Vaisse, Jonathan Laurence, Jeremy Shapiro, and Daniel Benjamin were also generous with their time and provided helpful feedback on early drafts of the manuscript. The authors would also like to acknowledge Strobe Talbott, James Steinberg, and Lael Brainard for their unwavering support of this book project.

The manuscript also benefited from the expertise of the following individuals: John Steinbruner, a former Brookings scholar and director of foreign policy who is now professor of public policy at the School of Public Policy, University of Maryland, and director of the Center for International and Security Studies at Maryland; Harley Feldbaum of the Paul H. Nitze School of Advanced International Studies; Stephen Morrison of the Center for Strategic and International Studies; Geoff Dabelko of the Woodrow Wilson International Center for Scholars; Cullen Hendrix of the University of North Texas; Nicholas Sambanis of Yale University and Brookings; Papia Debroy of the University of Michigan; Michael Lund of Creative Associates; Sharon Morris of Mercy Corps; Janet Lewis of Harvard University; and Kameron Kordestani of McKinsey & Company.

The authors are grateful to the participants in a workshop, Development in Fragile States: The Toughest Cases, held at Brookings in January 2009. This seminar informed the concluding chapter of the book. The editors also wish to extend special thanks to Nicki Alam for her extensive editorial assistance, and to Devorah West. The authors extend their appreciation to Robert Faherty, Larry Converse, Janet Walker, Susan Woollen, and other colleagues at the Brookings Institution Press for their excellent help in bringing the manuscript to publication.

Finally, I wish to acknowledge, with gratitude, that this book has been made possible by generous support from the Carnegie Corporation of New York, the William and Flora Hewlett Foundation, and the Ford Foundation.

STROBE TALBOTT
President
The Brookings Institution

Washington, D.C.
December 2009

CHAPTER ONE

The National Security Implications of Global Poverty

SUSAN E. RICE

On a deserted, dusty patch of dirt outside Gulu, in northern Uganda, U.S. Secretary of State Madeleine Albright held Charity, an angelic baby girl barely one month old. Charity had been left for dead in a ditch beside a rural road, trapped in the arms of her murdered mother and wedged between deceased family members. The brutal rebels of the Sudanese-backed Ugandan Lord's Resistance Army (LRA) had raided Charity's village and slaughtered as many as they could. Miraculously, one of Charity's siblings, her five-year-old brother, survived the assault. He had been shielded by his mother, who threw him to the ground when the shooting started and covered his little body with her own. The boy played dead until the killers moved on and then wriggled free. Hearing his infant sister crying, he pried her loose from his mother's arms and, cradling her carefully, walked for miles to the safety of a World Vision compound in Gulu.[1]

That was December 1997, when Gulu was ground zero for the LRA's reign of terror. As recently as 2006, children known as night commuters fled regularly every evening into Gulu from the bush to take refuge in ramshackle schools or hospitals. They sought safety in numbers and at least minimal protection from the Ugandan People's Defense Forces against marauding LRA rebels, who kidnapped children for conscripts and threatened them with death if they refused to kill their own.[2] Today,

I thank Nicki Alam for her research support.

1

millions who were displaced by the conflict remain haunted by the LRA's atrocities and vulnerable to yet more rounds of brutal violence.[3]

Despite multiple failed efforts to achieve military and negotiated solutions over the past two decades, the ongoing conflict rooted in northern Uganda has claimed at least 100,000 lives and displaced more than 1 million people.[4] Charity and her brother were victims of senseless but routine atrocities committed by and against the Acholi people, an ethnic group based in northern Uganda. The LRA's campaign of indiscriminate killing began shortly after President Yoweri Museveni took power in 1986.[5] To date, the government of Uganda has been unable to decisively defeat the LRA or negotiate an end to its insurgency of more than twenty years.[6]

Though war-torn and landlocked between East and Central Africa, Uganda is no basket case. At times it has been heralded by the World Bank as a model of economic growth and proof of the potential for economic transformation even in the toughest parts of Africa. Under President Museveni, Uganda achieved not only impressive economic growth rates but also unusual success in slowing the tide of HIV/AIDS and luring foreign investors. It remains a large and favored recipient of U.S. and European foreign assistance and a reliable regional security partner of the United States.

Uganda illustrates the potential consequences for U.S. national security of states affected by poverty, corruption, and weak institutional capacity. In Uganda, as elsewhere, poverty has helped fuel civil conflicts like those that devastated the young lives of Charity and her brother. Uganda's gross national income (GNI) per capita in 2008 was just $420, the world's fifteenth lowest.[7] The northern region, the epicenter of Uganda's civil war, has the country's highest poverty rate, highest population growth, and highest fertility levels.[8]

Uganda's internal strife has spilled over its borders, drawing in the forces of neighboring countries and contributing to the destabilization of an entire resource-rich region. Ugandan government forces have frequently raided neighboring southern Sudan in hot pursuit of the LRA, which has operated freely there and received military backing and material support from the Sudanese government in Khartoum.[9] For years, until the war in southern Sudan was halted in 2005 with the signing of the Comprehensive Peace Agreement, Uganda provided military support to Sudanese People's Liberation Army/Movement forces in their generation-long battle for self-determination and against the religious and racial oppression of the Arab Islamist regime in the Sudanese capital of Khartoum. Meanwhile, the LRA remains active in Sudan as well as the Democratic Republic of the Congo (DRC) and the Central African Republic where it is regularly responsible for mass atrocities and has joined in illegal exploitation and trade of gems, gold, and ivory.[10]

In 1998 Uganda joined neighboring Rwanda in invading the DRC, purportedly to halt uprisings from the Rwandan Hutu rebels in Congo who took refuge there after the 1994 Rwandan genocide, and from the LRA and Allied Democratic Forces (ADF), another Ugandan rebel group that was active from 1996 to 1999 and terrorized foreign tourists and Ugandans. These rebels benefited from the acquiescence, if not the active backing, of the Kinshasa government in the DRC. Once in the DRC, Uganda, like Rwanda, found the lure of lucrative minerals too great to abandon and occupied a substantial swath of that vast country for five years.[11] In 2007 oil was discovered in the Lake Albert Basin along the border between Uganda and the DRC, which further strained ties between the two countries.[12] Since early 2009, relations have begun to improve between Congo and both Uganda and Rwanda.

Like its neighbors, Uganda must contend with terrorism by Islamic extremists. On August 7, 1998, when nearly simultaneous bombs destroyed the U.S. embassies in Nairobi and Dar es Salaam, al Qaeda intended to hit a third target—the U.S. embassy in Kampala.[13] Only good luck in the form of alert border guards prevented another explosive-laden vehicle from reaching its target.

In addition, Uganda's poverty exacerbates its vulnerability to climate change and deadly disease. Although Uganda is not a significant source of greenhouse gas emissions, the effects of global climate change could increase the risk of future instability. Climatic changes that are consistent with scientific predictions of global warming—including rising temperatures, more intense rains and storms, more frequent droughts, and more erratic rainfall patterns—are already apparent in Uganda.[14] In 2007 severe floods and water logging destroyed up to 90 percent of crops in some parts of the country, leading to widespread food insecurity. Coffee, a major Ugandan export crop that employs over 500,000, is especially vulnerable to climate variations. Coffee beans could become unsuitable for export from Uganda if average annual temperatures rise by as little as 2 degrees, causing massive unemployment and intense hardship among

Uganda's small-scale coffee producers. A sharp reduction in coffee production could also intensify latent tensions in Uganda and stoke further conflict as well as extremism.

The 2007 rainfalls not only felled the coffee crop; they also contaminated protected water sources and destroyed latrines, posing a significant health risk. The World Health Organization (WHO) reported a massive increase in malaria and dysentery that year, while a new strain of the deadly Ebola virus was also discovered in December 2007.[15]

In short, the experiences of Uganda reflect the deadly consequences of poverty and strife in the world's poorest and most fragile states. They also emphasize that poverty and state weakness in faraway countries can ultimately have implications for the security of Americans.

A CHANGED SECURITY PARADIGM

Throughout the cold war period, successive U.S. administrations defined the vital national security interests of the United States in narrow strategic and geographic terms. Their aim was clear: to avert the existential threat of nuclear annihilation through deterrence and containment, and to counter Soviet and communist influences in key regions—chiefly Europe, the Middle East, and Asia. Only to the extent that superpower competition spread to more distant battlefields did the United States evince much strategic interest in parts of Africa and Latin America. Major threats were those that risked the very survival of the country, and such threats emanated almost exclusively from other states: the Soviet Union and its communist proxies. The post–cold war world is fundamentally different, and so is the nature of the threats Americans face. The Soviet Union is gone. The cold war proxy wars fought across the globe have ended. The risk of nuclear annihilation is reduced, though by no means eliminated. The world is in this regard a much safer place.

Yet it is still a dangerous world. It is more complex and less predictable. Real threats persist, but their origins and consequences are more diffuse. Fewer of the principal threats to U.S. national security today are existential in the cold war sense, with the crucial exception of nuclear terrorism. Furthermore, fewer derive primarily from nation-states.

In today's world, risks to U.S. national security extend well beyond a handful of hostile states. Foremost among them are transnational security threats that, by definition, are not limited to any individual state.

They include terrorism, weapons proliferation, the global economic crisis, conflict, infectious disease, international crime and narcotics flows, climate change, and environmental degradation. These transnational phenomena can threaten U.S. national security because they have the potential to kill significant numbers of Americans—whether swiftly or over an extended period of time.

With the advent of globalization and the rapid international movement of people, goods, funds, and information, transnational security threats can arise from and spread with dangerous speed to any part of the planet. They can emerge from remote regions and poor, weak states, turning them into potentially high-risk zones that may eventually, often indirectly, pose significant risks to distant peoples. In 2008 alone, more than 900 million travelers crossed an international border each day.[16] Over the past four decades, total seaborne trade more than quadrupled, reaching in excess of 8 billion tons in 2007.[17] The risk that weak states will inadvertently function as incubators of transnational security threats to their own people as well as to others becomes exponentially magnified in a highly interconnected world.

Such threats can potentially take various forms: a mutated, highly contagious and deadly flu virus that jumps from animals to humans, and from human to human, in Cambodia or Cameroon; a case of deadly hemorrhagic Marburg fever unwittingly contracted by a U.S. expatriate in Angola who returns to Houston on an oil company charter; terrorist cell attacks on a U.S. navy vessel in Yemen or Djibouti; the theft of biological or nuclear materials from poorly secured facilities in some forty countries around the world;[18] narcotics traffickers in Tajikistan and criminal syndicates from Nigeria; or flooding and other effects of global warming, exacerbated by extensive deforestation, in the Amazon and Congo River basins. Dangerous spillovers from fragile states could result in major damage to the global economy. In a worst-case scenario, millions of lives could be lost.

THE THREAT OF GLOBAL POVERTY

When Americans see televised images of bone-thin children with distended bellies, typically their humanitarian instincts take over. Few look at such footage and perceive a threat that could destroy their way of life. Yet global poverty is not solely a humanitarian concern. Over the long term, it can threaten U.S. national security. Poverty erodes a state's capacity to prevent the spread of disease and protect forests and watersheds. It creates conditions conducive to transnational criminal and terrorist activity, luring desperate individuals into recruitment and, more significant, undermining the state's ability to prevent and counter those violent threats. Poverty can also give rise to tensions that can erupt into full-blown civil conflict, further taxing the state and allowing transnational predators greater freedom of action. In the twenty-first century, poverty is an important driver of transnational threats.

Americans can no longer realistically hope to erect the proverbial glass dome over their homeland and live safely isolated from the killers—human or otherwise—that plague poorer countries. Al Qaeda has had training camps in conflict-ridden Sudan, Somalia, and Afghanistan and a presence in the diamond markets of Sierra Leone and Liberia.[19] A global pandemic or a mutated, deadly virus causing human-to-human contagion could also have an alarming impact.[20]

Low-income states tend to be fragile and in poor control of their territory and resources. Ill-equipped and poorly trained immigration and customs officials along with weak police, military, judiciary, and financial systems create vacuums readily invaded by transnational predators. Conflict, difficult terrain, and corruption render such states even more vulnerable. Terrorist groups are able to raise funds through tactical alliances with transnational criminal syndicates, smugglers, and pirates operating in lawless zones, from the Somali coast and Central Asia to the triborder region of South America. Not surprisingly, the human pawns drawn into global criminal enterprises—the narcotics couriers, sex slaves, and petty thieves—frequently come from the ranks of the unemployed or desperately poor. Transnational crime syndicates reap billions each year from illicit trafficking in humans, drugs, weapons, hazardous waste, and endangered species—all of which reach American shores.

Conflict

Among the most significant consequences of country-level poverty is a heightened risk of conflict. Poor countries are much more likely than rich ones to experience civil war. Their average gross domestic product (GDP) per capita is usually less than half that of countries free of conflict.[21] Indeed, per capita GDP is known to have a statistically significant relationship to the likelihood of civil war.[22] Economic decline heightens the risk even further.[23] The link between poverty and conflict, an area of rare scholarly consensus, is probably the most robust finding in the econometric literature on conflict.[24]

Put simply, increasing a country's GDP—without changing other important factors such as the degree of democratization or number of ethnic groups—reduces the chance of civil war in that country. An otherwise "average" country with $250 GDP per capita has a 15 percent risk of experiencing a civil war in the next five years, whereas for a country with per capita GDP of $5,000, the risk of civil war drops to less than 1 percent over the same period.[25] Other poverty-related factors that foment conflict include shrinking economic growth, low levels of education, and high child mortality rates.

Poverty also helps perpetuate the fighting and once a conflict has ended may increase the likelihood that war will recur.[26] This was the case in East Timor, where violence resumed in 2006, displacing an estimated 150,000 and necessitating the redeployment of UN forces, and in 2008 when an attempt was made on President José Ramos-Horta's life.[27] Since then, the security situation has improved. Ten years into the postconflict period, however, poverty remains high, unemployment is still rampant, and GDP growth has languished.[28] In 2009 half the country's population lived below the poverty line, compared with 36 percent in 2001.[29] Despite substantial inflows of international aid, East Timor's child mortality rate remains among the highest in the world, and unemployment hits nearly half the young people in urban areas, now a cauldron of disaffected youth.[30] Unless East Timor's economy improves and poverty is reduced, peace and stability will be difficult to sustain.

Civil wars tend to be long, averaging sixteen years by one estimate.[31] Their resolution often falters: one-third later reignite.[32] The ensuing vicious cycle is termed a "conflict trap."[33] Further conflict cannot be avoided unless economic performance improves, as occurred in Mozambique, one of the world's poorest nations. After civil war ended there in 1994, GDP increased by nearly 8 percent.[34] Furthermore, gross primary school enrollment jumped from 60 percent at the end of the war to roughly full enrollment in 2005.[35] In the wake of sustained economic growth and investments in social services, rural poverty declined 16 percent from 1997 to 2003.[36] Once an epicenter of subregional conflict, Mozambique is now among the more stable societies in southern Africa.

When conflicts ignite, they function as the ultimate killer of innocents, and can destabilize entire regions (as Liberia did in West Africa, the DRC and Darfur in Sudan), requiring costly international peacekeeping and humanitarian interventions. At the same time, conflict zones provide the optimal anarchic environment for transnational predators: Haiti and West Africa now host international criminals and drug traffickers; Afghanistan, Tajikistan, and Colombia, drug producers and smugglers; West Africa and Chechnya, weapons traffickers; and Congo, Angola, and Uganda, deadly pathogens. As conflicts in Bosnia, the Philippines, Kashmir, Afghanistan, Somalia, and Sudan have shown, war zones can provide fertile operating environments for international terrorist networks.

Terrorism

Most dangerous are conflict zones that collapse into failed states with no control over much of their territory, a classic example being Somalia. Anarchy has facilitated the operation of transnational terrorist networks, allowed Islamic extremists to grow powerful, and fueled the rise of piracy. Al Qaeda leaders have long believed Somalia could be "another Afghanistan . . . , a low-cost recruiting ground where disaffected people in a failed state would readily join its ranks."[37] Foreign jihadis operate terrorist training camps in Somalia.[38] Al Qaeda's cells in Somalia provided essential support to the perpetrators of the 1998 U.S. embassy bombings in the capitals of Kenya and Tanzania.[39] With the collapse of Siad Barre's government in 1991 and ensuing endemic violence, local militants also emerged. By December 2006, the Islamic Courts had gained control of large parts of the former Somali Republic. Although Ethiopian troops subsequently helped Somalia's Transitional Federal Government to reestablish control, the al Qaeda–linked al Shabaab movement maintains control over large swaths of southern Somalia, where al Qaeda leaders operate training bases and al Shabaab consistently threatens the fledgling transitional government in Mogadishu. Somalia's long-standing poverty and instability have also fostered piracy, now well established in the major shipping routes off the Horn of Africa.

Yet weak states need not collapse and fail before they can be exploited by terrorists. Al Qaeda has preyed on the territory, cash crops, natural resources, and financial institutions of low-income but somewhat more stable states, from Senegal to Yemen. Militants have exploited poor immigration, security, and financial controls to plan and carry out terrorist operations in Kenya, Tanzania, and Indonesia. Al Qaeda operatives have been detained in more than 100 countries worldwide.[40]

One such state is Mali. Ninety percent Muslim and a multiparty democracy since 1992, Mali remains an extremely poor state with a per capita GNI of approximately $500.[41] An estimated 36 percent of its 12 million people live on less than $2 a day, and income inequality remains high.[42] Mali's human development score is the eleventh lowest in the world.[43] Land-locked and bordering seven states—Mauritania, Algeria, Côte D'Ivoire, Guinea, Senegal, Burkina Faso, and Niger—Mali is roughly the size of Texas plus California. Malian authorities face an invigorated nomadic Tuareg rebellion in the north and have failed to expel terrorists associated with al Qaeda in the Islamic Maghreb (AQIM), formerly the Algerian-based Salafist Group for Preaching and Combat (GSPC).[44] The GSPC's leader, Amari Saifi (known as Al Para), and his associates evaded capture in the northern Malian desert for six months in 2003 before releasing thirty-two European hostages seized in southern Algeria.[45] Al Qaeda in the Islamic Maghreb has been involved in numerous instances of kidnapping and killing foreign nationals in Mali and the region and utilizes Mali's centuries-old, trans-Saharan Tuareg trading routes to smuggle cigarettes and other contraband to raise cash for its terrorist operations.[46]

Mali's poverty renders it vulnerable to terrorist infiltration in another critical way. Like several poor states, Mali's government lacks the resources and institutional capacity to provide adequately for its citizens. Large numbers do not have enough to eat or access to potable water, basic medical care, or educational opportunities for their children. To fill the social services gap in Mali and elsewhere, it relies on outsiders, including extremist Wahhabist charities and mosques funded by groups in Gulf states. Wahhabists are setting up mosques across northern Mali, often right next door to the indigenous Sufi mosques, and offering what the Sufi cannot: food, clothing, medical care, schools, and the opportunity to send young men to Saudi Arabia for religious training. When those newly minted Wahhabist clerics return, they draw additional adherents to their extremist ideology.

Evidence that al Qaeda strategists deliberately target weak, poor states appears in a work titled *The Management of Savagery: The Most Critical Stage through Which the Umma Will Pass,* which the Combating Terrorism Center of the U.S. Military Academy at West Point calls "one of the most recent and significant" extremist strategic texts.[47] In it, author Abu Bakr Naji outlines the successive stages in establishing an Islamic caliphate. A key stage, what he calls "the management of savagery," consists of laying the foundation, which entails bringing order, security, and Islamic sharia rule to formerly chaotic states—those of first "priority" being "Jordan, the countries of the Maghrib, Nigeria, Pakistan, and the countries of the Haramayn and the Yemen." The "common links between states in which the regions of savagery can come into being" include "the weakness of the ruling regime and the weakness of the centralization of its power in the peripheries of the borders of its state and sometimes in internal regions, particularly those that are over-crowded" and "the presence of jihadi, Islamic expansion being propagated in these regions."[48] Similarly, an article in *Sada al-Jihad*, an online extremist magazine, cites the weakness of Africa's states and pervasive corruption as an advantage, making them an easier place to operate than "in other countries which have effective security, intelligence and military capacities."[49] Africa's poverty and social conditions, it states, "will enable the mujahadeen to provide some finance and welfare, thus, posting there some of their influential operatives."

Disease

Compounding their vulnerability to terrorism, poor weak states typically lack a substantial capacity to monitor and control emerging disease pandemics. Poverty not only increases the risk of human exposure to deadly pathogens but also severely constrains a state's capacity to prevent, detect, and treat disease outbreaks or to contain them before they spread abroad. The WHO notes that although the world has made great strides in reducing child mortality since 1975, "the rate of decline in under-five mortality rates has been much slower in low-income countries as a whole than in the richer countries." The challenges to improving health standards and life expectancy are greatest in the poorest countries, which "were among those with the lowest life expectancy at birth in 1975 and have experienced minimal increases since then."[50] Of the roughly thirty new infectious diseases that have emerged globally over the past three decades, many (such as SARS, West Nile virus, HIV/AIDS, Hepatitis C, and H5N1 avian flu virus) originated in poor countries that had a rudimentary disease-surveillance capability. In the United States, the incidence of some infectious diseases has been on the rise since 1990, and influenza and pneumonia remain major causes of death.[51]

Population pressure impels poor people seeking arable land, firewood, and water to move deeper into previously uninhabited areas, increasing the risk of exposure to animal-borne or zoonotic diseases. Moreover, many live in close proximity to their livestock, at times a dangerous source of sustenance and income. Some deadly diseases of chickens and pigs, including pandemic influenza, are known to jump from animal to human. With the mortality rates of current strains exceeding 50 percent, a mutated avian flu (H5N1) virus of equal virulence that becomes readily transmissible from human to human could kill tens of millions world-wide. Since 2003 the H5N1 virus has been confirmed in 417 humans and has resulted in 257 deaths in some of the most impoverished, remote, and poorly governed parts of Asia and Africa (notably Nigeria, Sudan, Côte D'Ivoire, Niger, Burkina Faso, Myanmar, Cambodia, Laos, Viet-nam, and Indonesia), adding to the fear of possible mutation following contact between animals and humans.[52] If a deadly mutation first occurs in a country with weak health care infrastructure, the odds of detecting and swiftly containing the outbreak are reduced.

The DRC is one of several epicenters of disease. In 1976 Congo experienced its first known outbreak of hemorrhagic Ebola fever, which the WHO characterizes as "one of the most virulent diseases known to mankind." The fatality rate was roughly 90 percent. Outbreaks continue to occur periodically, the most recent in 2009 resulting in fifteen docu-mented fatalities.[53] An Ebola strain that first emerged in the DRC spread to Gabon, Uganda, and South Africa. Ebola has the potential to travel anywhere in the world because it is highly transmissible by contact with bodily fluids (including blood, sweat, and saliva) and has an incubation period of two to twenty-one days.[54]

The DRC is ill equipped to detect, treat, and contain disease. Its population is extremely vulnerable (nearly one-third of children are underweight, almost half of deaths among children under age five are caused by malnutrition, and children under five suffer a 13 percent mortality rate).[55] The DRC's per capita expenditure on the health sec-tor is the one of the lowest in the world ($26 per person).[56] The con-tinuing conflict in eastern Congo and the presence of over 18,000 UN peacekeepers increases the possibility that foreign military, police, or aid workers could contract infectious agents and transport them abroad.[57] A June 2006 outbreak of pneumonic plague in the violent Ituri region sickened 144 people and killed 22.[58] If detected early enough, antibiotics can treat the disease, which is contracted through contact with infected rodents or fleas or transmitted by airborne bacteria. However, DRC's poor surveillance and control mechanisms make early treatment less likely, particularly since violence impedes the access of international health workers.

While Ebola and the similar Marburg virus have not spread beyond Africa, other new or reemergent infectious diseases have. These include polio, which was almost eradicated until it spread from northern Nigeria to Indonesia in 2004–05. The West Nile virus, a potentially deadly mosquito-borne disease that originated in Uganda, reached New York City in 1999 (presumably by aircraft) and is now found throughout the continental United States. Rift Valley fever, which can cause blindness and, rarely, death, spread from East Africa to Yemen and Saudi Arabia in 2000, infecting hundreds. Lassa hemorrhagic fever, endemic in West Africa, particularly in the Mano River region, infects an estimated 300,000–500,000 people each year with flu-like symptoms and results in 5,000 deaths.[59] Fatality rates can reach 15–20 percent, especially among hospital patients, where human-to-human transmission can occur via blood or human secretions. Several fatal cases have occurred among UN peacekeepers deployed to Liberia and Sierra Leone.[60] An estimated twenty cases of Lassa fever have been reported outside of Africa, one victim being an American businessman who perished upon return to the United States. Before he died, he came into direct contact with 188 people in this country during the time his fever was believed to be contagious. Although none of them died, this demonstrates how quickly diseases can spread from remote regions to the United States.[61]

Inadequate health care infrastructure hampers disease detection and containment not only in Africa but also in the poorest states around the world. Among these, Bangladesh has made important gains in some aspects of its social infrastructure but still spends relatively little per capita on health (about $12 in 2006, less than half of Burkina Faso's expenditure).[62] The health sector's lack of capacity may have hampered the investigation of five outbreaks of the Nipah virus in Bangladesh in 2004, which first appeared in Malaysia in 1999 and has resulted in fatality rates as high as 50 percent.[63] The virus is not known to have spread from Bangladesh, though it is fairly contagious and has a relatively long incubation period.

In Latin America and the Caribbean, mosquito-borne dengue fever, including the deadly hemorrhagic variety, is resurgent, afflicting locals and foreign travelers in growing numbers. The Centers for Disease Control and Prevention now deems dengue's global distribution and impact on humans to be comparable to malaria, except in Africa. Dengue is believed to have first appeared in the Western Hemisphere in Brazil, arriving via mosquito-infested ships from Southeast Asia in the 1990s. Urbanization, population growth, and deteriorating public health infrastructure have increased the prevalence of dengue in Central and South America.[64] The Aedes mosquito, which carries the virus, is now common in parts of the U.S. South and Southwest. And as the U.S. climate warms, dengue will likely spread further within the United States.[65]

Global Climate Change

The relationship between poverty, state weakness, and global climate change is complex and mutually reinforcing. In its 2007 report, the Intergovernmental Panel on Climate Change (IPCC) concluded that as sea surface temperatures continue to rise, the odds are "better than 2 to 1" that hurricanes and tropical storms "will become more intense, with larger peaks and wind speeds and more heavy precipitation."[66] In poor countries, tropical storms and hurricanes can wreak devastation on a massive scale. In May of 2008, cyclone Nargis reached peak winds of 135 miles an hour as it approached the coast of Burma, causing widespread death and destruction. The autocratic government's negligent response to the storm increased the number of deaths and injuries exponentially, and the damage from the storm was estimated at over $10 billion, an astronomical amount for a country that ranks among the world's poorest. In some towns, up to 95 percent of buildings were destroyed by the wind, rain, and storm surge, leaving broad swaths of the country looking like a "war zone."[67] The UN Food and Agriculture Organization estimates that 65 percent of the country's rice paddies were impacted and that this may have caused long-term food shortages in Burma and neighboring countries. These and other recent natural disasters are a stark reminder of the staggering loss and destruction that can befall countries lacking the will, capacity, and resources to prepare for and respond to severe climate events.

There is perhaps no better illustration of vulnerability to climate change than the small island nation of Haiti. With more than two-thirds of the labor force unemployed and an estimated 78 percent of its population living on less than $2 per day, Haiti is the poorest country in the Western Hemisphere (GNI per capita is $520, almost half of the next poorest country, Nicaragua).[68] It may also be the most vulnerable to severe storms and weather events. Lacking an alternative source of energy, Haiti's farmers continue to cut down trees to provide fuel and to sell as charcoal; as a result, Haiti has lost more than 90 percent of its forest cover. The ground is largely incapable of absorbing rain, which triggers frequent deadly floods. In Haiti's vast slums, houses are pieced together out of corrugated tin, oil drums, wood, and cardboard and lack a foundation. These houses, so the local saying goes, "can fool the sun but they cannot fool the rain."[69] Whole communities are often washed away in the aftermath of a storm. Yet there are no regulations to prevent people—mainly the poor—from settling in precarious, low-lying areas and few efforts to prepare the population for looming storms, or to provide government relief in their aftermath. Haiti lacks even a minimal capacity to account adequately for the dead and injured.

Haiti lies just 100 miles east of Puerto Rico in an area exposed to frequent severe weather events because of weather patterns of the North Atlantic Basin. Its topography—especially its mountainous landscape—makes it especially prone to flooding and landslides. Yet in stark contrast to wealthier neighboring countries, the government in Haiti has taken few steps to protect its citizens from severe storms. When Hurricane Jeanne barreled across the Caribbean in 2004, making landfall in Puerto Rico, the Bahamas, and Florida and just skimming the eastern tip of the Dominican Republic, it caused relatively few fatalities: two dozen in the Dominican Republic, eight in Puerto Rico, and three in Florida, all of which experienced severe winds, torrential rains, and flooding. Haiti, by contrast, was never struck directly by the storm yet the peripheral heavy rain, flooding, and mudslides left over 3,000 people dead.

Poor states are also less able to cope with other likely impacts of climate change and environmental degradation. According to scientific projections, as the earth's surface temperature continues to rise, not only will storm activity increase, but some regions of the world will probably experience more severe droughts, rainfall variability, and a rise in sea level. A 2005 study by the National Oceanic and Atmospheric Administration (NOAA) suggests that the Sahel drought of the late twentieth century—which affected countries from Mauritania to Sudan—was at least in part a consequence of warming sea temperatures and climate change.[70] Current studies show that sea level is already rising, with impacts particularly severe in countries that have coastal deltas, such as Bangladesh, although the extent and rate of sea-level rise have not been precisely determined.[71] From Bangladesh to Nigeria to Tajikistan, low-income countries are no better equipped to face droughts, increased rainfall variability, or sea-level rise than they are to cope with a tropical storm or a hurricane. Disruptive and destructive within the developing world, the consequences of such climate events are unlikely to remain confined to poor states and could have significant implications for U.S. security.

The intelligence community's 2009 annual threat assessment warns that although global warming will have severe effects on the U.S. homeland, "the most significant impact . . . will be indirect and result from climate-driven effects on many other countries."[72] Should poor states like Haiti experience more frequent or severe storms, they will be further weakened and impoverished as a result, with possible wide-scale social unrest. Humanitarian emergencies related to climate events could also prompt calls for international (including U.S.) military interventions. Severe storms, droughts, or a sudden rise in sea level because of a storm surge could create large population displacements in countries like Sudan and Bangladesh, which could in turn contribute to civil conflict and even destabilize entire regions.

THIS BOOK

Intuition suggests that pervasive poverty and stark disparities in income can breed resentment, hostility, and insecurity. Nevertheless, a significant amount of effort has been devoted to discrediting the notion that global poverty has any security consequence for Americans. This book explains how, and why, global poverty affects American national security, and why poverty alleviation must be part of U.S. strategies to tackle transnational security threats, including conflict, terrorism, disease, and climate change. Reducing poverty alone will not suffice to address these transnational threats, but efforts to combat these challenges that do not include significant poverty reduction components are unlikely to produce sustainable outcomes.

Some have downplayed the links between poverty and national security, arguing that poverty does not cause terrorism and noting that the 9/11 hijackers were mainly educated, middle-class Saudis. If poor people were prone to be terrorists, they add, then Africa not the Middle East would be the major hot bed of terrorism. In addition, it has been alleged, poor people are too busy just trying to survive to do anyone harm.

Suppose, for the sake of argument, that such remarks are correct, and that an individual's personal economic circumstances and the plight of others have nothing to do with his or her decision to engage in acts of violence. Would that be a rational basis for concluding that global poverty has no security significance to the United States? Many would have the public believe so, but they would be mistaken.

Even if poverty at the household level did not make individuals more likely to take up arms against perceived government oppressors or to join terrorist groups, low national income and lack of employment opportunities are highly significant at the country level.[73] Poor states are often weak states that fail to meet the basic needs of many of their citizens—for food, clean water, health care, or education. Where human needs are great and service gaps persist, people tend to accept help from almost anyone willing to provide it. Sometimes help comes from multilateral or bilateral aid agencies. Sometimes it comes from secular NGOs. But in many parts of Africa and South Asia, food, clothing, schools, and health care are often provided by foreign-funded religious entities: NGOs, Christian missions, and Islamic charities or mosques. In many instances, as with the World Vision in Uganda or the Muslim Aga Khan Development Network, faith-based assistance is benign and well intended. In some cases, however, life-saving support comes only with religious, even extremist, strings attached, and potential recipients face the Hobson's choice of accepting it or suffering without.

The same poor states that cannot fulfill their core responsibilities to provide security or sustenance to their own people also sometimes fail to exercise effective sovereign control over their territory. Poor states often lack the legal, police, intelligence, and security sector capacity to control their borders and remote areas effectively, and to prevent the plundering of their natural resources. Indeed, such states pose the most immediate and deadly risks to their own citizens, including violence, corruption, and governmental neglect or abuse. Yet in a globalizing world that must contend increasingly with transnational security threats even more often than state-based threats, the consequences of poverty and state weakness can and do spill over borders into neighboring countries and to far-flung regions of the world, ultimately affecting Americans at home and America's interests abroad.

Chapter 2 of this book examines the world's poor and the relationship between poverty and state weakness. To understand how poverty is a threat, one must first determine how it impedes the capacity of states to fulfill their basic functions, which is to provide security for their populations, to deliver basic services, and to create conditions for economic growth and political participation. To develop and implement effective strategies to break the links between poverty, state weakness, and transnational threats, one must understand why and how weak states are weak and adjust the strategies accordingly. The impact of poverty and state weakness on U.S. and global security is not simple, linear, or swift—nor are the solutions.

Chapters 3 through 6 provide in-depth assessments of the relationship between poverty, state weakness, and specific transnational threats: terrorism, civil conflict, global climate change, and disease. Each of these threats is complex in its own right, and to address them will require investments in people, technology, and institutional capacity. A question given close attention in these chapters is how poverty drives the threat or exacerbates other drivers and risks. Drawing on case studies, the authors illustrate how poverty and state weakness combine to heighten the spread of threats or impede the capacity to control them.

Chapter 7 returns to a core challenge identified in this analysis: if there is a downward spiral of poverty and state weakness, how can it be broken? The United States must embrace long-term strategies, in partnership with other countries, to counter transnational security threats. The overriding imperative of such strategies must be to strengthen the legitimacy of weak states and to increase their capacity to control their territory, fulfill the basic human needs of their people, and, above all, continue promoting sustainable democracy *and* development. But it is equally important to recognize the limitations of foreign assistance if weak states do not make a sustained commitment to national development and effective policies. This is perhaps the toughest challenge for policymakers: to find ways to target external support for development so as to produce results in states that show little commitment to responsible governance. Solving this puzzle and designing effective strategies to build the capacity of weak states and reduce poverty is a core U.S. national security imperative in the twenty-first century.

NOTES

1. World Vision is an American Christian NGO that has provided social services and support to victims in Uganda since 1986 (see www.worldvision.org/worldvision/wvususfo.nsf/stable/globalissues_uganda).

2. UN Office of the Special Representative of the Secretary General for Children and Armed Conflict, "DRC: UN Calls for the Unconditional Release of 90 LRA-Abducted Children in the DRC," press release, October 1, 2008.

3. UN Office for the Coordination of Humanitarian Affairs, "OCHA in 2009: Uganda" (ochaonline.un.org/ocha2009/uganda.html).

4. UN Refugee Agency, *Statistical Online Population Database Uganda* (Geneva, 2007).

5. International Crisis Group, "Northern Uganda: Understanding and Solving the Conflict," Africa Report 77 (Washington, April 14, 2004).

6. International Crisis Group, "Northern Uganda: The Road to Peace, with or without Kony," Africa Report 146 (Washington, December 10, 2008).

7. World Bank, *World Development Indicators 2009* (Washington, 2009).

8. Overseas Development Institute, "Regional Inequality and Primary Education in Northern Uganda," Policy Brief 2, prepared for *World Development Report 2009*.

9. International Crisis Group, "Crisis Watch: Uganda" (Washington, January 1, 2009), and "Northern Uganda: Understanding and Solving the Conflict," p. 7.

10. International Crisis Group, "Northern Uganda: The Road to Peace."

11. UN Security Council, "Final Report of the Panel of Experts on the Illegal Exploitation of Natural Resources and Other Forms of Wealth of the Democratic Republic of the Congo," S/2002/1146 (New York, October 16, 2002), pars. 97–131.

12. Francis Kwera, "Analysis: Race for Oil Pumps up Deadly Uganda-Congo Tension," Reuters AlertNet, September 28, 2007.

13. James Risen, "U.S. Directs International Drive on Bin Laden Networks," *New York Times*, September 25, 1998; Neely Tucker, "U.S. Deals Serious Blow to Bin Laden's Network," *New Orleans Times-Picayune*, September 20, 1998.

14. Oxfam, "Turning Up the Heat: Climate Change and Poverty in Uganda," 2008 (www.oww.be/documenten/campagne/ugandan_climate_change.pdf).

15. Andrew Ehrenkranz, "Ebola Rising: A New Strain of the Deadly Virus Has Doctors Scrambling to Contain the Disease," *Newsweek* Web Exclusive, December 6, 2007 (www.newsweek.com/id/74101).

16. UN World Tourism Organization, *World Tourism Barometer* (Madrid, Spain, January 2009), p. 1.

17. UN Conference on Trade and Development, *Review of Maritime Transport* (Geneva, 2007), p. 5.

18. Matthew Bunn, "Securing Nuclear Stockpiles Worldwide," in *Reykjavik Revisited: Steps toward a World Free of Nuclear Weapons,* edited by George P. Shultz and others (Stanford, Calif.: Hoover Press, December 2008), p. 248.

19. Douglas Farah, *Blood from Stones: The Secret Financial Network of Terror* (New York: Broadway Books, 2004). See also Government Accountability Office, "Terrorist Financing: U.S. Agencies Should Systematically Assess Terrorists' Use of Alternative Financing Mechanisms" (Government Printing Office, November 2003), p. 21.

20. Paul Carless and Yuanyuan Cheng, "Proposal for the Inclusion of Zanamivir for the Treatment and Prophylaxis of Avian Influenza in the WHO Model List of Essential Medicines," paper prepared for WHO Seventeenth Expert Committee on the Selection and Use of Essential Medicines (Geneva, March 2009) (www.who.int/selection_medicines/committees/expert/17/expert/Zanamivir_Rev1.pdf), p. 4.

21. See Susan E. Rice, Corinne Graff, and Janet Lewis, "Poverty and Civil War: What Policymakers Need to Know," Global Economy and Development Working Paper (Brookings, December 2006).

22. Two of the most widely cited studies that established this finding are Paul Collier and Anke Hoeffler, "Greed and Grievance in Civil War," *Oxford Economic Papers* 56 (October 2004): 563–95; and James D. Fearon and David D. Laitin, "Ethnicity, Insurgency, and Civil War," *American Political Science Review* 97, no. 1 (2003): 75–90. See also Paul Collier, *The Bottom Billion: Why the Poorest Countries Are Failing and What Can Be Done about It* (Oxford University Press, 2007).

23. Collier, *The Bottom Billion,* pp. 17, 19.

24. See Rice and others, "Poverty and Civil War." Also Macartan Humphreys and Ashutosh Varshney, "Violent Conflict and the Millennium Development Goals: Diagnosis and Recommendations," paper prepared for the meeting of the Millennium Development Goals Poverty Task Force Workshop, Bangkok, June 2004; Nicholas Sambanis, "Poverty and the Organization of Political Violence: A Review and Some Conjectures," in *Brookings Trade Forum 2004,* edited by Susan Collins (Brookings, 2004); and Nicholas Sambanis, "What Is Civil War? Conceptual and Empirical Complexities of an Operational Definition," *Journal of Conflict Resolution* 48, no. 6 (2004): 814–58.

25. See Rice and others, "Poverty and Civil War."

26. On poverty and the duration of conflict, see Paul Collier, Anke Hoeffler, and Mans Soderbom, "On the Duration of Civil War," *Journal of Peace Research* 41, no. 3 (2004): 253–73; and James D. Fearon, "Why Do Some Civil Wars Last So Much Longer than Others?" *Journal of Peace Research* 41, no. 3 (2004): 275–301. On poverty and the recurrence of conflict, see Barbara F. Walter, "Does Conflict Beget Conflict? Explaining Recurring Civil War," *Journal of Peace Research* 41, no. 3 (2004): 371–88.

27. UN Security Council, "Report of the Secretary-General on Timor-Leste Pursuant to Security Council Resolution 1690 (2006)," S/2006/628 (August 8, 2006), par. 26 (www.un.org/Docs/sc/sgrep06.htm).

28. World Bank, *World Development Indicators 2009.*

29. Mark Dodd, "Warning on East Timor Instability by World Bank," *The Australian,* April 29, 2009.

30. Lawrence Korb and Arnold Kohen, "The World Must Heed the Harsh Lessons of East Timor," *Financial Times,* June 30, 2006; and United Nations

Development Program (UNDP), *Timor-Leste Human Development Report 2006* (http://hdr.undp.org/docs/reports/national/TIM_TIMOR_LESTE/TIMOR_LESTE_2006_en.pdf).

31. Fearon, "Why Do Some Civil Wars Last So Much Longer Than Others?"

32. Walter, "Does Conflict Beget Conflict?"

33. World Bank, "Breaking the Conflict Trap: Civil War and Development Policy," Policy Research Report (Washington, 2003).

34. World Bank, *World Development Indicators 2009*.

35. Ibid.

36. U.K. Department for International Development, "Monitoring and Evaluating Poverty Reduction Strategies in Mozambique, Study 2," CMI Brief, vol. 7, no. 3 (January 2008).

37. David Shinn, "Al-Qaeda in East Africa and the Horn," *Journal of Conflict Studies* 27, no. 1 (2007): 47–75.

38. Ibid.

39. Thomas Dempsey, "Counterterrorism in African Failed States: Challenges and Potential Solutions," U.S. Army War College, Strategic Studies Institute (April 2006) (www.strategicstudiesinstitute.army.mil/pdffiles/pub649.pdf).

40. Cofer Black, "Al-Qaeda: the Threat to the United States and Its Allies," Testimony to U.S. House Committee on International Relations (April 1, 2004).

41. World Bank, *World Development Indicators 2009*.

42. Ibid.

43. UNDP, *Human Development Index 2008* (http://hdrstats.undp.org/2008/countries/country_fact_sheets/cty_fs_MLI.html).

44. Heidi Vogt, "West Africa's Disenfranchised Groups a Potential Recruiting Target for Terrorists," Associated Press Worldstream, June 13, 2007.

45. "Suspected Leader of Algerian Hostage Takers Arrested in Chad," Agence France-Presse, May 18, 2007.

46. International Crisis Group, "Islamic Terrorism in the Sahel: Fact or Fiction?" Africa Report 92 (March 31, 2005), p. 18.

47. Abu Bakr Naji, "The Management of Savagery: The Most Critical Stage through Which the Umma Will Pass," translated by William McCants (West Point, N.Y.: Combating Terrorism Center, May 2006) (www.ctc.usma.edu/naji.asp), pp. 15–16.

48. Ibid.

49. Abu Azzam al-Ansari, "Al Qaeda Moving to Africa," quoted in Douglas Farah, "Jihadists Now Targeting Africa," June 19, 2006 (www.douglasfarah.com/).

50. WHO, *World Health Report 2008*.

51. Centers for Disease Control and Prevention, "Health, United States, 2008" (www.cdc.gov/nchs/hus.htm), pp. 4, 268.

52. WHO, "Cumulative Number of Confirmed Human Cases of Avian Influenza A/(H5N1) Reported to WHO," Epidemic and Pandemic Alert

Response, April 9, 2009 (www.who.int/csr/disease/avian_influenza/country/cases_table_2009_04_08/en/index.html).

53. WHO, "End of Ebola Outbreak in the Democratic Republic of the Congo," February 17, 2009 (www.who.int/csr/en/).

54. Centers for Disease Control and Prevention, "Interim Guidance about Ebola Virus Infection for Airline Flight Crews, Cargo and Cleaning Personnel, and Personnel Interacting with Arriving Passengers" (www.cdc.gov/ncidod/dvrd/spb/mnpages/dispages/ebola/Ebola_airline.pdf); and U.S. Army Medical Research Institute of Infectious Diseases, *USAMRIID's Medical Management of Biological Casualties Handbook*, 5th ed. (August 2004) (http://usamriid.detrick.army.mil/education/bluebookpdf/USAMRIID%20Blue%20Book%205th%20Edition.pdf). See also WHO, "Ebola Haemorrhagic Fever," Fact Sheet 103 (December 2008).

55. UN Children's Fund, *Basic Indicators and Statistics 2007* (www.unicef.org/); and World Bank, *World Development Indicators 2009*.

56. WHO, *Statistics, Core Health Indicators 2008* (www.who.int/whosis/database/core/core_select.cfm).

57. UN Department of Peacekeeping Operations, "MONUC Facts and Figures," February 28, 2009 (www.un.org/Depts/dpko/missions/monuc/facts.html).

58. Médecins sans Frontières, "No End in Sight as Pneumonic Plague Outbreak Increases in Ituri, DRC," June 22, 2006 (www.reliefweb.int/rw/rwb.nsf/db900sid/EVOD-6QZDFY).

59. WHO, "Lassa Fever," Fact Sheet 179 (April 2005); and WHO, "Nipah-like Virus in Bangladesh—Update," Epidemic and Pandemic Alert and Response Report, February 26, 2004.

60. WHO, "Weekly Epidemiological Record," March 11, 2005 (www.who.int/wer/2005/wer8010.pdf).

61. Centers for Disease Control and Prevention, "Morbidity and Mortality Weekly Report," October 1, 2004 (www.cdc.gov/mmwr/preview/mmwrhtml/mm5338a2.htm).

62. World Bank, *World Development Indicators 2009*.

63. WHO, "Nipah Virus," Fact Sheet 262 (September 2001).

64. Center for Infectious Disease Research and Policy, "Dramatic Dengue Spike among U.S. Tropics Travelers," July 7, 2006 (www.cidrap.umn.edu/cidrap/content/bt/vhf/news/jul0706dengue.html). See also Centers for Disease Control and Prevention, "Division of Vector-Borne Infectious Diseases: Dengue," April 24, 2008 (www.cdc.gov/ncidod/dvbid/dengue/index.htm#history).

65. Intergovernmental Panel on Climate Change (IPCC), "Summary for Policymakers," in *Third Assessment Report, Working Group II: Impacts, Adaptation, and Vulnerability* (Milan, December 2003), p. 12.

66. IPCC, "The Physical Science Basis," in *Fourth Assessment Report, Working Group I: Climate Change 2007* (Valencia, Spain, November 2007), p. 15.

67. Grant McCool, "Myanmar Cyclone Stirs More Rice Supply Fears," *Reuters India*, May 5, 2008 (http://in.reuters.com/article/domesticNews/idINSP 13877220080505).

68. Central Intelligence Agency (CIA), *World Factbook, Haiti* (https://www.cia.gov/library/publications/the-world-factbook/); and World Bank, *World Development Indicators 2009*.

69. Amy Wilentz, "Hurricanes and Haiti," *Los Angeles Times*, September 13, 2008.

70. I. M. Held and others, "Simulation of Sahel Drought in the 20th and 21st Centuries," *Proceedings of the National Academy of Sciences* (Washington, October 17, 2005) (www.gfdl.noaa.gov/bibliography/related_files/ih0502.pdf).

71. German Advisory Council on Global Climate Change, "Special Report: The Future Oceans—Warming Up, Rising High, Turning Sour," 2006 (www.wbgu.de/wbgu_sn2006_en.pdf).

72. Dennis Blair, Director of National Intelligence, "Annual Threat Assessment of the Intelligence Community for the Senate Select Committee on Intelligence," February 12, 2009.

73. Parts of this chapter have been adapted from Susan E. Rice, "Strengthening Weak States: A 21st Century Imperative," in *Power and Superpower: Global Leadership in the 21st Century*, edited by Morton H. Halperin and others (New York: Century Foundation, 2008). See also Susan E. Rice, "The Threat of Global Poverty," *National Interest* 83 (Spring 2006): 76–82.

CHAPTER TWO

Poverty and State Weakness

SUSAN E. RICE

Grinding poverty is the lot of nearly half of the world's population. More than 2.5 billion human beings subsist on less than $2 a day—$730 a year—the equivalent of seven pairs of quality sneakers in the United States.[1] Poverty is more widespread than previously thought. Even before the recent global financial crisis, an estimated 1.4 billion people lived in extreme poverty (defined by the World Bank as less than $1.25 a day), up from the previous estimate of 1 billion.[2] The percentage of people in the developing world living below the international poverty line has dropped from 52 to 26 percent since 1981.[3] Nonetheless, in absolute terms, that number is increasing, and so is the gap between those living in extreme poverty and the rest of the world.[4] In sub-Saharan Africa, the world's poorest region, the number living in poverty has almost doubled in the past twenty years. If current trends continue, the African continent will be home to one-third of the world's poor by 2015. Although the complete impact of the recent food, energy, and financial crises on global poverty rates has yet to be determined, it has hit low-income countries hard.[5]

This chapter examines poverty's global prevalence and its relationship to weak states. Poverty and state weakness often interact in a vicious, destructive cycle, further entrenching poverty and in turn compromising the capacity of states to provide for their citizens and uphold their responsibilities to the international community.

THE WORLD'S POOR

While most of the world has become wealthier over recent decades, notes economist Paul Collier, the one billion poorest people live in countries where income has actually declined. The "average person in the societies of the bottom billion now has an income only around one-fifth that of the typical person in the other developing countries."[6] Since 2005 the developing world has been hit by a series of crises that threaten to derail recent progress toward alleviating poverty and achieving the Millennium Development Goals (MDGs) in the developing world. The food, fuel, and global financial crises are having a severe impact on poor countries because poor and weak states lack the resources necessary to adapt to such shocks. The increase in worldwide food prices from 2005 to 2008 has in itself forced 200 million more people into extreme poverty, most of whom will remain in poverty through 2009, even as food prices stabilize.[7] Of the additional 30 million expected to face unemployment in 2009 as a result of the financial crisis, 23 million live in the developing world.[8] The goal of halving 1990 poverty levels by 2015 will almost certainly not be reached in sub-Saharan Africa and South Asia, except in India.[9]

In the developing world, poverty does not just promise misery; it is often a sentence to death. Hunger, malnutrition, and easily preventable diseases like diarrhea, respiratory infections, neonatal tetanus, measles, malaria, and cholera thrive in fetid slums that have no basic sewerage, clean water, or electricity. Desolate rural areas lack basic health infrastructure to provide prenatal care or life-saving vaccines. Despite notable progress in recent years, 9.2 million children under five years of age died in 2007, mainly from preventable illnesses.[10] In total, 25,205 children worldwide die *each day*—almost ten times the number of people who perished in the attacks of September 11, 2001. Most succumb, in effect, to poverty. The large majority of these children—7.5 million—live in South Asia and sub-Saharan Africa.[11] In Sierra Leone, which has the world's highest rate of child mortality, more than one-quarter of all children die before their fifth birthday.[12] With the lagging progress in human development, infant deaths in developing countries are expected to increase by up to 2.8 million between 2009 and 2015.[13] The United Nations Children's Fund (UNICEF) blames undernutrition for more than one-third of under-five deaths.[14] By World Bank estimates, access to improved sanitation facilities could save the lives of 1.5 million children a year.[15] Taken for granted across America, such facilities are unknown to 72 percent of the people in Cambodia.[16]

The preponderance of the world's poor live in the most populous countries: China (106 million) and India (266 million). However, both countries have made tremendous progress in reducing extreme poverty.[17] Between 1981 and 2007, more than half a billion people moved out of poverty in China, while the percentage in extreme poverty dropped by approximately one-third during roughly the same period in India (figure 2-1, pp. 26–27).[18] The challenge of poverty in countries with comparatively effective states is quite different from that of weak states.

Latin America and the Caribbean (with the exception of Haiti) have made significant strides as well over the past two decades, with 17 million fewer people suffering dire privation.[19] Nicaragua is the region's second poorest country with per capita gross national income (GNI) at $1,000, while Bolivia, Guyana, Honduras, and Paraguay are each in the $1,000 to $1,700 range.[20] By contrast, Central Asia remains mired in extreme poverty, with Afghanistan, Tajikistan, Uzbekistan, and the Kyrgyz Republic all having per capita GNI of $730 or less.[21]

Still, it is Africa that continues to lag substantially behind the rest of the world. In 2005, 51 percent of sub-Saharan Africa's working poor lived on less than $1.25 a day.[22] After decades of stagnation and decline, Africa, too, had begun to make progress in reducing extreme poverty, witnessing a 6 percent drop since 2000.[23] Tanzania, for one, had started making some progress, with annual gross domestic product (GDP) rising at a rate of roughly 2 percent during the early 1990s and accelerating to over 7 percent annually in this century.[24] Sierra Leone, for another, moved from low and even negative annual GDP growth in the early 1990s, in the midst of civil war, to over 6 percent now that it is recovering from the conflict.[25] At the same time, the African continent is home to thirty of the world's forty-three poorest countries.[26]

In the wake of the financial crisis, sub-Saharan Africa expects economic growth to drop from 5.5 percent in 2008 to 1.7 percent in 2009 owing to reduced exports and deteriorating terms of trade.[27] Thirteen countries in the region are likely to see per capita income decline by about 11 percent.[28] Dwindling economic activity further exposes weak states to market shocks, leaving sub-Saharan Africa and its high percentage of economically vulnerable countries at particular risk.[29] Not surprisingly, the 2009 Annual Threat Assessment of the U.S. intelligence community warns that "the primary near-term security concern of the United States is the global economic crisis and its geopolitical implications," especially in sub-Saharan Africa, but also in Latin America and the states of the former Soviet Union, where poor countries lack the capacity and coping mechanisms to mitigate the impacts of the crisis.

FIGURE 2-1. Percent of Population Living on Less than $1.25 per Day

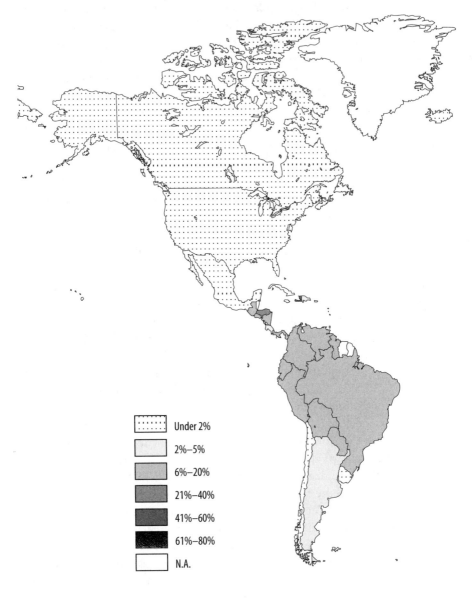

Under 2%

2%–5%

6%–20%

21%–40%

41%–60%

61%–80%

N.A.

Source: UN Human Development Indexes, 2008.

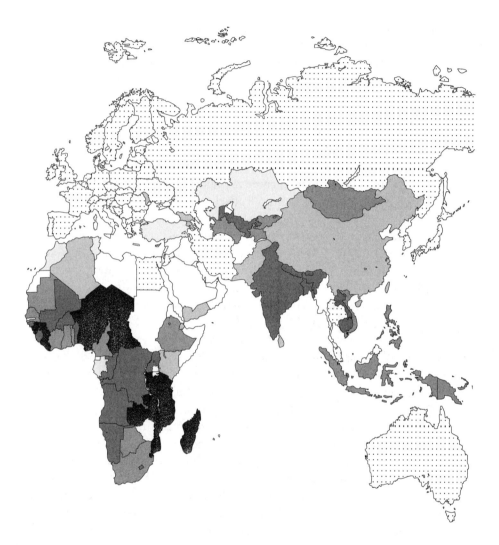

STATE WEAKNESS

A substantial majority of the world's poorest countries, with per capita GNI in the bottom quintile of developing nations, are also the world's weakest states—countries like Somalia, Afghanistan, and Haiti. Conversely, few of the best performing countries have incomes of those in the bottom two quintiles of per capita GNI.

Descriptions of the world's weakest states vary. The U.S. Agency for International Development (USAID), the British Department for International Development, the Fund for Peace, the World Bank, and others have defined substantially overlapping but differing sets of "weak," "fragile," "failing," or "low-income . . . under stress" states.[30] In February 2008 Susan Rice and Stewart Patrick published the Index of State Weakness in the Developing World, an analytical tool that utilizes twenty indicators in four key areas of state function to measure state performance and rank developing countries according to their relative capacity.[31] It defines weak states as those that lack the essential capacity or will, or both, to *(1) foster an environment conducive to sustainable and equitable economic growth; (2) establish and maintain legitimate, transparent, and accountable political institutions; (3) secure their populations from violent conflict and control their territory; and (4) meet the basic human needs of their population.*[32] Fifty-six states fall in the bottom two quintiles of the index (pp. 30–31).[33]

Although the Brookings Index of State Weakness was published in 2008, much of the data underpinning the index—such as GNI per capita as a measure of economic performance, control of corruption as a measure of democratic governance, and life expectancy as an indicator of social welfare—can be expected to change very little from one year to the next.[34] These indicators suggest that Somalia, the Democratic Republic of the Congo (DRC), and Afghanistan will likely remain near the bottom of the index in 2009, whereas Tanzania is likely to be in or near the top of the second quintile. A few countries on the list may change rank, however, particularly if they have experienced a sudden increase in violence (as Kenya did following the disputed general elections there) or are especially vulnerable to the global financial crisis (as in the case of the DRC and Haiti).

Although the drivers of weakness vary enormously from state to state, poverty is the predominant factor eroding state capacity—by fueling violence and sapping human capital, by hollowing out or impeding the development of effective state institutions and markets, and by creating environments especially conducive to corrupt governance. Notwithstanding the many country exceptions across the developing world, stronger economic performance often goes hand in hand with better provision of social welfare and effective governance. The few weak states in which extreme poverty (as measured by per capita GNI) is not a predominant characteristic are oil-producers with an extremely uneven distribution of wealth, such as Equatorial Guinea. Not surprisingly, most of the world's weakest countries have experienced conflict in recent decades. Poor, conflict-ridden states may be condemned to arrested development for years, if not decades. Poor governance is also an important element of state weakness; yet it is not the only one. If all weak states were to become democracies tomorrow, they would not necessarily become capable states. The link between poverty and weakness is neither simple nor direct but takes the form of a spiral: poverty drives weakness, and capacity deficits can, in turn, exacerbate poverty.[35]

Not surprisingly, given the importance of poverty, the weakest states are geographically concentrated in sub-Saharan Africa and, to a lesser extent, in South Asia and Central Asia (figure 2-2, pp. 32–33). There are, of course, high performers in sub-Saharan Africa—including Botswana and Mauritius. Nonetheless, most countries in sub-Saharan Africa, even the top performers, fail to deliver adequate welfare services to their citizens, compared with countries in other regions, in part owing to the devastating impact of the HIV/AIDS pandemic. The world's weakest countries include the subset that are failed states or are embroiled in conflict. They encompass, in addition, many fragile states emerging from conflict within the past fifteen years, several illegitimate regimes, and states that are newly legitimate but still lack the ability to achieve sustained gains in human development.

In South Asia, the second poorest region in the world, countries tend to perform more poorly in providing security, primarily because of an ongoing or recent conflict. Afghanistan, Nepal, Pakistan, and Sri Lanka all receive among the world's lowest security scores.

Countries in Central Asia typically perform more poorly on political indicators than in other areas of governance. Uzbekistan and Tajikistan are by far the worst performers in this regard. Even relatively stronger performers in the region, including Kyrgyzstan, score low in government effectiveness and legitimacy.

The poorest and weakest states in the index can be differentiated by their relative rank. Critically weak states include the countries that rank

Index of State Weakness in the Developing World

							Bottom quintile

Black, white, and gray blocks and quintiles are based on full sample of 141 countries.

Only the 56 weakest states with their overall and basket scores are presented below. A basket score of 0.00 represents the worst score in the 141-country sample; a score of 10.00 signifies the best. The full index with 141 weak states can be found at www.brookings.edu/reports/2008/02_weak_states_index.aspx.

Second quintile
Third quintile
Fourth quintile
Top quintile

Rank	Country	Overall score	Economic	Political	Security	Social welfare	GNI per capita (dollars)
1	Somalia	0.52	0.00	0.00	1.37	0.70	226
2	Afghanistan	1.65	4.51	2.08	0.00	0.00	271
3	Democratic Republic of the Congo	1.67	4.06	1.80	0.28	0.52	130
4	Iraq	3.11	2.87	1.67	1.63	6.27	1,134
5	Burundi	3.21	5.01	3.46	2.95	1.43	100
6	Sudan	3.29	5.05	2.06	1.46	4.59	810
7	Central African Republic	3.33	4.11	2.90	5.06	1.25	360
8	Zimbabwe	3.44	1.56	1.56	6.81	3.84	350
9	Liberia	3.64	3.39	3.91	6.01	1.25	140
10	Côte d'Ivoire	3.66	5.23	2.12	3.71	3.56	870
11	Angola	3.72	5.42	2.67	5.32	1.45	1,980
12	Haiti	3.76	3.90	2.62	5.21	3.31	480
13	Sierra Leone	3.77	5.04	3.87	5.43	0.76	240
14	Eritrea	3.84	3.09	2.78	7.01	2.48	200
15	North Korea	3.87	0.52	0.95	7.28	6.73	n/a
16	Chad	3.90	5.80	2.42	6.18	1.21	480
17	Burma	4.16	4.72	0.89	3.96	7.07	n/a
18	Guinea-Bissau	4.18	5.22	3.83	5.96	1.69	190
19	Ethiopia	4.46	6.14	4.03	5.91	1.75	180
20	Republic of the Congo	4.56	5.08	2.77	6.45	3.95	1,100
21	Niger	4.60	5.45	4.69	7.33	0.94	260
22	Nepal	4.61	5.17	3.84	2.94	6.50	290
23	Guinea	4.67	5.00	2.64	7.43	3.61	410
24	Rwanda	4.68	5.33	4.26	6.62	2.51	250
25	Equatorial Guinea	4.77	7.51	1.73	7.95	1.91	8,250

Rank	Country	Overall score	Eco-nomic	Political	Security	Social welfare	GNI per capita (dollars)
26	Togo	4.80	4.78	2.68	7.38	4.38	350
27	Uganda	4.86	5.78	4.55	4.89	4.23	300
28	Nigeria	4.88	5.39	3.51	5.37	5.24	640
29	Cameroon	5.12	5.78	3.09	7.54	4.07	1,080
30	Yemen	5.18	5.80	3.64	6.43	4.85	760
31	Comoros	5.20	4.24	4.20	8.18	4.20	660
32	Zambia	5.23	5.08	4.59	8.15	3.11	630
33	Pakistan	5.23	6.58	3.52	4.69	6.13	770
34	Cambodia	5.27	6.33	3.00	7.18	4.57	480
35	Turkmenistan	5.27	5.05	1.40	7.88	6.75	1,700
36	Uzbekistan	5.30	5.20	1.78	6.66	7.54	610
37	Mauritania	5.30	6.23	4.34	6.38	4.24	740
38	Djibouti	5.31	5.05	3.69	8.21	4.29	1,060
39	Mozambique	5.32	5.60	5.33	8.35	1.98	340
40	Papua New Guinea	5.32	5.13	4.62	7.45	4.08	770
41	Swaziland	5.33	5.57	3.65	8.28	3.80	2,430
42	Tajikistan	5.35	6.18	3.03	6.39	5.82	390
43	East Timor	5.51	3.93	4.41	7.74	5.98	840
44	Burkina Faso	5.51	6.30	4.87	8.30	2.59	460
45	Laos	5.53	5.88	2.56	7.98	5.71	500
46	Malawi	5.60	5.68	4.83	8.11	3.77	170
47	Colombia	5.63	5.84	5.79	1.78	9.11	2,740
48	Bangladesh	5.64	6.08	3.97	6.55	5.98	480
49	Madagascar	5.65	5.24	5.95	7.65	3.76	280
50	Kenya	5.65	5.77	4.72	6.95	5.15	580
51	The Gambia	5.79	5.26	4.54	8.29	5.06	310
52	Mali	5.85	6.33	6.16	8.49	2.43	440
53	Lesotho	5.88	4.59	6.40	8.35	4.18	1,030
54	Solomon Islands	5.92	4.59	5.05	7.66	6.39	680
55	Tanzania	5.94	6.38	5.41	8.08	3.89	350
56	Sri Lanka	5.94	6.32	5.47	3.38	8.59	1,300

FIGURE 2-2. Map of Weak States

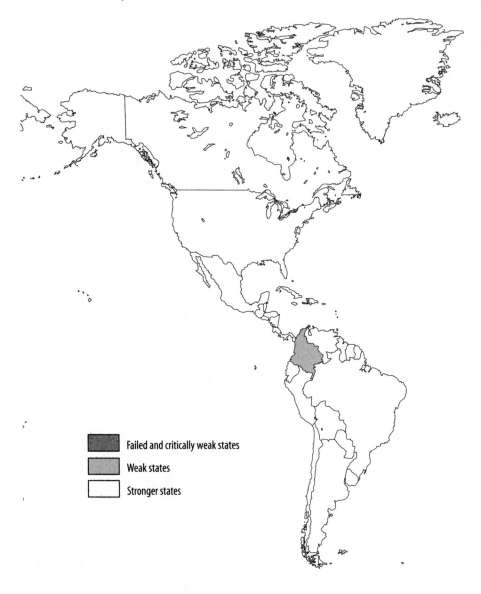

Source: Susan E. Rice and Stewart Patrick, *Index of State Weakness in the Developing World* (Brookings, 2008), p. 5.

in the bottom quintile and are least capable of fulfilling most, if not all, of the four critical functions of government. The second-quintile countries are weak, yet suffer fewer severe capacity gaps than the bottom quintile. They tend to perform poorly in some areas and score variably across the four dimensions of state function.

CRITICALLY WEAK STATES

The twenty-eight critically weak states in the bottom quintile of the Index of State Weakness cover most of sub-Saharan Africa, stretching over 2,000 miles from southwestern Africa, across the Great Lakes Region, parts of West Africa, and into East Africa. This large swath of state failure and critical weakness condemns more than 480 million people to sustained violence, deprivation, and hopelessness. Nigeria, number 28 and the most populous country in sub-Saharan Africa, garners an especially low security score and does not perform above the two bottom quintiles in any area of state function. Nigeria's performance matters enormously to the West African region, and its further faltering or even potential failure would have far-reaching regional and international ramifications. Five critically weak states are located outside sub-Saharan Africa (index rankings are indicated in parentheses): Iraq (4),[36] Haiti (12), North Korea (15), Burma (17), and Nepal (22).

Extreme poverty is a predominant characteristic of most critically weak states. Nine of the ten poorest countries in the world—Burundi (5), the DRC (3), Liberia (9), Ethiopia (19), Guinea-Bissau (18), Eritrea (14), Somalia (1), Sierra Leone (13), and Rwanda (24)—are critically weak. Malawi (46) is the one exception. All but five of the twenty-eight critically weak states are low-income countries, the exceptions being oil producers with an uneven distribution of wealth: Iraq (4), the Republic of the Congo (20), Angola (11), Equatorial Guinea (25), and Cameroon (29). More than 85 percent of the critically weak states have experienced conflict in the past fifteen years. Among those that have not yet failed but are wracked by long-standing violent conflict are Burma (17) and Yemen (30). In Nigeria (28), communal violence and a history of political instability place it at risk of wider conflict.

The international community has intervened militarily in many failed and critically weak states. In the past fifteen years, the United Nations (and in some cases also the African Union) has deployed peacekeepers or observers to half of the failed or critically weak states. The United States has deployed forces to five: Afghanistan (2), Haiti (12), Iraq (4),

Liberia (9), and Somalia (1).[37] France and the European Union have also deployed forces to Côte d'Ivoire (10) and the DRC (3), respectively, and the United Kingdom has sent troops to Sierra Leone (13) and Angola (11).[38]

WEAK STATES

Like the critically weak states, most of the world's weak states, with overall scores in the second quintile of the index, are impoverished. Twenty-one of the twenty-eight in this second quintile are low-income countries (with a per capita GNI of $905 or less). Being poorer states with smaller tax bases, most lack the resources to effectively meet their population's needs. Yet even among this group some underperformers enjoy higher income but fail to use their resources to deliver essential public goods. Two are Algeria (57) and Turkmenistan (35), both energy producers.[39] Two others are Swaziland (41) and Colombia (47), although in the latter case, recent government efforts have improved social service delivery. On the flip side, a handful of states perform better than their low incomes would predict. These include The Gambia (51), Malawi (46), and Tanzania (55).

Weak states tend to exhibit more variable scores across all four areas of state function than do countries in the first quintile. Some score poorly in one or more areas, while others demonstrate mediocre performance across the board. A number of weak states are plagued by insecurity—especially recent or ongoing conflict—which lowers their overall scores despite their above-average performance in other categories. Examples include Zambia (32), Pakistan (33),[40] Sri Lanka (56), and Algeria (57). Particularly striking, Colombia (47) ranked as the fifth most insecure country in the world in 2008 but was a far stronger performer on political and social welfare indicators. The country's overall ranking will rise if it sustains security gains achieved in 2008–09. Among the more stable and secure countries in this cohort are Malawi (46), Mali (52), Mozambique (39), Tanzania (55), and Zambia (32).

Poor political performers among the weak states include Cameroon (29), Laos (45), and Turkmenistan (35), which ranks between North Korea (15) and Zimbabwe (8) on political indicators. Its neighbor, Uzbekistan (36), also places within the bottom ten.

On economic performance, Comoros (31), Djibouti (38), East Timor (43), Lesotho (53), and the Solomon Islands (54) each score in the bottom quintile owing to factors ranging from sluggish growth and high income inequality to a weak regulatory environment. On the social welfare indicator, Mozambique (39) and Mali (52) score poorly across the board.

FIGURE 2-3. Weak States Differ Dramatically

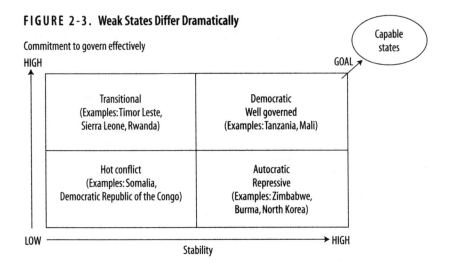

WEAK STATES REQUIRE DIFFERENT POLICY APPROACHES

Weak states that cannot control their resources or territory effectively or provide for the essential needs of their citizens create actual or potential security voids. Much can be accomplished by strengthening and sustaining the capacity of weak states to govern legitimately and effectively. Building the capacity of weak states to be effective partners in combating transnational threats is a central security imperative for the United States in the twenty-first century. Unfortunately, there is no consensus on how to do so.

Understanding how the elements of state weakness reinforce one another both in generic terms and in specific states is a crucial first step in designing effective policy responses. At the same time, it is essential to differentiate among the several types of weak states. Policymakers must define with greater precision the distinct characteristics of this disparate collection of potentially problematic countries, which range from the fully failed to the poor but relatively stable and well governed. Weak states can be arranged in four categories: autocracies, conflict countries, countries transitioning from conflict or autocracy, and fragile democracies that are embarked on the path to sustainable security, if not yet broadly based development (figure 2-3). Admittedly, some states may not fall squarely into any single category, but the objective of U.S. and international policy should be to help weak states move from conflict and autocracy, through postconflict or postautocratic transitional periods, to the more

FIGURE 2-4. Weak States Require Different Policy Approaches

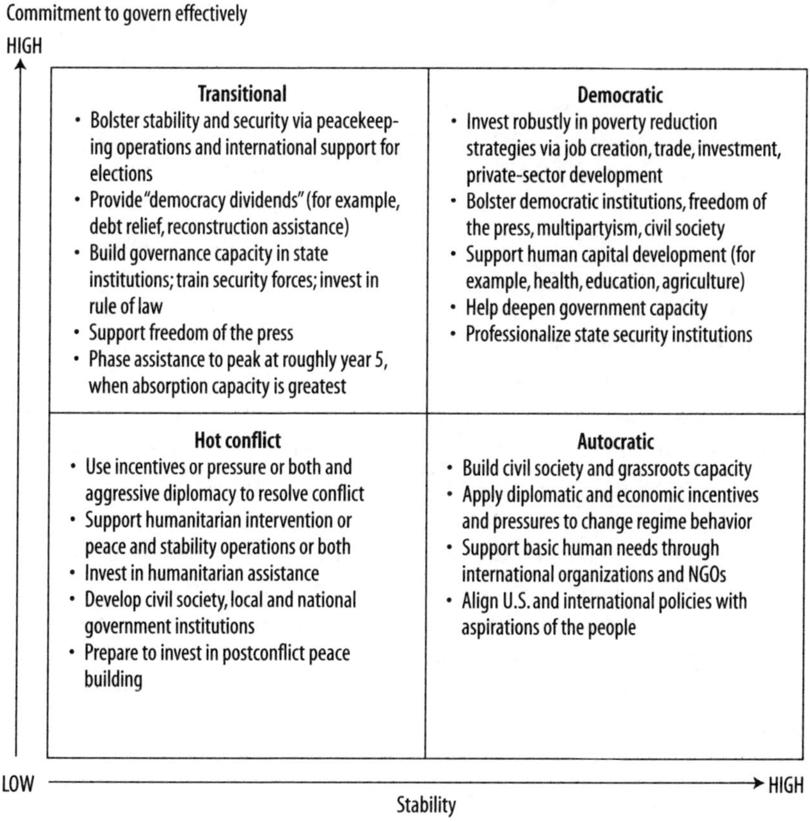

Commitment to govern effectively

HIGH

Transitional	Democratic
• Bolster stability and security via peacekeeping operations and international support for elections • Provide "democracy dividends" (for example, debt relief, reconstruction assistance) • Build governance capacity in state institutions; train security forces; invest in rule of law • Support freedom of the press • Phase assistance to peak at roughly year 5, when absorption capacity is greatest	• Invest robustly in poverty reduction strategies via job creation, trade, investment, private-sector development • Bolster democratic institutions, freedom of the press, multipartyism, civil society • Support human capital development (for example, health, education, agriculture) • Help deepen government capacity • Professionalize state security institutions
Hot conflict	**Autocratic**
• Use incentives or pressure or both and aggressive diplomacy to resolve conflict • Support humanitarian intervention or peace and stability operations or both • Invest in humanitarian assistance • Develop civil society, local and national government institutions • Prepare to invest in postconflict peace building	• Build civil society and grassroots capacity • Apply diplomatic and economic incentives and pressures to change regime behavior • Support basic human needs through international organizations and NGOs • Align U.S. and international policies with aspirations of the people

LOW ⟶ HIGH

Stability

stable stage of fragile, functioning democracy. The ultimate goal should be to build the ranks of capable states like Romania, Botswana, and Mauritius, helping them attain at least middle-income status, consolidate democracy, and achieve lasting peace (for at least a generation), while contributing constructively to the international system.

The nature of the state capacity-building challenge and appropriate international policy strategies also differs among the four types of states (figure 2-4), which are at various stages of stability and commitment to effective governance. Hence, the United States and international policy-makers should construct agreed-upon theories of state capacity building in different contexts that are based on a shared policy framework. Thereafter they must work together to apply those theories flexibly, tailoring them to individual political and security circumstances. For instance, the

World Bank cannot successfully support long-term development projects in a hot conflict zone. The United States cannot credibly fund development through state organs in a dictatorship. Nor would it typically be appropriate for the United States to build the security sector of an autocracy or state at war, though it may be wise to help do so in a postconflict environment or a nascent democracy. Immediate postconflict states have different capacity-building challenges than those with some track record of stability and democracy. In short, policymakers must adapt international security, political, and economic assistance to the nature of the state they seek to strengthen.

Particularly intractable are the challenges posed by autocratic, highly corrupt states whose leaders are masters of maintaining the status quo. It may be tempting to write such states off as too difficult or too unsavory to address in any constructive way. Yet that approach may be shortsighted. However odious a given regime, it may be foolish to consign its people to perpetual purgatory. Working with nongovernmental organizations (NGOs), multilateral institutions, and others, the United States and the international community could pursue ways to seed positive change within the very real constraints imposed by repressive regimes. Such strategies could combine humanitarian assistance and support for basic human needs with the application of appropriate diplomatic and economic pressures and incentives, as well as investments in civil society, grass-roots organizations, and local institutions.

TOWARD VIABLE POLICIES

Ultimately, building effective states in the developing world, focusing both on their will and capacity to deliver essential public services to their citizens, must become a significant component of U.S. national security policy. Yet, the Index of State Weakness suggests that there are numerous profiles of weakness among developing countries. Some states, like Mozambique, are weak primarily in one area (social welfare and security, respectively). Others, like Yemen, suffer from multiple deficiencies. U.S. development assistance often fails to respond to specific country needs. The objective should be to target new assistance to address the specific performance gaps manifest in individual weak states. U.S. policy must take into account each state's unique performance gaps. Moreover, some weak states are more significant as real or potential incubators of transnational security threats than are others and have varying resource and policy constraints. The international community cannot expect to influence positive change with equal intensity or effect in each weak state. Clear analysis is needed to ensure rational choices about policy and country priorities. Unfortunately, this kind of analysis has long been lacking.

To better understand the national security consequences of poverty and state weakness, as well as the policy challenges that lie ahead in weak states, it is helpful to take a closer look at specific countries and threats. Only then can we duly appreciate poverty's role in fueling transnational threats, and the critical role that aid and other forms of external assistance can play in building the capacity and will of weak states to bring security, good governance, economic growth, and social welfare to their inhabitants.

NOTES

1. World Bank, "Poverty at a Glance" (Washington, April 2009) (http://web.worldbank.org/WBSITE/EXTERNAL/NEWS/contentMDK:20040961~menuPK:34480~pagePK:64257043~piPK:437376~theSitePK:4607,00.html).

2. In 2008 the World Bank proposed a revised figure that defines poverty as living on less than $1.25 a day. See Shaohua Chen and Martin Ravallion, "The Developing World Is Poorer Than We Thought, But No Less Successful in the Fight against Poverty," Policy Research Working Paper 4703 (Washington: World Bank, 2008).

3. World Bank, "Poverty at a Glance."

4. World Bank and International Monetary Fund (IMF), *Global Monitoring Report 2009: A Development Emergency* (http://siteresources.worldbank.org/INTGLOMONREP2009/Resources/5924349-1239742507025/GMR09_book.pdf).

5. World Bank, "Rising Food and Fuel Prices: Addressing the Risks to Future Generations," Human Development Network (HDN) and Poverty Reduction and Economic Management (PREM) Network (Washington, 2008); IMF, "The Implications of the Global Financial Crisis for Low-Income Countries" (Washington, 2009); World Bank, "Swimming against the Tide: How Developing Countries are Coping with the Global Crisis," Staff Background Paper for the G20 Finance Ministers and Central Bank Governors Meeting, Horsham, United Kingdom, March 13–14, 2009.

6. Paul Collier, *The Bottom Billion: Why the Poorest Countries are Failing and What Can Be Done about It* (Oxford University Press, 2007), p. 10.

7. World Bank and IMF, *Global Monitoring Report 2009*.

8. Ibid., p. 2.

9. Ibid., p. 14.

10. UNICEF, "Releasing Declining Numbers for Child Mortality, UNICEF Calls for Increased Efforts to Save Children's Lives," press release, September 12, 2008 (www.unicef.org/media/media_45607.html).

11. UNICEF, "Statistics by Area: Child Survival and Health" (December 2008) (www.childinfo.org/mortality.html).

12. UNICEF, "Releasing Declining Numbers for Child Mortality."

13. World Bank and IMF, *Global Monitoring Report 2009*.

14. UNICEF, "Releasing Declining Numbers for Child Mortality."

15. World Bank, "The Economic Impacts of Poor Sanitation," press release, March 20, 2008.

16. World Bank, *World Development Indicators 2006* (Washington, 2006); World Health Organization (WHO), *Water, Sanitation and Hygiene Links to Health* (Geneva, 2004) (/www.who.int/water_sanitation_health/publications/facts2004/en/).

17. See Chen and Ravallion, "The Developing World Is Poorer Than We Thought," table 8.

18. World Bank, "Estimates for China from 1981 to 2007" (http://web.world bank.org/WBSITE/EXTERNAL/COUNTRIES/EASTASIAPACIFICEXT/ CHINAEXTN/0,menuPK:318956~pagePK:141159~piPK:141110~theSite PK:318950,00.html).

19. Socioeconomic Database for Latin America and the Caribbean, Poverty Data, Regional estimates, 2007 (www.depeco.econo.unlp.edu.ar/cedlas/sedlac/ statistics.htm#poverty).

20. World Bank, *World Development Indicators 2007* (Washington, 2007).

21. Ibid.

22. World Bank, *World Development Indicators 2005* (Washington, 2005).

23. Africa Progress Panel, "Africa's Development: Promises and Prospects" (Geneva, 2008), p. 7.

24. U.S. Central Intelligence Agency (CIA), "Tanzania," in *World Factbook* (Washington, 2008).

25. CIA, "Sierra Leone," in *World Factbook* (2008).

26. UN-OHRLLS, "Country Profiles," *Least Developed Countries* (www. unohrlls.org/en/ldc/related/62/).

27. World Bank and IMF, *Global Monitoring Report 2009*, p. 25.

28. Ibid., p. 33.

29. Ibid., p. 32.

30. Susan E. Rice and Stewart Patrick, *Index of State Weakness in the Developing World* (Brookings, 2008), p. 5.

31. Ibid.

32. The index includes all countries classified by the World Bank as low-income, lower-middle-income, or upper-middle-income in its 2007 *World Development Report*. The index excludes countries with a population below 100,000 and also excludes the West Bank and Gaza, which is not a sovereign state. Since publication of the 2007 *World Development Report*, four countries have graduated from the category of upper-middle-income countries and in 2009 were no

longer considered developing countries by the World Bank: Equatorial Guinea, Hungary, Oman, and the Slovak Republic.

33. For the full list of 141 countries included in the index, see Rice and Patrick, *Index of State Weakness.*

34. The datasets that underpin the index to measure economic performance are per capita GNI, 2006 (World Bank, *World Development Indicators*); GDP growth, 2002–06 (World Bank, *World Development Indicators*); income inequality, 2006 (World Bank, *World Development Indicators*); inflation, 2002–06 (IMF, *International Financial Statistics*); and regulatory quality, 2006 (World Bank, *Governance Matters VI*). Those used to measure democratic governance are government effectiveness, 2006 (World Bank, *Governance Matters VI*); rule of law, 2006 (World Bank, *Governance Matters VI*); voice and accountability, 2006 (World Bank, *Governance Matters VI*); control of corruption, 2006 (World Bank, *Governance Matters VI*); and Freedom Ratings, 2006 (Freedom House). Performance in the area of security is measured by conflict intensity, 1992–06 (Center for Systemic Peace, *Major Episodes of Political Violence*); political stability and absence of violence, 2006 (World Bank, *Governance Matters VI*); incidence of coups, 1992–06 (Archigos 2.8 and Economist Intelligence Unit); gross human rights abuses, 1992–06 (Political Terror Scale); and territory affected by conflict, 1991–05 (Political Instability Task Force). The measures of social welfare were child mortality, 2005 (UNICEF, *State of the World's Children*); primary school completion, 2005 (World Bank, *World Development Indicators*); undernourishment, 2004 (Food and Agriculture Organization); percent of population with access to improved water sources and improved sanitation facilities, 2004 (World Bank, *World Development Indicators*); and life expectancy, 2005 (World Bank, *World Development Indicators*).

35. The causal relationship between poverty, conflict, and state failure is undoubtedly complex, as poverty both fuels conflict and deepens as a result of conflict. See World Bank, *Breaking the Conflict Trap: Civil War and Development Policy* (Washington, 2003).

36. Iraq's rank in the index is likely to have risen since 2008, given improvements in security and governance.

37. The United Nations has deployed to Angola, Burundi, Central African Republic, Chad, the DRC, Côte d'Ivoire, Republic of the Congo, Ethiopia, Eritrea, Liberia, Rwanda, Sierra Leone, Somalia, and Sudan (www.un.org/Depts/dpko/dpko/).

38. Postconflict countries with an international peacekeeping presence are likely to score better than their internal performance or capacities warrant. Their scores reflect the support they receive from international institutions or foreign governments in fulfilling one or more government functions. Examples include Bosnia and Herzegovina (113), East Timor (43), and Lebanon (93).

39. Not all energy-producing weak states have an annual per capita income above $905. Among the poorest oil-producing states are Nigeria, Sudan, and Uzbekistan.

40. Pakistan's score does not reflect the country's increased instability since 2007.

CHAPTER THREE

Poverty, Development, and Violent Extremism in Weak States

CORINNE GRAFF

In October 2000, a 35-foot craft approached the U.S.S *Cole,* docked in Aden Harbor, Yemen. Operated by two Saudi suicide terrorists, the small boat was packed with about 600 pounds of powerful explosives. Within minutes, the bombers triggered a blast that ripped through the metal hull of the 9,100-ton vessel, a U.S. Navy destroyer. The explosion killed seventeen American sailors and injured thirty-nine others. It was powerful enough to rattle buildings surrounding the port. While responsibility for the attacks was initially unclear, law enforcement agencies eventually traced them to Osama bin Laden, who, according to the 9/11 Commission, directly supervised, helped plan, and funded the operation.[1]

Immediately after the U.S.S. *Cole* attack, the Clinton administration assigned high priority to counterterrorism cooperation in Yemen. After 9/11, U.S. policy focused on special operations missions in Yemen to help track and capture or kill al Qaeda suspects. U.S.-Yemeni intelligence prompted a 2002 U.S. missile strike in Yemen that blew up a car occupied by a top al Qaeda leader. Yemen received U.S. security assistance, including funding to help rebuild its coast guard and monitor land borders, as well as financial and operational support for Yemeni special operations and other military forces, which resulted in numerous arrests.[2]

Initially, U.S. and Yemeni counterterrorism initiatives seemed to pay off: several terrorist plots were foiled, and the capture of al Qaeda leaders was hailed as a serious blow to the group's leadership and capabilities in Yemen.[3] Yet by 2006 the tide had begun to turn back. Analysts warned of a second generation of al Qaeda–inspired militants taking root in Yemen. A sharp increase in terrorist attacks soon followed.[4] In 2008 a local cell calling itself al Qaeda in Yemen (AQY) twice attacked the U.S. embassy compound in the capital of Sana, killing two Yemenis in a March rocket attack and seventeen people—including one American—in a September bombing plot.[5] Other plots linked to al Qaeda have targeted foreign oil workers and facilities, a residential compound housing Americans and other foreign residents, army checkpoints, and tourists visiting the country.[6] Saudi Arabia announced in 2009 that many of its most-wanted militants had taken refuge in neighboring Yemen, including the regional leader of al Qaeda.[7]

Why, eight years after the 9/11 attacks and despite ongoing and initially effective U.S. and Yemeni counterterrorism operations against al Qaeda's leadership, does the country remain a hot spot for violent extremism? This question has implications far beyond Yemen and bears on Islamic violent extremism globally. Violent extremism should not be construed as the only important transnational threat to U.S. security, as other chapters in this book indicate. Yet the U.S. fight against violent extremism remains a top foreign policy priority and is one we must get right. As even hawkish Secretary of Defense Donald Rumsfeld remarked in 2003, our current approach begs the question: is the United States "capturing, killing or deterring more terrorists every day than the madrassas and the radical clerics are recruiting, training and deploying against us?"[8]

To understand why terrorist activity persists in countries like Yemen, one must move beyond intercepting terrorist leaders and bombers, and examine the conditions that allow violent extremists to operate and attract lower-level recruits and build popular support. Yemen country experts point to numerous drivers and enablers of terrorism, but the one that is increasingly gaining attention is poverty.[9] Though situated on the oil-rich Arabian Peninsula, Yemen ranks among the most impoverished places in the world (it is poorer than Côte d'Ivoire, Cameroon, and the Republic of Congo) and is the world's sixth fastest-growing country (the population is set to double by 2020).[10] The human development challenges that plague much of the Muslim world today—from low-quality education to lack of jobs, corruption, and a deficit of political liberties—all seem to be particularly acute in Yemen. Some warn that diminishing resources are undermining the government's capacity to mount effective counterterrorism operations and could cause the state to collapse.[11]

Yet the challenge for U.S. policymakers is how to reconcile the view of country experts who believe low income contributes to terrorism with that of terrorism experts who tend to dismiss poverty's role? Much has been written by country experts about the perils of persistent poverty in weak states such as Pakistan and in Central Asia, Southeast Asia, and the Horn of Africa.[12] Yet since 9/11, terrorism experts have invoked empirical evidence that poverty does not correlate with a higher incidence of terrorist attacks and participation. The consensus appears to be that poverty does not motivate individuals to participate in terrorism, and that development assistance, therefore, has no place in a long-term counterterrorism strategy. On the contrary, policymakers would be well advised to pay far greater attention to development's role in a long-term U.S. strategy against terrorism.

The reality is that there simply is no robust empirical relationship between poverty and terrorist attacks, making it largely impossible to draw policy conclusions from this literature. To be sure, extremist groups exploit a variety of conditions across the world, even in wealthy industrialized states, where attacks have often involved educated, middle-class recruits. However, new evidence suggests that weak and failed states—many of which are among the world's poorest countries— are at increased risk of harboring violent extremists, that terrorist attacks are more deadly in poor countries, and that more attacks targeting Americans are occurring in the developing world. This chapter focuses on the vulnerabilities of weak states to extremism as a first step toward formulating more adequate, long-term strategies against violent extremism in the developing world.

The United States must take the lead in making effective capacity building and poverty alleviation in weak states a priority. This has not been the case to date, except in Iraq and Afghanistan. Rather, U.S. global counterterrorism strategy aims primarily at intercepting individual terrorists, at the expense of long-term gains in the wider fight against violent extremism. With extremist groups gaining ground across the Muslim world—not only in Yemen but also in North Africa and parts of Asia—this security-based approach appears to be backfiring. The recent global financial crisis may give violent extremists an additional boost, making even clearer the link between poverty, weak states, and terrorism in key parts of the developing world.[13]

In 2004 the 9/11 Commission concluded that a comprehensive counterterrorism strategy must "include economic policies that encourage development . . . and opportunities for people to improve the lives of their families."[14] Yet five years on, the United States is still far from such a strategy.[15] In Yemen, for example, U.S. foreign assistance spending for several years amounted to roughly $12 per person, less than aid to comparably poor countries in Africa, and substantially less than assistance to Iraq and Afghanistan.[16] Half of the approximately $20 million annual budget for Yemen in fiscal 2005–08 was spent on military and intelligence cooperation.[17] What little the U.S. government did provide in nonmilitary assistance in 2008 was tied to the extradition of terrorists, including several U.S.S. *Cole* bombers.[18] In a country whose population consistently ranks among the most anti-American in the world, this approach is not working.[19] U.S. policy in Yemen continues to be largely one-sided, lacking a long-range plan to dissuade youths from joining extremist groups. As discussed in chapter 7 of this book, donor agencies must redouble their efforts to identify policy solutions that are effective in countries that lack institutional capacity and are unable to maintain or establish domestic security.

WHAT WE REALLY KNOW ABOUT POVERTY AND VIOLENT EXTREMISM

Research on poverty and terrorism has grown into a cottage industry since 9/11, but much of it claims there is no connection between the two. Some studies of economic and demographic conditions—such as income per capita, gross domestic product (GDP) growth, unemployment rates, and income inequality—and their relationship to terrorist attacks go so far as to treat the link between poverty and terrorism as a "myth," to paraphrase one recent headline.[20] In the view of former Princeton economist Alan Krueger, now U.S. assistant secretary of the treasury for economic policy, "There is little reason for optimism that a reduction in poverty or increase in educational attainment will lead to a meaningful reduction in the amount of international terrorism."[21] This sentiment is widely echoed in both academic and journalistic circles.[22] Like Krueger, al Qaeda specialist and television journalist Peter Bergen argues that economic deprivation inspires neither political nor terrorist violence.[23]

Yet these and other similar findings do not comport with circumstances on the ground. In Yemen, for example, one official recently observed that "most young people have no prospects in life" and "fanatics offer them the illusion that they can take power."[24] Substantial anecdotal evidence from a broad swath of countries suggests that poverty does bear on terrorist activity and cannot be overlooked.

Througout the Muslim world, violent extremists take refuge and gain support among the poor. From Yemen to Kashmir, Chechnya, and across the Middle East, uneducated and often impoverished young men with few employment prospects often are being recruited to join violent extremist groups in exchange for financial rewards.[25] From Mali to Yemen, Pakistan, and the Philippines, poverty undermines government capacity and allows violent extremists to use ungoverned territories as staging grounds for international attacks.[26]

Even in wealthier Muslim-majority countries like Morocco and Lebanon, squalid slums or refugee camps provide fertile grounds for terrorist recruiters. The Moroccan Islamic Combatant Group (GICM), an al Qaeda ally, recruited mainly unemployed and uneducated young men from the slums of Casablanca to carry out simultaneous bombing attacks in that city in May 2003, killing forty-five people.[27] One of the masterminds of the 2004 Madrid train bombings was a Moroccan national who grew up in a shantytown outside of the Moroccan city of Tetouan.[28] Similarly, many of Lebanon's Islamist militia groups such as al Qaeda–inspired Fatah al Islam originate in and draw support from the country's downtrodden Palestinian refugee camps.[29] Furthermore, many of the bombers in recent terrorist attacks in Western Europe and North America have roots in regions rife with inequality and lacking access to services and economic opportunities. A 2004 U.K. assessment of the threat of young Muslim radicals in Europe finds two categories of extremists there: one is well-educated, and the other consists of "under-achievers with few or no qualifications, and often a criminal background." In the United Kingdom, "Muslims are more likely than other faith groups to have no qualifications (over two-fifths have none) and to be unemployed and economically inactive, and are over-represented in deprived areas."[30]

Indeed, one would be hard-pressed to name a single major recent attack in the developing world in which household poverty, lack of employment opportunities, or lack of state capacity did not play some role. Pakistan-based Lashkar-e-Taiba—the group suspected of carrying out the attacks in Mumbai in 2008—recruits largely from the poor southern Punjab region of Pakistan. While the ongoing conflict in Kashmir motivates many to participate in Lashkar attacks, poverty is a common grievance of young recruits.[31] Jemaah Islamiyah—the Southeast Asian militant Islamist group with ties to al Qaeda that killed 200 people in an October 2002 car bombing in Bali—preys on the poor and powerless, offering religious education as well as room and board to children whose families lack the means to pay for school.[32]

From their public statements and texts, it is clear that al Qaeda and other violent extremists deliberately exploit conditions of poverty. Osama Bin Laden has issued fatwas, religious rulings, describing terrorist attacks as a response to "severe oppression, suffering, excessive iniquity, humiliation and poverty."[33] Radical ideologues associated with violent extremists have also spelled out the advantages of poor, weak states in Africa, where operatives are encouraged to seek refuge.[34] The message seems to resonate widely: public opinion polls in places like Pakistan show that significant percentages of the population believe poverty and lack of jobs are a strong cause of violent extremism.[35] People in developing countries who suffer from widespread attacks themselves see poverty as an important factor.

Anecdotal evidence thus seems to contradict the recent consensus among experts. Which interpretation is correct?

The first step in answering this question is to recognize that the different explanations of violent extremism may not be mutually exclusive. One common factor to emerge from various investigations is that zealous religious leaders, Islamic fundamentalists, and particularly violent Salafi ideologues have played a key role in mobilizing violent extremists throughout the Muslim world. There is also the argument that foreign military occupation and authoritarian regimes are a strong predictor of suicide attacks.[36] In addition, it has been shown that individuals who join violent extremist groups develop an overriding allegiance to the group that is manifested in suicide attacks. In this respect, violent extremists operate like exclusive clubs that select and initiate members, encouraging them to develop a fierce allegiance to each other.[37] This may be why some of the most high-profile recruits are alienated from their homeland: they joined violent extremist groups in their quest for social integration. Members are highly skilled, not because less educated individuals do not volunteer to become violent extremists, but because these groups select only the most skilled candidates.[38]

All of these factors are compatible with poverty's role. As counterterrorism expert Daniel Byman warns, the global financial crisis could "make many people around the world more willing to believe that the current system is corrupt and more open to ideologies—first steps toward embracing violent extremism."[39] Others would agree that "radicalism, separatism and other ideological motivations for terrorism that appear to be intrinsically noneconomic may actually stem from underlying economic conditions."[40] According to research on the background and status of Guantanamo Bay detainees, terrorist activity in some cases was motivated by religious conviction or for political reasons and in others by lack of opportunity. A Taliban driver held at Guantanamo explained: "I didn't know the Taliban was an enemy of the United States. I used to think the Taliban was an opportunity for me to work, to avoid being with no money and to eat."[41] Clearly, violent extremists are motivated by a variety of factors, a prominent one being poverty.

Moreover, the empirical research on poverty and terrorism has been accepted without careful scrutiny. For the most part, this research relies on a simplistic conception of violent extremism. Yet terrorism is merely a technique of violence that can be used for a wide variety of ends. It is defined as intentional and politically motivated violence perpetrated by non-state groups against civilians or noncombatants, or both.[42] The fact that poverty does not correlate or seem to explain all attacks against civilians should not come as a surprise, since such attacks can have widely differing objectives. The late scholar Charles Tilly questioned the scientific legitimacy of scholarship that seeks to identify the "root cause" of all terrorist incidents everywhere.[43]

The research that has been most widely cited in the press—cross-country empirical analysis of terrorist incidents—represents just one strand of work among at least three different approaches. A close examination of empirical research reveals three types of terrorism studies to date (table 3-1): country case studies, cross-country analysis, and studies of al Qaeda membership. Taken as a whole, this literature reflects little agreement on the role of poverty. It certainly does not rule out poverty as a contributing factor.

In the cross-country empirical literature, poverty and its relationship to terrorism are often too narrowly conceived, and the longer-term impacts of household poverty and low national income on societies overlooked. This research focuses almost exclusively on whether poverty directly motivates individual terrorist recruits or popular support for terrorist leaders. Yet poverty can make governments less responsive to their citizens, and less legitimate. The resulting vacuums tend to be filled by non-state organizations. Moreover, while most Muslim charities have noble intentions and seek to provide desperately needed welfare services, some have aided and abetted violent extremists—notably in Afghanistan, Bosnia, and around Pakistan's refugee camps. Poverty also increases the likelihood of conflict. War zones from Chechnya to Iraq, Bosnia, the

TABLE 3-1. Three Types of Studies on Poverty and Terrorism

	Country case studies	Cross-country analysis	Al Qaeda studies
Examples	Alam (2003); Angrist (1995); Berman (2003); Honaker (2005); Khashan (2003); Livingstone and Halevy (1988); Moghadam (2003); Saleh (2004); Thompson (1989); Toth (2003); White (1993)[a]	Abadie (2006); Blomberg, Hess, and Weerapana (2002); Burgoon (2004); Krueger and Laitin (2003); Krueger and Maleckova (2003); Li and Schaub (2004); Piazza (2006); Santos Bravo and Mendes Dias (2006)[b]	Sageman (2004)[c]
Subject	Terrorist activity in Egypt, Israel, the Palestinian Territories, Lebanon, and Northern Ireland	Terrorist activity across all countries	Al Qaeda members
Economic variables tested	Level of schooling, literacy, income, and employment status of terrorist bombers and supporters	GPD per capita, GDP growth, unemployment rate, income inequality, HDI, literacy, life expectancy, school enrollment, health and education spending	Level of schooling, literacy, income and employment status of al Qaeda members
Measure of terrorism	Individuals who participate in or voice support for terrorist attacks	Number of terrorist attacks in a country and/or number of violent extremists from that country	Al Qaeda members
Agree on economic root causes of terrorism?	No	Debate largely ongoing; emerging consensus that a rise in unemployment or sharp recession increases participation in terrorist attacks	Indicate that al Qaeda members are generally not poor or under-educated
Main weaknesses	Findings may not apply to violent extremism in the Muslim world	Research conflates different forms of terrorism; findings may not apply to violent extremism in the Muslim world	Sample of al Qaeda members may not be representative of rank and file

a. Joshua D. Angrist, "The Economic Returns to Schooling in the West Bank and Gaza Strip," Working Paper 95-5 (Massachusetts Institute of Technology, 1995); Anwar Alam, "The Sociology and Political Economy of 'Islamic Terrorism' in Egypt," *Terrorism and Political Violence* 15, no. 4 (2003): 114–42; James Honaker, "Unemployment and Violence in Northern Ireland: A Missing Data Model for Ecological Inference," paper presented at the annual meeting of the Midwest Political Science Association, Chicago, April 15, 2005; Hilal Khashan, "Collective Palestinian Frustration and Suicide Bombings," *Third World Quarterly* 24, no. 6 (1995): 1049–67; Neal Livingstone and David Halevy, "The Perils of Poverty," National Review 40, no. 8 (1988): 28; Basel Saleh, "Economic Conditions and Resistance to Occupation in the West Bank and Gaza Strip: There Is a Causal Connection," paper presented to the Graduate Student Forum, Kansas State University, April 4, 2003; J. L. P. Thompson, "Deprivation and Political Violence in Northern Ireland, 1922–1985: A Time-Series Analysis," *Journal of Conflict Resolution* 33, no. 4 (1989): 676–99; James Toth, "Islamism in Southern Egypt: A Case Study of a Radical Religious Movement," *International Journal of Middle East Studies* 35, no. 4 (2003): 547–72; Robert W. White, "On Measuring Political Violence: Northern Ireland, 1969 to 1980," *American Sociological Review* 58 (August 1993): 575–85.

b. Alberto Abadie, "Poverty, Political Freedom, and the Roots of Terrorism," *American Economic Review* 96, no. 2 (2006): 50–56; S. Brock Blomberg and others, "Terrorism from Within: An Economic Model of Terrorism," Working Papers in Economics (Claremont Colleges, 2002); Brian Burgoon, "On Welfare and Terror: Social Welfare Policies and Political-Economic Roots of Terrorism," *Journal of Conflict Resolution* 50, no. 2 (2006): 176–203; Alan B. Krueger, and D. D. Laitin, *"Kto Kogo?* A Cross-Country Study of the Origins and Targets of Terrorism," in *Terrorism, Economic Development, and Political Openness,* edited by Philip Keefer and Norman Loayza (Cambridge University Press, 2003); Alan B. Krueger and Jitka Maleckova, "Seeking the Roots of Terrorism," *Chronicle of Higher Education,* 2003; Quan Li and Drew Schaub, "Economic Globalization and Transnational Terrorism: A Pooled Time-Series Analysis," *Journal of Conflict Resolution* 48, no. 2 (April 2004); James Piazza, "Rooted in Poverty? Terrorism, Poor Economic Development and Social Cleavages," *Terrorism and Political Violence,* http://www.informaworld.com/smpp/title~content=t713636843~db=all~tab=issueslist~branches=18 - v1818, no. 1 (March 2006): 159–77; Ana Bela Santos Bravo and Carlos Manuel Mendes Dias, "An Empirical Analysis of Terrorism: Deprivation, Islamism and Geopolitical Factors," *Defense and Peace Economics* 17, no. 4 (2006): 329–41.

c. Marc Sageman, *Understanding Terror Networks* (University of Pennsylvania Press, 2004).

Philippines, and Somalia have been exploited by violent extremists seeking refuge from the law or easy recruits among a battle-hardened, idle population of youths.

Once violent extremism has taken root in poor states, poverty further exacerbates the threat by crippling states and hampering their ability to mount and implement effective counterterrorism programs, as is the case in Yemen. Moreover, low national income may limit the reach of the state so severely that its political regime may have no choice but to form an alliance with radicals or permit jihadis into its midst in order to ensure its survival (as in Pakistan and Yemen). The few studies that have explored the far-reaching consequences of poverty in weak and failed states find that a complex brew of poverty-related conditions leave their citizens more prone to violent extremism. The limitations of recent research on poverty and terrorism has important policy implications, as explained in the following sections.

Country Case Studies

As table 3-1 indicates, country case studies on terrorist activity focus primarily on the Palestinian Territories, Lebanon, Egypt, and Northern Ireland, examining the backgrounds of individual bombers there, as well as the level of popular support for violent extremism among certain groups during terrorism campaigns (for example, among the inhabitants of the West Bank and Gaza during the Second Intifada). Some concentrate on the personal backgrounds of bombers, especially their employment status and level of literacy and schooling compared with that of the general population.[44] Others focus on public opinion polls in countries undergoing a surge in terrorist attacks and seek to identify the demographic profile of respondents strongly supportive of acts of terrorism.[45] Still others examine the relationship between economic opportunities among particular religious or ethnic groups and the incidence of terrorist attacks (for example, the relationship between unemployment rates among Irish Catholics in Northern Ireland and the number of deaths resulting from Irish Republican Army attacks).[46]

Although many of these studies find low income, economic shocks, and unemployment to be associated with higher numbers of attacks, some are unclear on this point. It also remains unclear whether violent extremism thrives for the same reasons in different countries, whether in the context of foreign occupation, a struggle for national liberation, or opposition to American policies. Another drawback of this research is that it focuses on suicide attacks, which are relatively rare and may have different underlying causes than other types of terrorist attacks.[47]

Cross-Country Statistical Analysis

Cross-country research on terrorist activity seeks to establish the profile of countries in which attacks are most prevalent. The method of analysis consists of examining the statistical relationship between certain country characteristics (such as income level, degree of social welfare, or absence of democratic governance) and either the number of terrorist attacks in the country or the perpetrators' country of origin. The economic indicators of primary interest are national income per capita, GDP growth, unemployment rates, income inequality, the United Nations Development Program's Human Development Index, illiteracy, infant mortality, life expectancy, school enrollment rates, and health and education spending as a percentage of total public expenditures. Some scholars also examine the relevance of certain political variables, including Freedom House's Political Rights Index and Civil Liberties Index, and the Polity IV Project's overall Polity Index, which measures the level of democracy in a country.

By and large, studies of this nature suffer some of the same shortcomings as the work on specific countries, with similarly controversial results, except for considerable agreement on the likelihood that a significant drop in employment opportunities, or a severe economic recession or shock, will render violent extremism more attractive to potential recruits, especially educated young men. Even "poverty skeptic" Alan Krueger acknowledges that in an average country a "sharp increase in the unemployment rate," particularly when it affects "college graduates relative to high school graduates," can result in a spike in terrorist attacks, as it has in countries with large youth bulges, such as the West Bank and Gaza Strip.[48]

Beyond this, however, the literature is inconclusive. Some studies see no significant relationship between low per capita income or underdevelopment and the likelihood of attacks in a country.[49] Others find evidence to the contrary.[50] Similarly, some studies find that fewer democratic rights increase the likelihood of attacks, whereas others see no relationship between the two. A few suggest that the risk of violent extremism is greatest in countries in transition toward democracy.[51]

Perhaps one reason for the contradictory findings from essentially the same cross-country approach and data is the tendency to concentrate on terrorist attackers themselves and to ignore the larger pool of volunteers and behind-the-scenes foot soldiers involved in the less visible planning of terrorist bombings. Nobel prize–winning criminologist Gary Becker, whose work forms the basis of much cross-country analysis, has noted that the evidence would be more convincing if it also included bombers who failed or were captured before accomplishing their missions. The unsuccessful bombers, says Becker, are likely to be significantly less educated and skilled than the perpetrators of successful attacks: "The sample of bombers or other terrorists must be representative of all terrorists . . . before reliable conclusions can be drawn about the relation between economic opportunities and the recruitment of terrorists."[52]

A second and more serious shortcoming is the cross-country literature's reliance on a catchall definition of "terrorism." Charles Tilly complains: "A remarkable array of actors sometimes adopt terror as a strategy, and therefore no coherent set of cause-effect propositions can explain terrorism as a whole."[53] Because these studies focus on many different kinds of terrorist attacks globally, they shed little light on the specific attacks prevalent today, namely, violent extremism in the Muslim world targeting American interests.

Profile of al Qaeda Members

Yet another analytical approach, demonstrated by former intelligence analyst Marc Sageman, is to consider the demographic profile of participants in al Qaeda attacks. Sageman finds that al Qaeda leaders and high-profile participants in large-scale attacks are not less educated, more impoverished, or more underemployed than the average citizen in their country of origin. Such evidence, he argues, "refutes the widespread notion that terrorism is a result of poverty and lack of education."[54] The problem here, however, is that the results may be biased because the primary source of information on violent extremists is the press, which is more likely to focus on the masterminds and bombers. Hence the individuals selected for study may not be representative of all al Qaeda operatives. Rank-and-file members tend to receive far less attention in the press. Recent profiles of al Qaeda's membership based on unclassified sources may not include sufficient information on the larger pool of willing volunteers and lower-tier recruits.

Weak States: Missing Link between Poverty and Violent Extremism in the Muslim World

Some studies instead look at weak states and their vulnerability to violent extremist ideologies and attacks. As the 9/11 Commission reported in 2004, violent extremists "have fled to some of the least governed, most lawless places in the world . . . areas that combine rugged terrain, weak governance, room to hide or receive supplies, and low population densities."[55] This work is an important complement to studies of the causes of recruitment and has received little attention to date.

Poor, weak, or conflict-prone states provide an ideal environment for a global organization in the business of producing large-scale terrorist attacks.[56] To mount attacks on a global scale, al Qaeda and its affiliates have had to maintain a presence—in the form of local recruiters—across many countries. In view of its considerable infrastructure needs, the organization has sought appropriate locales in which to train bombers and store contraband, set up communication hubs, coordinate the activities of local cells in various countries, and establish at least rudimentary business operations, transshipment points, and traffic routes to generate income.

Poor, weak states with inadequate border and territorial controls fit the bill. They serve as a sanctuary for violent extremist groups and their cells and hubs and lack legitimacy in the eyes of their citizens. Particularly susceptible are underserviced regions, such as the Federally Administered Tribal Areas in Pakistan, the southern Philippines, northern Mali, or parts of southern and northern Yemen. Also vulnerable are refugee camps, such as those in the Middle East and Pakistan. As history has shown, when central governments fail to deliver basic services, disgruntled citizens succumb more readily to offers to address their grievances, even from violent extremist groups. The Taliban gained a foothold in Afghanistan in the 1990s in part because they were able to establish security, law, and order and reopen major trade routes after years of civil war.[57] The Muslim Brotherhood moved into Egypt and the West Bank and Gaza by establishing a "broad network of mosques, boys' and girls' schools, youth groups, clinics, hospitals, charities, trade unions, night schools for workers, and even factories," whereas the state had failed to do so.[58] In Pakistan, the lack of will and capacity to fund the state school system permitted madrassas to flourish. Although some would disagree that madrassas fuel extremist ideologies or violence in Pakistan, the sorry state of its public schools did foster militancy and help polarize society.[59]

Being prone to conflict, poor and weak states easily intersect with terrorism. Conflict zones not only exacerbate inadequate service delivery and lack of territorial control, but they also provide an arena in which extremists can acquire military and organizational skills.[60] Guerrilla wars and insurgencies in places from Iraq to Afghanistan and Chechnya have provided al Qaeda and its affiliates with a constant flow of battle-hardened recruits. Afghanistan's war against the Soviet Union gave rise to al Qaeda, which began as a recruiting and financial support platform for Afghanistan's jihadists. Thousands of Muslim radicals from countries in the Middle East, North and East Africa, Central Asia, and the Far East morphed into the base that became Osama bin Laden's transnational terrorist organization. Likewise, young Muslim radicals from Western Europe, Indonesia, and Yemen rallied to al Qaeda's cause as a result of the U.S. invasion of Iraq.

These observations are supported by compelling empirical evidence, which has led some to conclude that state weakness "is a significant predictor of transnational terrorism."[61] Countries categorized as being at the highest risk for state failure according to the Fund for Peace's Failed States Index are three times more likely to suffer an attack than are the two categories of strongest states. The five states at the bottom of the index—in 2009 these were Somalia, Zimbabwe, Sudan, Chad, and the DRC—are among the poorest in the world and "are substantially more likely to be the location and source of transnational terrorist attacks than any other category of state rated" by the index, which covers nearly every country in the world.[62] In addition to the Failed States Index, which looks only at factors that are *predictors* of violence and conflict, other evidence has shown that the risk of transnational terrorist activity also rises with political instability, civil wars, and guerrilla warfare."[63]

Compelling as it is, analysis of this nature still rests on poor-quality data and would greatly benefit from further investigation, particularly of individual countries. Moreover, the findings do not show a causal relation between state weakness and terrorist activity, only an empirical one. Nor does this research demonstrate that state weakness is the most important driver inasmuch as strong states may also be vulnerable, but in different ways.[64] Nonetheless, this literature provides specific insights into the mechanisms that render weak states more vulnerable to violent

TABLE 3-2. Vulnerabilities of Poor, Weak States to Violent Extremists[a]

Vulnerability	Operational needs of violent extremist groups	
	Territory/base of operations	Recruits/popular support
Lack of control over territory	Can establish factories, training facilities, storehouses, communication hubs Can evade counterterrorism efforts	Allows organized recruitment activities
Porous borders	Facilitate trafficking in and transshipment of weapons, people, narcotics, dirty money, other contraband	Allow passage of recruits into and out of the country
Lack of effective regulation/weak rule of law	Have easy access to falsified documents Can raise and transfer funds Can establish front businesses, charities, and so on to generate/transfer funds	Perception of injustice leading to increased recruitment or passive support Few or no conflict resolution mechanisms (small claims courts) Unregulated madrassas/mosques/charities can radicalize population
Inadequate social welfare	Widespread passive support for violent extremism complicates counterterrorism operations	Inadequate social welfare creates vacuum, which can be filled by radical NGOs Dissatisfaction with government creates grievances, passive support, or recruitment Government lacks legitimacy
Poverty (for example, unemployment)	State lacks adequate tax base for counterterrorism	Cost of recruitment drops, as legitimate sources of income decrease
Corruption	Officials vulnerable to bribery (falsification of documents)	Perception of injustice/lack of government legitimacy can increase recruitment or passive support
Lack of democratic governance		Lack of voice/accountability reinforces perception of violent extremism as only solution, as individuals increasingly turn to illegitimate modes of expression
History of violence/conflict	Conflict-besieged government is prone to striking Faustian bargain with violent extremists Can operate more freely in fog of war	Culture of violence renders individuals more prone to recruitment Lack of security renders citizens more vulnerable to violent extremists that offer them protection

a. See Ray Takeyh and Nikolas Gvosdev, "Do Terrorist Networks Need a Home?" *Washington Quarterly* 25 (Summer 2002): 97–108.

extremist ideologies and attacks and can help guide development policy. As table 3-2 indicates, weak states meet the needs of violent extremist groups as a base of operations, as well as a source of manpower and popular support. But does this apply throughout the developing world? Which weak states are of particular concern, and why?

VIOLENT EXTREMISM IN THE DEVELOPING WORLD

Events in Yemen suggest that eight years after 9/11, there is no room for complacency in poor, Muslim countries where U.S. interests may be directly at stake. Although the number and lethality of attacks worldwide declined in 2008, most databases show a steady increase in attacks since 2003, and most agree with data from the National Counterterrorism Center suggesting as much as a threefold increase since 2004 (figure 3-1). If the rise since the U.S. invasion of Iraq is factored out, however—attacks in Iraq accounted for 79 percent of total global fatalities from terrorist attacks in 2006—the global average shows a slight decline.[65] Reports focusing exclusively on al Qaeda terrorist activity confirm that violent extremism—except in Iraq—may be decreasing. By one estimate, attacks around the world declined by 65 percent from the high point in 2004, while the resulting fatalities dropped by more than 90 percent.[66] Lack of popular support for terrorist tactics and al Qaeda in key Muslim countries may help explain why global violent extremism is losing steam, as may recent successes in foiling attacks.[67]

These trends lead some observers to argue that the danger of terrorist attacks has been wildly exaggerated since 9/11. It is true that the aggregate number of casualties from terrorist attacks is low in comparison with other life-threatening global dangers, particularly in poor countries. In 2008 a person had about a 1 in 1 million chance of dying in a terrorist attack. The odds of dying from such an attack were slightly higher than the chance of being struck by lightning. According to critics of the Bush administration's "war on terrorism," other global threats—including the proliferation of weapons of mass destruction, global climate change, and the spread of infectious disease—should outrank terrorism on the global agenda. In their view, counterterrorism is essentially a narrow concern of the developed world.

It is certainly useful to keep the threat of terrorist attacks in perspective and not let it overshadow other serious global challenges. As other chapters in this book argue, climate change, disease, and civil conflict pose enormous risks to people in poor countries, and to international security. Even so, the threat of terrorist attacks does continue to worry Americans, particularly in the developing world. So far, the threat is concentrated in a handful of countries, but violent extremists may well seek refuge in increasingly poor, weak countries in the face of counterterrorism campaigns in places like Indonesia and the Philippines. Moreover,

FIGURE 3-1. Global Fatalities from Terrorist Attacks, 1998–2006

Number of fatalities

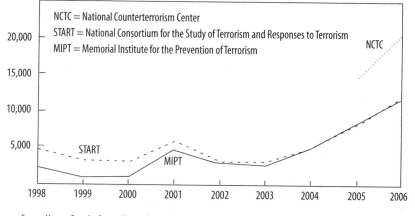

Source: Human Security Center, *Human Security Report 2007* (www.humansecurityreport.info/).

developing countries have more to lose from violent extremism than do their wealthier counterparts.

The most tragic and dramatic attacks of 2008 occurred in Mumbai, India, and were on a scale similar to the 1998 attacks on the U.S. embassies in Kenya and Tanzania, which killed 235 civilians. Other large-scale attacks have occurred in Bali, Indonesia (2002); Madrid, Spain (2004); Amman, Jordan (2005); and the London underground (July 2005). Several potentially large-scale attacks appear to have been foiled, including an attack on JFK airport and on the Fort Dix Army base in New Jersey, as well as on underground transit links in New Jersey in 2006. Aside from these high-profile and foiled attacks, many in Western capitals, the vast majority of incidents tend to be smaller and heavily concentrated in just a few countries that are mired either in conflict or poverty, or both.

There were approximately 11,800 terrorist attacks in the world in 2008, resulting in more than 54,000 deaths, injuries, and kidnappings.[68] Since 2004 twenty-five countries have experienced a high-fatality attack by Sunni extremists, the groups that most concern U.S. officials (figure 3-4). The overwhelming majority were concentrated in about seven countries. Iraq topped the list, followed by Pakistan, Afghanistan, Somalia, and India (figure 3-2). Somalia reported 442 incidents in 2008, with a staggering 1,278 deaths, which included international peacekeepers. Yemen had 71 attacks and 201 deaths. Many of the states on this list

FIGURE 3-2. Countries with Most Terrorism Fatalities

Number of fatalities

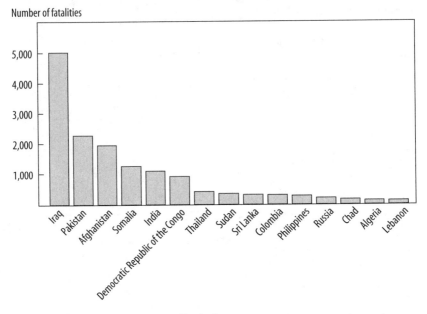

Source: National Counterterrorism Center, *2008 Terrorism Report.*

were in conflict in 2008, and most were either low-income or lower-middle-income countries.[69] By contrast, high-income states of the Organization for Economic Cooperation and Development (OECD) had far fewer attacks on their soil that year: there were several dozen attacks in France, Greece, and Spain, with only a handful in Germany, Italy, and the United States. This variation in the number of attacks across countries merits far more attention.

Far from focusing narrowly on U.S. targets or those just in rich countries, terrorist attacks kill primarily in developing countries around the world. Since 9/11, low-income countries as classified by the World Bank have seen the steepest rise in casualty-causing terrorist attacks, when compared with wealthier countries (figure 3-3).[70] Furthermore, the occurrence of suicide attacks, reported in only a handful of countries before 9/11, is now more common across a broad spectrum of developing countries ranging from Afghanistan, Uzbekistan, and Pakistan to Somalia and Yemen.[71] Policymakers and experts are deeply concerned

FIGURE 3-3. Casualty-Causing Terrorist Attacks by Income Group, 1968–2001

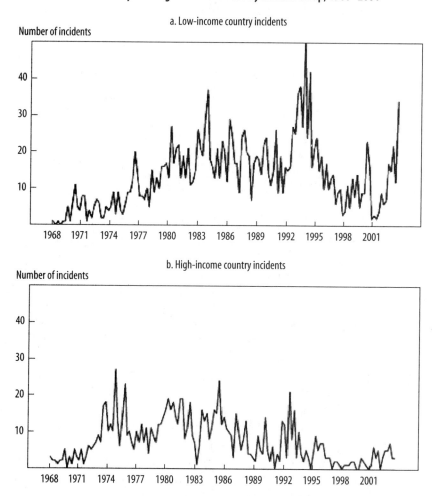

a. Low-income country incidents

Number of incidents

b. High-income country incidents

Number of incidents

Source: Walter Enders and Todd Sandler, "Distribution of Transnational Terrorism among Countries by Income Class and Geography after 9/11," *International Studies Quarterly* 50, no. 2 (2006): 367–93.

about the rise and spread of suicide attacks, as these tend to be particularly lethal and destructive.

Policymakers in the United States in particular should care about the occurrence of attacks in developing countries because many of the targets are Americans (figure 3-5), and violent extremist groups in key

FIGURE 3-4. Rise of High-Fatality Sunni Attacks in Afghanistan and Iraq Compared with the Rest of the World, 2004–08

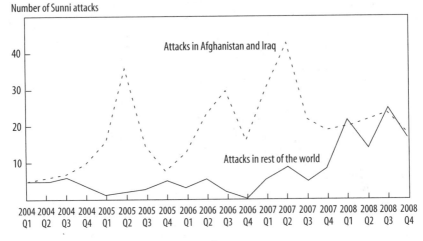

Number of Sunni attacks

Source: National Counterterrorism Center, *2008 Terrorism Report.*

countries around the world pose a threat to the U.S. homeland. Indeed, "there was a greater concentration of deadly post-9/11 incidents involving a U.S. target" in low-income countries than in any other category of countries.[72] The rise of extremism in the Muslim world is a recent phenomenon arising in the late 1970s. Since then the number of religion-based extremist groups has increased as a share of all types of terrorists.[73] New evidence shows that "the rise of fundamentalism is associated with a large and statistically significant increase in transnational terrorism attacks" in low-income states, and fundamentalism has had "virtually all of its impact" in these countries, not in wealthier countries.[74]

The threat of a terrorist attack involving a weapon of mass destruction (WMD) may also be enhanced in the developing world. As a recent British government report on political instability explains, "Leakage of WMD technology, trafficking and further proliferation [are] facilitated by systemic corruption, the presence of organized criminals and terrorists, poor governance, lack of territorial control and state failure, all of which are associated with instability."[75] Thirteen of the seventeen states with current or suspended WMD programs in 2006 (beyond the permanent five of the UN Security Council) were at risk of instability.[76] Weak states are even more likely to serve as the source, transit, and destination

FIGURE 3-5. Terrorist Attacks with a U.S. Target, by Income Group, 1968–2001

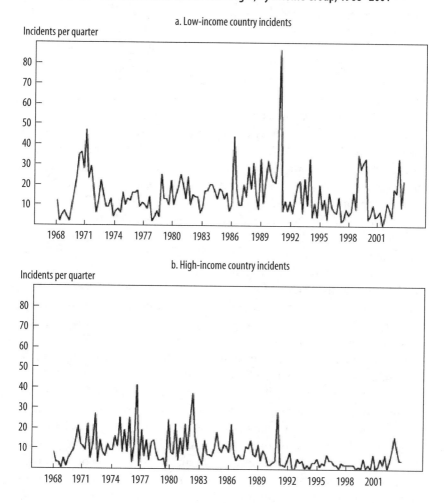

a. Low-income country incidents

b. High-income country incidents

Source: Enders and Sandler, "Distribution of Transnational Terrorism among Countries by Income Class and Geography after 9/11."

of conventional weapons in the illegal arms trade.[77] Because weak states lack the capacity to control the flow of weapons, it is easier to obtain small arms for illicit purposes, including terrorism.

The most serious terrorist threat to U.S. national security today comes from a handful of countries in the developing world, most notably the remote border area between Pakistan and Afghanistan, over which

Pakistan exercises limited control.[78] In July 2007 the U.S. intelligence community released a special report warning that al Qaeda "has protected or regenerated key elements of its Homeland attack capability"[79] operating from a safe haven in the Pakistan Federally Administered Tribal Areas, and possibly building capabilities in Iraq in order to recruit and plan for attacks elsewhere, including perhaps the United States, although "al-Qa'ida today is less capable and effective than it was a year ago."[80] Other high-risk areas include Iraq, Indonesia, the Sahel, Yemen, and East Africa. The 2009 assessment mentions wealthier countries in Europe, as well as Saudi Arabia and "home-grown" extremist groups in the United States, but hastens to warn that developing countries are involved even there. For instance, cells in Europe and the United States benefit from al Qaeda affiliates returning from Pakistan. Key terrorist leaders in the Gulf region have sought refuge in Yemen, thereby posing a threat to Saudi Arabia. Other reports on terrorist havens confirm this list of developing country hot spots, adding places like the Philippines (Mindanao), Somalia, and the Caucasus.[81]

Confronting the threat of violent extremism in the developing world must be a high priority precisely because poor countries that have the least capacity to prevent or respond to terrorist attacks can easily become locked in a doom spiral. Attacks can stretch their already limited resources and capacity, which in turn can make these countries more vulnerable to future attacks. There is strong evidence to suggest that terrorism campaigns such as the one currently under way in Yemen make economic growth even more elusive in such countries.

As is now well known, violent extremists, including al Qaeda, aim not just to take lives but also to strike at the engines of economic growth. The attacks of 9/11 succeeded in wreaking massive economic devastation, causing between $80 billion and $90 billion in lost wages, workers' compensation, and reduced commerce.[82] The per capita cost of such an attack on poor countries whose governments are unable to cushion the blow would be far greater. Following the attacks of September 11, the U.S. Federal Reserve reacted to a surge in liquidity demand by cutting the Federal Funds rate, keeping funds available for investment. The U.S. Congress approved a $40 billion supplemental appropriation for emergency spending on search and rescue efforts at the crash sites, tighter security at airports and other public venues, and disaster relief.[83] The increase in government spending acted as a powerful stimulus to consumer demand. Economists believe the economic cost of the attacks could have been much higher and of longer duration if the government had been unable to implement monetary and fiscal policies in response.

Because most poor countries lack these capabilities, they are much more likely to suffer long-term economic consequences such as higher unemployment or a recession. Following the attacks on the U.S.S. *Cole* and the French supertanker *Limburg,* to cite one example, maritime insurance jumped 300 percent and put Yemen's shipping industry in jeopardy as ships were diverted away from the port of Sana to neighboring ports in Djibouti and Oman.[84] Economists have shown that the countries least able to cope with the economic impact of a terrorist attack are small, poor countries exposed to protracted terrorism campaigns. Somalia and Yemen are two prime examples, but with slightly different policy challenges.

The challenge in Yemen, a country edging toward collapse but still having a modicum of control over parts of its territory, is to help promote development and strengthen capacity in key areas despite widespread public corruption. In Somalia, perhaps the world's only fully collapsed state, it is essential to find a political solution to the conflict and to strengthen the weak transitional government, particularly at the subnational level. In each case, it is critical that U.S. assistance bolster the legitimacy of the state.

YEMEN

Yemen faces perhaps the most difficult challenges of any developing country in which al Qaeda–inspired extremists maintain a presence. While the official poverty rate has declined slightly over the past decade, experts warn that the number of people living below the poverty line is increasing and could reach 55 percent of the population in the wake of the global food crisis.[85] Thirty-five percent of the population was undernourished in 2003–05, and the food shortages are more serious than they are in Angola, Chad, and Rwanda.[86] The 2007 food crisis and ensuing massive food riots could easily recur. Entwined with these economic woes is steep population growth, which now requires Yemen to import over 90 percent of its domestic wheat and rice consumption. Because much of the income used to finance these imports stems from oil revenues, as is the case in many other oil-dependent Muslim countries, Yemen's troubles are now compounded by the decline in crude prices. With oil production dwindling, it is estimated that oil will no longer provide sufficient revenue to pay government workers in a matter of five years or less.[87] Furthermore, Yemen, an extremely arid country located at the southern tip of the Arabian Desert, is running out of water. At current rates of consumption, the groundwater source that supplies the capital city of Sana—with approximately 2 million inhabitants—will be exhausted within twenty years.[88]

Economic trends of this nature intensify the risk of violent extremism. As table 3-3 shows, one of Yemen's main vulnerabilities in this regard is the lack of public financing to enforce border controls and exercise authority over remote parts of the country. As General Anthony Zinni, former commander in chief of the U.S. Central Command, has pointed out, Yemen's "coast is porous. It's a sieve, as are their land borders."[89] Yemen's 1,000-mile border with Saudi Arabia and its shorelines are notoriously dangerous, allowing smugglers to clandestinely transfer people and contraband goods. Throughout the hinterlands, the military's reach is limited, and the government relies mainly on tribesmen who are more committed to meeting the needs of regional tribes than to maintaining national peace and security.[90] What manpower the government does have at its disposal is of limited use, given the shortages of equipment, training, and good intelligence.[91] Where the Saudis can spend $200 million on communications equipment for security if they need to, says Yemeni president Ali Abdullah Saleh, "if we need to spend $1 million, we have to squeeze and save."[92] In the north and northeast, local tribal leaders exercise control largely independently of the central government. The central government's presence over much of Yemen's territory is further hampered by its mountainous and desert terrain.

Porous borders and lack of counterterrorism capacity are precisely the problems that the United States has thus far sought to address in its post-9/11 approach to Yemen. However, the U.S. approach has focused too narrowly on tactical counterterrorism initiatives, largely ignoring the many other significant gaps in state capacity that render Yemen vulnerable to terrorist activity. What little U.S. foreign aid has been provided over and above security assistance (figure 3-6) has been delivered mainly through "carrots-and-sticks" funding to entice the Yemeni government to cooperate in fighting terrorist activity. The investments of other donor countries increasingly dwarf U.S. foreign assistance, diminishing U.S. influence over Yemeni policy.

U.S. foreign assistance spending amounted to just under $20 million in 2008.[93] By contrast, the British government has committed to

TABLE 3-3. Yemen's Vulnerability to Violent Extremism[a]

Weakness	Operational needs of violent extremists in Yemen	
	Territory/base of operations	*Recruits/popular support*
Lack of control over territory	Al Qaeda terrorist training camps Difficulty intercepting terrorism suspects in north Al Qaeda communications hubs	
Porous borders	Availability of weapons	Recruits flow in and out of the country, evading border controls and joining the jihad in other countries
Lack of effective regulation/weak rule of law	Falsified documents available Al Qaeda established front businesses to channel profits and weapons	Few or no conflict resolution mechanisms (small claims courts) Unregulated madrassas and mosques have been used to recruit
Inadequate social welfare	Local tribal leaders, lacking support from central government, ally with al Qaeda and extremists	Interviews reveal Yemenis do not trust their government, which lacks legitimacy
Poverty (for example, unemployment)		Recruits cite lack of jobs as reason for joining violent extremists
Corruption	Shadow employees prevalent in Yemen Bribery widespread; de facto, government relinquishes oversight over funding	Recruits also cite injustices in the way government addresses needs of its citizens
Lack of democratic governance		
History of violence/ conflict	Saleh regime relies heavily on jihadi fighters to tamp down al-Houthi revolt in north	Between 5,000 and 40,000 Yemenis joined jihad in Afghanistan, with many returning to Yemen after Soviet withdrawal An estimated 17 percent of foreign fighters in Iraq were from Yemen, and many have returned

a. This table merely illustrates Yemen's vulnerabilities to al Qaeda terrorism and should not be considered an exhaustive list.

increasing assistance by 400 percent between 2006 and 2011, which amounts to more than $220 million through 2011. As a result, the U.S. government yields very little leverage over Yemen, and "it is no surprise that the Saleh government will not make painful compromises to secure fairly minor U.S. rewards."[94]

U.S. policy in Yemen would be more effective if it were grounded in a better understanding of the entire range of the state's capacity deficits and constraints—including ongoing conflict. In addition to porous

FIGURE 3-6. U.S. Bilateral Economic Assistance to Yemen, 1998–2007

Millions of constant 2007 US$

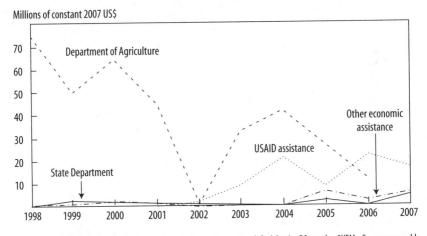

Source: USAID (http://qesdb.usaid.gov/cgi-bin/broker.exe?_service=default&unit=R&cocode=3YEM+&_program=gbk progs.report_country_plot.sas&x=20&y=7).

borders and lack of territorial control, these conditions include the absence of local government capacity, especially in the areas of health and education, lack of employment opportunities, and an ongoing rebellion, as well as domestic unrest (table 3-3).

Absence of Local Government Capacity

Basic public services, especially in the areas of health and education, are virtually nonexistent in Yemen. Aside from roadblocks and military checkpoints along major roadways that lead to oil fields and pipelines, the central government's presence in rural Yemen is hardly perceptible.

Between 2003 and 2006, the latest year for which data are available, public spending on health and education services declined from 8.6 percent of GDP to 7 percent. Health spending is only about 2 percent of GDP. That works out to a meager $11 per person, meaning Yemen ranks almost last in the world in terms of spending on health as a proportion of total expenditures.[95] By contrast, the U.S. government spent about 15.2 percent of its GDP on health care in 2007, or about $6,966 per capita, while Canada spent $3,173 per head and the United Kingdom, $2,560.[96] It is estimated that only 25 percent of Yemen's rural population has access to basic health services and that 30 percent has no access to clean water.[97]

Doctors' salaries are so low that many leave to practice in neighboring countries, such as the United Arab Emirates. Yemen has only 3 doctors per 10,000 people and only 6.1 hospital beds per 10,000 people.[98]

The health and education vacuum in Yemen is often filled by nongovernmental organizations that are difficult to regulate. The country has at least 4,000 underground religious schools serving 330,000 children without any government oversight.[99] The increase in unlicensed religious schools is a concern because some appear to promote a militant ideology.[100] Many of the schools—along with a variety of Islamic welfare institutions such as orphanages, vocational training centers, mosques, charitable societies, hospitals and clinics—are funded by wealthy Saudi patrons and Saudi-based charities. Since the oil boom of the 1970s, Saudi Arabia has spent more than 4 percent of its GDP on overseas aid each year, with two-thirds of that amount going toward "Islamic activities"—essentially, to Saudi proselytizing.[101] Unable to address the needs of their citizens, low-income states like Yemen—as well as Sudan, Mauritania, Nigeria, Somalia, Bosnia, Bangladesh, and Afghanistan—have become the targets of Saudi largesse across the Muslim world.

The role of Islamic—mainly Saudi—charities in spreading radicalism and fueling attacks, especially through madrassas, remains somewhat unclear.[102] A 2002 report of the Council on Foreign Relations stated that charities based in Saudi Arabia have been the most important source of funds for al Qaeda.[103] However, the projects typically funded by these institutions in some of the poorest and most neglected parts of the developing world have had a substantially positive impact on the health and education sectors and advance worthy causes. Their potential to fuel attacks and extremism should not be overplayed. This is certainly true in poverty-stricken Yemen, which has cracked down on extremist schools by establishing a government-mandated curriculum and closing many of the institutions that deviated from this curriculum.[104] The Islah Charitable Society provides humanitarian assistance in every governorate of Yemen and has allocated funding to almost half a million orphans and poor families over the past decade.[105]

Yet the historical record shows that in the prelude to 9/11, extremist charities and schools did funnel resources and people toward al Qaeda, in some cases directly to individuals planning attacks. Some charities were used as safe houses. According to a 2002 report to the United Nations Security Council, Saudi charities and patrons channeled between $300 million and $500 million into al Qaeda and other jihadi outfits.[106] An example of what went on in the schools is provided by John Walker Lindh, the American student who was captured during the U.S.-led invasion of Afghanistan in 2001. Lindh had traveled to Yemen in the 1990s to learn Arabic and become familiar with Islamic culture. While studying at a hard-line Salafi school there, he came into contact with jihadis and was recruited to fight alongside the Taliban in Afghanistan.

Although the main function of unregulated charities may not be to provide direct support or recruits for violent extremists, these institutions help to fill a social vacuum and thus are a constant reminder to Yemenis that their government is failing them: "We don't hate our country. We hate our government. It doesn't take care of us," explains one tribal leader.[107] These attitudes create a hospitable environment for extremist groups in the country. Government officials acknowledge their incapacity to provide for the people: "There is a shortage in Yemenis' lives. . . . The state is really not capable of meeting those needs," explains Yemeni former interior minister Ali Mohammed Othrop.[108] As a result, tribal leaders and Yemeni citizens living in remote areas may be less likely to cooperate with the government on counterterrorism. This represents a significant obstacle to effective intelligence collection and other counterterrorism operations in that the government "needs the co-operation of the local tribes" to intercept terrorist operatives, "but the tribes do not much care for their own government."[109] As a result, "there are many . . . who side with the terrorist organization not so much because they share its goals but because they see it as an ally against an authoritarian and unresponsive regime," explains one Middle East expert.[110]

Lack of Employment Opportunities

When the lack of employment is factored into this equation, the risk becomes even clearer. Because the oil sector dominates Yemen's economy, as it does elsewhere in the developing world, oil-based growth does not generate many local employment opportunities and leaves most of the poor behind.[111] This dynamic will only worsen if oil prices decline again and Yemen's supply of oil dwindles. With employment opportunities scarce, unemployment reached 35 percent in 2003.[112] The oil sector itself makes matters worse by bringing laborers in from neighboring countries, which breeds resentment in the local population.

Several high-profile incidents attest to the link between unemployment and al Qaeda. Salim Hamdan, a Yemeni citizen captured during the invasion of Afghanistan and found guilty by a U.S. military tribunal in 2008 of providing material support to al Qaeda, was recruited for jihad in a Sana mosque, described as a "gathering place for the dispossessed," and thus "exerted an especially strong pull on the country's poor."[113] Hamdan eventually signed on to become bin Laden's driver because "working as a driver and mechanic in bin Laden's motor pool paid better than driving a dabab [minibus] in Sana."[114] As the former spokesman for Yemen's Islamic party explains, "Unless they are the sons of sheiks or political leaders, the young people have no way to use their energies. The one option that is in front of anyone who wants to achieve anything is jihad."

Civil Conflict

The risk of terrorist attacks is also heightened by the outbreaks of civil war dotting Yemen's recent history: a civil conflict in North Yemen between 1962 and 1968 (with 200,000 dead); sectarian violence in South Yemen in 1986 (10,000 dead); another civil war in 1994, this one pitting the recently unified north against the south (7,000 dead); and an ethnic insurgency against the central government that erupted in the north in 2004 and continues to simmer (thousands of deaths).[115] The latest conflict began when a contingent from the largely Sunni government of Saleh tried to arrest the Shia leader of a long-neglected sect based in northern Yemen, and his followers began clashing with government forces. Such clashes make clear the government's inability to hold this diverse country together.

President Saleh fears the conflict poses a threat to the sovereignty and perhaps the very survival of his regime. In an effort to maintain authority, he has formed alliances with and recruited soldiers from various tribal leaders and Sunni groups with a view to expanding his army. Saleh is also said to have turned to former jihadists to bolster the ranks of his security forces. Thus, one journalist observes, Yemen "not only welcomed back its own fighters, it opened its borders to jihadis from other Arab countries as well."[116] Poverty and conflict, added to Yemen's incapacity to provide services to its citizens at the local and regional level and to promote growth and create jobs, act as a powerful fuel for extremism.

The United States could help the government build capacity in the areas of health and education and create jobs through social investments, such as the World Bank Social Fund for Development is making. The United States currently provides some funding through multilateral and bilateral channels, but other agencies—including the British Department for International Development—are doing much more. The World Bank's fund, established over a decade ago, supports three main types of programs: community development, government and NGO capacity building to improve service delivery, and microfinance. With impressive early results, the fund has been hailed as a model of effective development in weak states.[117] By 2004–05 these initial accomplishments included:

—New loans to 25,588 active borrowers and savings accounts to 24,617 active clients

—The creation of 9.4 million man-days of employment through community subprojects

—Increased gross enrollment in basic education from 62.9 percent to 67.6 percent, and additional classes in public schools, rising from 116,788 to 123,322

—Increased access to primary health care for 1.1 million Yemenis, and training to about 730 health care workers and local health committees

—Increased access to water services in 312 communities through projects implemented directly by the communities

—Improved access to rural areas through new roads and other projects that have reduced journey costs and travel times by 40 percent and reduced the price of imported goods

—Training for 593,000 people at all levels of government and in communities through capacity-building interventions, with results including a National Strategy for Childhood and Youth, the development of school design standards, and manuals on rural road interventions.[118]

While it is too early to tell whether this type of program will have sustainable security benefits in Yemen, one thing is certain: reducing unemployment, increasing social service delivery (especially in rural areas), increasing the effectiveness of government, and removing some of the risk factors for conflict should reduce Yemen's vulnerability to terrorist activity in the short term. At the very least, promoting such concrete improvements in the day-to-day lives of ordinary Yemenis would send a clear message to a Yemeni citizenry skeptical of U.S. and Western interests and policy in the country and the region.

SOMALIA

As in Yemen, the incidence of terrorist attacks in Somalia has risen sharply in recent years. The number registered by the U.S. National

Counterterrorism Center jumped from 25 in 2005 to 442 in 2008, with 278 in the first six months of 2009. The rise of violent extremism is difficult to disentangle from the country's ongoing insurgency but is certainly being impelled by other forces as well in what has become the world's most emblematic failed state.

Somalia, located on the Horn of Africa, has a population of between 9 million and 10 million and has been without a central government since 1991. Somalia's capacity to govern through public institutions effectively ceased to exist nearly two decades ago. In the words of Sheik Sharif Ahmed, president of Somalia's Western-backed Transitional Federal Government (TGF) since January 2009, "The economy is non-existent. State institutions are non-existent. Essential services are non-existent."[119] Since the fall of strongman Siad Barre in 1991, Somalia has remained in chaos, although some clan-based, religious, and private institutions do provide much-needed governance and social services. Rivaling militias jostling for power have clashed violently over the course of the past two decades. Ironically, Somalia's deepening fragmentation has had a moderating effect on the intensity of armed conflicts. The violence has become more local and less lethal than the wars of the 1990s.[120] Yet violent anarchy still reigns over much of south and central Somalia. *New York Times* correspondent Jeffrey Gettleman graphically captures the living conditions in the capital city of Mogadishu:

> Death comes more frequently and randomly than ever before. I met one man . . . who was chatting with his wife on her cell-phone when she was cut in half by a stray mortar shell. Another man I spoke to went out for a walk, got shot in the leg during a crossfire, and had to spend seven days eating grass before the fighting ended and he could crawl away."[121]

When a state collapses and conflict simmers, the most tragic and immediate consequence is often humanitarian crisis. Somalia was the epicenter of the world's most severe humanitarian catastrophe in 2008 in terms of number of lives at risk and people dependent on emergency assistance. Over the years, 1 million refugees have fled the fighting.[122] Decades of war, internal displacement, and drought have caused widespread famine, with one out of every four Somalis malnourished. Malnutrition exceeds the level defined by the United Nations as the threshold for a humanitarian emergency. The country ranks lowest by almost every measure of development. About 73 percent live on less than $2.00 a day.

More than one out of every five children die before the age of five, and of those who survive, most will never be enrolled in any formal education program.

According to some intelligence analysts, there have been few risks to international security in Somalia, which has presented mainly a moral challenge of preventing further loss of life and improving the quality of life. Correspondence documenting al Qaeda's early operations in the Horn of Africa in the 1990s suggested that the environment there presented significant obstacles to the organization: "Foreign terror suspects operating in Somalia are prone to extortion and betrayal; can get caught up in clan conflicts; are easily visible in a context of few foreign visitors; and face difficulties of communication, transportation, disease and access to clean water."[123] As a result, Somalia appeared to be an unfavorable place "for foreign terrorists to operate in or from."[124] Argues Somalia expert Ken Menkhaus, terrorist cells prefer weak states over collapsed states.[125]

That was then. By 2009 al Qaeda–affiliated extremists had built a growing presence in the country. While the threat of violent extremism in Somalia should not be exaggerated, and viewing conditions in Somalia through a narrow counterterrorism lens has proved disastrous for U.S. foreign policy, the threat is real. The main risk in Somalia currently stems from a radical militant force called the al Shabaab, or youth movement. The group emerged in 2005 as a hard-line military force associated with the broader and generally more moderate Islamic Courts Union (ICU), a grass-roots movement that has formed the core of the Islamist insurgency in Somalia. More recently, al Shabaab has been blamed for suicide bombings and killings, as well as for hiding al Qaeda suspects involved in the 1998 bombings of the U.S. embassies in Kenya and Tanzania.[126] The State Department's *Country Reports on Terrorism 2006* states that al Shabaab consists of radicalized young men in their twenties and thirties, some having trained with al Qaeda in Afghanistan. Starting in 2006, a steady flow of foreign jihadi volunteers entered Somalia to join al Shabaab, now suspected of including several hundred foreigners. Suicide attacks have been on the rise, targeting UN facilities, government buildings, peacekeepers, and civilians. In its 2009 annual threat assessment, the U.S. intelligence community concluded that al Qaeda will continue to plot operations against U.S., Western, and other targets in the country, and that popular support for al Shabaab will likely grow.[127] Terrorism experts are particularly concerned, given the role of Somalia-based cells in helping to carry out the 1998 U.S. embassy bombings, the bombing of a Mombasa, Kenya, hotel in 2003, and an attempted attack on the U.S. embassy in Nairobi in 2003.[128]

Another transnational threat stemming from Somalia's anarchy that has grabbed world attention is the growing epidemic of Somali-based piracy attacks, now occurring almost daily off the country's long coast. In April 2009 Somali pirates captured the U.S. captain of the container ship *Maersk Alabama*, who was later rescued by Navy SEALs. In 2008 alone, Somali pirates hijacked forty-two vessels, earning $100 million in ransom and threatening international shipping lanes in one of the world's most heavily traveled waterways.[129] By June 2009, these attacks had already reached 114, surpassing the 111 attempted attacks in 2008. For some, Somalia's pirates are "just the current iteration of the country's infamous warlords, making millions off the chaos around them and spreading some of the wealth to the grunts beneath them." [130]

To be sure, most Somalis have little appetite for salafi ideology and jihad, yet violent extremism persists in their midst for a variety of reasons (see table 3-4)—one being anti-American and anti-Western sentiment, which terrorist leaders exploit in motivating recruits to launch attacks. Long-standing political repression is another factor, which makes terrorist attacks difficult to disentangle from local, clan-based violence and insurgency. Still, poverty and state collapse have played a critical role in transforming Somalia into an attractive haven.

Absence of Rule of Law

Lacking a national system of rule of law, Somalia has given regional al Qaeda cells a secure location "practically opaque to Western and regional security forces," as well as to criminal justice systems and counterterrorism initiatives. The al Qaeda cells that carried out attacks in East Africa were based in and operated from Somalia.[131] From this safe haven, they marshaled funding, facilitated planning, provided expertise to attackers, and procured weapons for the attacks.

Persistence of Conflict, Absence of Public Services and Unemployment

Equally important, the war zone that has ravaged many parts of Somalia provides a refuge to renegades hiding from the law. On several occasions, U.S. drone attacks have missed their intended targets in part because the conflict zone is difficult to penetrate. Al Qaeda operatives

TABLE 3-4. Somalia's Vulnerability to Violent Extremism[a]

	Operational needs of violent extremist groups in Somalia	
Weakness	Territory/base of operations	Recruits/popular support
Lack of control over territory	Potential training ground for Saudi recruits to extremist violence Training camps based around Mogadishu Difficult for United States to intercept terrorist suspects	Al Qaeda operatives move freely in and out of Somalia Influx of foreign jihadi volunteers
Porous borders	Transfer weapons, which can be obtained at lowest international market price Channel funds across border	Al Qaeda operatives move freely in and out of Somalia Influx of foreign jihadi volunteers
Lack of effective regulation/weak rule of law	Violence extremists evade government authority	
Inadequate social welfare	Private charities have channeled funds to al Qaeda	Provision of social welfare buys the allegiance of citizens
Poverty (for example, unemployment)	No state apparatus and no financing for counterterrorism	No legitimate means of employment
Corruption		Loyalty can be bought by just about anyone with the means
Lack of democratic governance		
History of violence/ conflict	Territory is opaque to external security forces	Insurgency against Western-backed government serves as international rallying cry Provision of security increases popular support

a. This table merely illustrates Somalia's vulnerabilities to Islamist terrorism and should not be considered exhaustive.

have been able to move freely around Somalia "with little or no visibility by external security and intelligence agencies."[132]

In addition, the persistent insecurity plaguing south and central Somalia has rendered ordinary Somalis more likely to support and join radical groups like al Shabaab. The Islamic Courts Union, initially a moderate clan-based movement that has recently been radicalized, gained broad popular appeal after bringing an element of peace and security to Mogadishu and its surroundings. Much as the Taliban had done in Afghanistan a decade earlier, the ICU garnered the loyalty of the population and seized hold over the country in 2006 largely by providing health care, education, and security. Most visitors to Mogadishu in this period were struck by the ICU's accomplishments: "Road-blocks were removed and even the ubiquitous piles of rubbish that had blighted the city for a decade or more were cleared. The main Mogadishu airport and seaport were reopened and rehabilitated for the first time in a decade. Squatters were made to vacate government buildings, illegal land grabs were halted, and special courts were opened to deal with the myriad claims for the restitution of property."[133]

Although most nongovernmental service providers operating in Somalia and substituting for the government have benevolent intentions, some have channeled and raised funds for al Qaeda.[134] Owing to religious and cultural differences, many ordinary Somalis are wary of radical groups like al Shabaab. Yet many young, unemployed men have few options other than to join the extremists. One al Shabaab recruit acknowledged he joined because the group's leaders promised him an income of $300 a month.[135]

What can be done in Somalia to help turn the situation around? Clearly, addressing the above vulnerabilities is a tall order since public institutions must be built from the ground up. Despite nearly two decades of engagement in the country, donors have made few inroads. Since the 1993 Black Hawk Down incident and death of eighteen American soldiers, Western military engagement has become politically unsellable and is highly unlikely. The recent surge in anti-Americanism only serves to complicate matters.

As in Yemen, U.S. policy toward Somalia has been off balance, focusing primarily on a short-term, tactical counterterrorism strategy that has not yielded results and, if anything, appears to have been counterproductive. The U.S.-sanctioned 2006 Ethiopian military incursion into the country "succeeded in ousting an increasingly radical Islamist movement, the Islamic Courts Union, but provoked a brutal cycle of insurgency and counterinsurgency that plunged the country into new depths of misery."[136] U.S. airstrikes against al Qaeda regional leaders have failed to hit many of their designated targets and only served to radicalize the population. The U.S. policy of supporting corrupt, violent Mogadishu-based warlords in 2005 is widely believed to have fueled the rise of al Shabaab and helped the ICU garner broadly based support and win the state.[137] U.S. and Western support of successive transitional governments that have relied on harsh tactics and that focus on narrow clan politics merely helps build support for radical Islamists.[138] Likewise, other countries have dealt with the surge in piracy largely through naval operations, including international armed convoys and rescue missions off the shores of Somalia. Such security-based approaches tend to ignore the underlying problems that invite terrorism, piracy, and other kinds of criminality. The resulting challenges are daunting—but must be met.

The ultimate goal in Somalia must include an effort to build and strengthen a viable central government that can begin to provide adequate security and welfare to its people. Because central and southern Somalia are in the midst of a hot conflict, however, the process must consist of two steps, the first focusing on stabilization and the second on conflict-sensitive development and state-building activities.

Somalia specialist Ken Menkhaus and others find it difficult to see how progress can be made on the stabilization front without the presence of a robust international peacekeeping force.[139] The African Union Mission to Somalia (AMISOM), a regional peacekeeping force of 4,300 soldiers approved by the UN Security Council in 2006, is mandated to support the Transitional Federal Government and to assist in providing security for humanitarian assistance. But in a country of 9 million people, this puny force can barely step out beyond Mogadishu. As a result, aid agencies on the ground have been unable to distribute much aid. Not surprisingly, a recent report on U.S. strategy in Somalia found that despite receiving $242 million in American food aid between 2001 and 2007, "the country's acute malnutrition rates, which remain above the emergency threshold in some parts of the country," have not dropped.[140]

Beyond bolstering the international force, other important steps to improve security on the ground should include a strategy to draw neighboring countries involved in the conflict into the process of political reconciliation; significantly better analysis of conditions on the ground, and of the country's social, political, and cultural dynamics; a diplomatic effort to promote peace that takes in all influential domestic groups; a focus on human rights and accountability in the transitional government; and less reliance on covert U.S. military intervention, which is decimating America's standing in the country.

When the level of violence begins to drop, the United States and other donors should continue to provide humanitarian assistance, especially conflict-sensitive aid. From the outset, the aim should be to help build sustainable security and to reduce the incentives for individuals to support and join violent extremist groups. Among the lessons the World Bank and other donors have learned about this type of assistance, a primary one is the importance of identifying the aid recipients who are the potential winners and losers.[141] Priority should also be given to aid programs that avoid strengthening one clan at the expense of another. Small-scale projects tend to be less susceptible to lineage-based competition and division. Programs that help to manage natural resources and resource revenues in a transparent and fair manner would also help.

Once the violence subsides, much can be done to begin rebuilding Somalia's institutions, even before an effective government is restored in Mogadishu. As in Yemen, community-driven projects and initiatives should be emphasized from day one to help restore trust in the government's capacity to deliver desperately needed services to its citizens. But the trick will be to deliver aid without further polarizing different factions. The silver lining is that during the two-decade conflict, Somali communities have "been forced to employ a range of strategies to cope in a situation of extremely limited support from outside the lineage (that is, from government or domestic and international organizations)."[142] As a result, community-driven development is not only likely to be an effective way to circumvent the lack of capacity at the national level, but it is particularly well suited to local institutions and practices in this deeply fragmented country.

CONCLUSION

Despite much commentary to the contrary, there is little convincing evidence to suggest that poverty does not affect the incidence of terrorist attacks. The body of scholarly research thus far has failed to establish this, let alone explain how to measure terrorism. Hence the quantitative data and ensuing research disputing such a relationship remain a poor guide for policy.

More convincing is the mounting evidence confirming that poor, weak states are vulnerable to violent extremists. It helps explain why deadly attacks seem to occur mainly in the developing world, and why anti-American terrorist activity is concentrated in countries and regions that face daunting development challenges. Yemen and Somalia illustrate the difficulty of sustaining counterterrorism efforts in countries plagued by economic decline or dire poverty. Not only is the threat of attacks in these countries unlikely to disappear without some attempt to address poverty and weakness, but further poverty and violence are also in store for them unless donors help to break this vicious cycle. This does not mean that developed countries are not vulnerable, but simply that extremist violence is more likely to arise wherever governments are unable to provide for their citizens. Given the global reach of extremist groups today, the risk of terrorist activity even in distant countries has important implications for U.S. interests. Building consensus on this point is an important first step toward solving the operational question of what it will take to reduce support for and participation in violent extremism in poor, weak states.

In part what it will take is a more refined long-term approach to the threat of violent extremism, which can only be achieved through more in-depth analysis of terrorist activity and its parameters in weak states. Policymakers have had sound instincts on this subject for over a decade, with many officials warning especially since the attacks of 9/11 that weak and failed states represent a danger to security in the twenty-first century. Data show that attacks are particularly lethal, prevalent, and likely to target Americans in the developing world. Yet how and why such states increase the risk of transnational attacks and pose a risk to neighboring countries remains poorly understood. The factors that make poor states vulnerable to extremists need to be fleshed out to better inform preventive policies.

It also needs to be recognized that the fight against terrorist activity as conducted under previous administrations, particularly the Bush administration, is not serving the nation well, as illustrated in Yemen and Somalia. Targeted assassinations, precision strikes against so-called high-value targets, and other tactical measures may have removed some of al Qaeda's leadership in key developing countries, but in the absence of a wider strategy, such tactical measures will not produce sustainable progress. These countries are a concrete reminder that the United States needs to craft a long-term plan to dissuade the next generation of violent extremists from taking up arms. In this vein, President Barack Obama has refashioned the U.S. approach to Afghanistan and Pakistan, placing more emphasis than his predecessor on a military strategy for stabilizing Afghanistan and providing more economic assistance to Pakistan with a view to jump-starting that country's economy.

By and large, U.S. policy since 9/11 has focused primarily on providing counterterrorism support to poor countries of strategic concern. Far too little thinking has gone into how to use U.S. foreign assistance policy and development to help prevent and diminish the appeal of violent extremism, and to help increase the legitimacy of key Muslim-majority states. Likewise, too few U.S. aid dollars are being invested in people and development in these countries.[143] For instance, 60 percent of the $10 billion spent on U.S. aid to Pakistan since 2001 has gone toward reimbursing U.S. partners for their assistance in counterterrorism operations, not to assistance programs.[144] And most of the $50 billion in U.S. aid invested in Egypt since 1979 has gone toward military assistance, while economic assistance to that country has not targeted Egypt's flailing economy and lack of opportunities.

Admittedly, many of the majority-Muslim states in which poverty intersects with violent extremism are "difficult partnership countries." The challenge of providing effective aid in such areas should not be underestimated (see chapter 7). Despite their considerable natural wealth, many countries in the Arab world have experienced limited economic and social progress, largely because democratic governance and political freedoms are unknown.[145] Poor countries there and throughout the developing world have suffered deep divisions and conflict. A lack of democracy and a history of conflict are precisely the conditions under which traditional aid is least effective, primarily because they preclude effective mechanisms for managing and absorbing aid. Investing in rule of law programs, including measures to provide or build police capacity, is one way to reestablish security and improve the effective delivery of aid.

Development agencies such as the World Bank, the British Department for International Development, and the U.S. Agency for International Development have tackled the challenge of aid to fragile states head on, and their work has yielded valuable lessons for U.S. policy. Donors must heed these lessons by committing the resources and policies necessary to address the threat of terrorist attacks in poor, weak states. One means to this end would be community-based development, which is particularly well-adapted to countries with very weak or nonexistent central institutions since grass-roots service providers often emerge spontaneously to fill the void in war zones. It will be important, however, to resist the temptation to exclude and alienate all Muslim charities and social welfare providers and to prevent further divisions in strife-ridden societies. Most of these are moderate institutions and play a critical role in the absence of state institutions. In poor regions where violent extremists have maintained a foothold, there are simply no good alternatives. A striking example is Afghanistan's program of National Solidarity, a joint effort by the international community and the Afghan government to reach the country's rural communities directly through a participatory approach to development. Community programs implemented at the village level have already reached 13 million rural people and have benefited from critical services, including access to an improved water source, new roads, and numerous other small infrastructure projects, which draw nearly 80 percent of their staff from local communities.[146]

The effectiveness of such programs has yet to be proved, given their novelty. As the Yemen case and initial evaluations by the World Bank suggest, however, these endeavors show promise. They not only address the vulnerabilities cited in this chapter but also help build international support for the United States, even in places where U.S. standing remains abysmally low. The surge of goodwill toward the United States in response to U.S. aid for the 2004 tsunami victims is but one reminder of this potential. Assistance in poor Muslim countries could go a long way toward showing U.S. commitment to the needs of people in these states, and could help rally more international partners to the cause of counterterrorism. Attacks are growing more numerous and deadly in the developing world, where security controls tend to be more lax; preventing terrorist attacks would save lives first and foremost in developing countries. In addition to protecting U.S. national security, incorporating development assistance into an international counterterrorism strategy is a long-overdue global solution to a global problem.

NOTES

1. National Commission on Terrorist Attacks upon the United States, *9/11 Commission Report: Final Report of the National Commission on Terrorist Attacks upon the United States* (New York: W. W. Norton, 2004).

2. Jeremy Sharp, "Yemen: Background and U.S. Foreign Relations," Report RL34170 (Congressional Research Service, January 22, 2009). It remains unclear whether and how the Obama administration will change course in Yemen. To date, Obama policy has focused primarily on Yemen's rehabilitation program for returning Yemeni detainees still held in the U.S. detention center in Guantanamo Bay, Cuba. See "CIA Deputy Chief Visits Yemen for Talks on Fighting Terrorism," Associated Press, May 28, 2009.

3. Gregory Johnsen, "Al Qaida in Yemen's 2008 Campaign," *CTC Sentinel*, April 2008.

4. Gregory D. Johnsen, "Al Qaeda in Yemen Reorganizes under Nasir al-Wahayshi," *Terrorism Focus* 5, no. 11 (Washington: Jamestown Foundation, March 18, 2008).

5. "Death Toll in Yemen Rises to 19," *International Herald Tribune*, September 21, 2008.

6. Yoram Schweitzer and Sari Goldstein Ferber, "Al-Qaeda and the Internationalization," JCSS Report 55 (Tel Aviv: Jaffee Center for Strategic Studies, November 2005); Council on Foreign Relations, "CFR Backgrounder: Terrorism Havens: Yemen," December 2005; "U.S. Moves Commandos to Base in East Africa," *New York Times*, September 18, 2002, p. A14; Mohammed Sudan, "Yemen Certain French Tanker Was Deliberately Hit," Reuters World News, October 13, 2002.

7. Donna Abu-Nasr, "Fears of Yemen Turning into Another Afghanistan," Associated Press, May 3, 2009.

8. Donald Rumsfeld, Secretary of Defense, "Memorandum on the Global War on Terrorism," October 16, 2003.

9. Michael Knights, "U.S. Embassy Bombing in Yemen: Counterterrorism Challenges in Weak States," Policy Watch 1404 (Washington Institute for Near East Policy, 2008), p. 2; Gregory Johnsen, "Al Qaeda's Generational Split," *Boston Globe*, November 9, 2007.

10. The population growth rate is estimated to be more than 3 percent. See World Bank, *World Development Indicators 2009* (Washington, 2009).

11. Gregory Johnsen, "Well Gone Dry: A Letter from Sana," *National Interest* 11, no. 2 (2006): 131–39; Abu-Nasr, "Fears of Yemen Turning into Another Afghanistan."

12. See Johnsen, "Well Gone Dry." See also David Shinn, "Al Qaeda in East Africa and the Horn," *Journal of Conflict Studies* 27 (Winter 2007): 47–75; Zacahry Abuza, *Militant Islam in Southeast Asia* (Boulder, Colo.: Lynne Rienner, 2003); and Ahmed Rashid, *Jihad: The Militant Islam in Central Asia* (Yale University Press, 2002).

13. Brookings counterterrorism expert Dan Byman warns of the possible consequences of the crisis for transnational terrorism. See "Global Financial Crisis and Counterterrorism," Middle East Strategy at Harvard blog (http://blogs.law.harvard.edu/mesh/2009/05/global-financial-crisis-and-counterterrorism/).

14. National Commission on Terrorist Attacks, *9/11 Commission Report*, p. 379.

15. Madeleine K. Albright and others, *Combating Catastrophic Terror: A Security Strategy for the Nation* (Washington: Center for American Progress Action Fund, 2005), p. ii.

16. Gregory Johnsen, "Empty Economic Reforms Slow Bid to Join the GCC," *Arab Reform Bulletin*, 2007.

17. Alfred B. Prados and Jeremy Sharp, "Yemen: Current Conditions and U.S. Relations," CSR Report RS21808 (Congressional Research Service, January 4, 2007).

18. Knights, "U.S. Embassy Bombing in Yemen."

19. Julie Ray and Mohamed Younis, "Approval of U.S. Leadership Up in Some Arab Countries," *Gallup,* June 1, 2009 (www.gallup.com).

20. Robert Barro, "The Myth That Poverty Breeds Terrorism," *Business Week,* June 10, 2002. See also Guy Giorno, "Blinding Ourselves to Ugly Truths," *Toronto Star,* September 22, 2002; Scott Atran, "Who Wants to Be a Martyr," *New York Times,* May 5, 2003; and "Hatred Drives Bombers," Editorial, *Washington Post,* September 16, 2004.

21. Alan B. Krueger and Jitka Maleckova, "Education, Poverty and Terrorism: Is There a Causal Connection?" *Journal of Economic Perspectives* 17 (Fall 2003): 119–44.

22. See, for instance, Alan B. Krueger and D. D. Laitin, "*Kto Kogo?* A Cross-Country Study of the Origins and Targets of Terrorism," in *Terrorism, Economic Development, and Political Openness,* edited by Philip Keefer and Norman Loayza (Cambridge University Press, 2003); Alberto Abadie, "Poverty, Political Freedom, and the Roots of Terrorism," *American Economic Review* 96, no. 2 (2006): 50–56; James Piazza, "Rooted in Poverty? Terrorism, Poor Economic Development and Social Cleavages," *Terrorism and Political Violence* 18 (March 2006): 159–77.

23. Peter Bergen and Michael Lind, "A Matter of Pride: Why We Can't Buy Off the Next Osama bin Laden," *Democracy: A Journal of Ideas* 3 (Winter 2007): 9.

24. Yemeni deputy prime minister, quoted in Ian Black, "Yemen Terrorism: Soft Approach to Jihadists Starts to Backfire as Poverty Fuels Extremism," (Manchester) *Guardian,* July 30, 2008.

25. Alistair Lyon, "Yemen Staring at Famine Next Year," Reuters, June 7, 2009; former Yemeni foreign minister Abdulkareem al-Eryani, "A Poverty Plan," *New York Times* June 2, 2009; Alex Perry, "Somalia's Crisis: Not Piracy, but Its People's Plight," *Time,* June 5, 2009; Shinn, "Al Qaeda in East Africa and the Horn"; Bill Keller, "Springtime for Saddam," *New York Times,* April 6, 2002; Jessica Stern, *Terror in the Name of God: Why Religious Militants Kill* (New York: Ecco, 2003).

26. Angel Rabasa and others, *Ungoverned Territories: Understanding and Reducing Terrorism Risks* (Santa Monica, Calif.: RAND, 2007).

27. Scheherezade Faramarzi, "In Slum Home to Suicide Bombers, the Desperation Continues," Associated Press Worldstream, May 15, 2005.

28. Andrea Elliott, "Where Boys Grow Up to Be Jihadis," *New York Times,* November 25, 2007.

29. Hassan Fattah, "Fighting in Lebanese Refugee Camp Rages, and Spreads," *New York Times,* June 4, 2007.

30. Elaine Sciolino, "Europe Confronts Changing Face of Terrorism," *New York Times,* August 1, 2005.

31. Emily Wax, "Calls Shed Light on Gunmen's Motives: Officials Say Two Mumbai Attackers Voiced Numerous Grievances," *Washington Post*, December 16, 2008.

32. "The Answer to Terrorist Bombs," *Sydney Morning Herald*, August 7, 2003.

33. Killian Clarke and Andrew Gordon, "Al Qaeda's Hypocrisy: The Globalization of Terrorism," Harvard College Globalization Project (www.harvard globalization.com/magazine/al-qaedas-hypocrisy-the-globalization-of-terrorism).

34. Douglas Farah, "Jihadists Now Targeting Africa," June 19, 2006 (www. douglasfarah.com/).

35. Pew Global Attitudes Project, "Islamic Extremism: Common Concern for Muslim and Western Publics" (Washington: Pew Research Center, 2005).

36. Robert Pape, *Dying to Win: The Strategic Logic of Suicide Terrorism* (New York: Random House, 2005).

37. Eli Berman, "Hamas, Taliban and the Jewish Underground: An Economist's View of Radical Religious Militias," Working Paper 10004 (Cambridge, Mass.: National Bureau of Economic Research, 2003).

38. On the selection of highly skilled individuals by terrorist organizations, see Diego Gambetta and Steffen Hertog, "Engineers of Jihad: Why Engineering Graduates Are Over-Represented among Radical Islamists," paper presented at the Peace Research Institute, Oslo, August 10, 2006; Effi Benmelech, Claude Berrebi, and Esteban F. Klor, "Economic Conditions and the Quality of Suicide Terrorism" (January 1, 2009) (http://ssrn.com/abstract=1367828). On the alienation of terrorist recruits, see Marc Sageman, *Understanding Terror Networks* (University of Pennsylvania Press, 2004).

39. Byman, "Global Financial Crisis and Counterterrorism."

40. S. Brock Blomberg and Gregory Hess, "From (No) Butter to Guns?" in *Terrorism, Economic Development and Political Openness,* edited by Keefer and Loayza, pp. 83–115 (Cambridge University Press, 2008).

41. Benjamin Wittes and Zaahira Wyne, "The Current Detainee Population of Guantanamo: An Empirical Study," Brookings Governance Studies (December 16, 2008) (www.brookings.edu/reports/2008/1216_detainees_wittes.aspx).

42. The U.S. government defines terrorism as any activity involving violent or life-threatening acts that are criminal and intended to intimidate or coerce civilians, or to influence policy or otherwise influence the conduct of government. See U.S. Federal Criminal Code, 18 U.S.C. sec. 2331.

43. Charles Tilly, "Terror, Terrorists, Terrorism," *Sociological Theory* 22 (March 2004): 5–13.

44. See, for instance, Basel Saleh, "Economic Conditions and Resistance to Occupation in the West Bank and Gaza Strip: There Is a Causal Connection," *Topics in Middle Eastern and North African Economies,* no. 6 (2004).

45. See Hilal Khashan, "Collective Palestinian Frustration and Suicide Bombings," *Third World Quarterly* 24, no. 6 (2003): 1049–67.

46. James Honaker, "Unemployment and Violence in Northern Ireland: A Missing Data Model for Ecological Inference," paper presented at the annual meeting of the Midwest Political Science Association, Chicago, April 15, 2005.

47. Pape, *Dying to Win.*

48. Krueger and Maleckova, "Education, Poverty and Terrorism."

49. See especially Krueger and Laitin *"Kto Kogo?"*; Abadie, "Poverty, Political Freedom, and the Roots of Terrorism"; and Piazza, "Rooted in Poverty?"

50. See S. Brock Blomberg and others, "Terrorism from Within: An Economic Model of Terrorism," Working Papers in Economics (Claremont Colleges, 2002); Brian Burgoon, "On Welfare and Terror: Social Welfare Policies and Political-Economic Roots of Terrorism," *Journal of Conflict Resolution* 50, no. 2 (2006): 176–203; Quan Li and Drew Schaub, "Economic Globalization and Transnational Terrorism: A Pooled Time-Series Analysis," *Journal of Conflict Resolution* 48 (April 2004): 230–58; and Ana Bela Santos Bravo and Carlos Manuel Mendes Dias, "An Empirical Analysis of Terrorism: Deprivation, Islamism and Geopolitical Factors," *Defense and Peace Economics* 17, no. 4 (2006): 329–41.

51. One study that has found weak evidence of a link between democracy and terrorism is Konstantinos Drakos and Andreas Gofas, "In Search of the Average Transnational Terrorist Attack Venue," *Defence and Peace Economics* 17 (April 2006): 73–93. For a study that claims political freedom explains terrorism, see Abadie, "Poverty, Political Freedom, and the Roots of Terrorism."

52. See "Terrorism and Poverty: Any Connection?" Becker-Posner blog, 2005 (www.becker-posner-blog.com/archives/2005/05/terrorism_and_p_1.html).

53. Tilly, "Terror, Terrorists, Terrorism."

54. See Sageman, *Understanding Terror Networks.*

55. National Commission on Terrorist Attacks, *9/11 Commission Report,* p. 366.

56. Ray Takeyh and Nikolas Gvosdev, "Do Terrorist Networks Need a Home?" *Washington Quarterly* 25 (Summer 2002): 97–108; Cristina C. Brafman Kittner, "The Role of Safe Havens in Islamist Terrorism," *Terrorism and Political Violence* 19, no. 3 (2007): 307–29; Rabasa and others, *Ungoverned Territories.*

57. Berman, "Hamas, Taliban and the Jewish Underground," p. 6.

58. Ibid., pp. 7–8.

59. Saleem Ali, "Pakistan's Madrassahs and Extremism: Is There a Connection?" (Brookings Doha Center, March 18, 2009); Omer Taspinar, *Fighting Radicalism with Human Development* (Brookings, forthcoming); C. Christine Fair, "Islamic Education in Pakistan" (Washington: United States Institute of Peace, 2006); Tariq Rahman, *Denizens of Alien Worlds: A Study of Education, Inequality and Polarization in Pakistan* (Oxford University Press, 2004).

60. Nauro F. Campos and Martin Gassebner, "International Terrorism,

Political Instability and the Escalation Effect," Discussion Paper (Bonn: Institute for the Study of Labor, 2009).

61. James Piazza, "Incubators of Terror: Do Failed and Failing States Promote Transnational Terrorism?" *International Studies Quarterly* 52, no. 3 (2008): 469–88. See also Brian Lai, "Draining the Swamp: An Empirical Examination of the Production of International Terrorism, 1968–1998," *Conflict Management and Peace Science* 24, no. 4 (2007): 297–310; and Burgoon, "On Welfare and Terror."

62. Piazza, "Incubators of Terror."

63. Campos and Gassebner, "International Terrorism, Political Instability and the Escalation Effect."

64. Joshua Sinai, "The Evolving Terrorist Threat: The Convergence of Terrorism, Proliferation of WMD, and Enabling Conditions in Weak and Strong States," *Journal of Counterterrorism and Homeland Security International* 13, no. 2 (2007): 10–16.

65. See Human Security Center, *Human Security Report 2007* (www.human securityreport.info/).

66. IntelCenter, *Jihadi Attack Kill Statistics (JAKS)*, vol. 8 (August 2007); and IntelCenter, *Jihadi Ops Tempo Statistics (JOTS)*, vol. 6 (July 2007).

67. PEW Global Attitudes Project, "A Rising Tide Lifts Mood in the Developing World: Sharp Decline in Support for Suicide Bombing in Muslim Countries" (Washington: Pew Research Center, July 24, 2007).

68. National Counterterrorism Center, *2008 Terrorism Report* (www.nctc. gov).

69. For conflict data, see Monty Marshall, *Major Episodes of Political Violence* (www.systemicpeace.org/warlist.htm). Income groups are based on the World Bank classification.

70. Walter Enders and Todd Sandler, "Distribution of Transnational Terrorism among Countries by Income Class and Geography after 9/11," *International Studies Quarterly* 50, no. 2 (2006): 367–93.

71. Assaf Moghadam, "Motives for Martyrdom: Al Qaida, Salafi Jihad and the Spread of Suicide Attacks," *International Security* 33, no. 3 (2008/2009): 46–78.

72. Enders and Sandler, "Distribution of Transnational Terrorism among Countries," p. 383.

73. Bruce Hoffman, *Inside Terrorism* (Columbia University Press, 1997).

74. Enders and Sandler, "Distribution of Transnational Terrorism among Countries," p. 383.

75. Prime Minister's Strategy Unit (Cabinet Office), "Investing in Prevention: An International Strategy to Manage Risks of Instability and Improve Crisis Response" (London: February 2005), p. 30.

76. Stewart Patrick, "Weak States and Global Threats: Fact or Fiction?" *Washington Quarterly* 29, no. 2 (2006): 27–53.

77. Ibid.

78. National Commission on Terrorist Attacks, *9/11 Commission Report*; and Bruce Riedel, "Pakistan and the Terror: The Eye of the Storm," *Annals of the American Academy of Political and Social Science*, 618 (July 2008).

79. National Intelligence Council, *The Terrorist Threat to the U.S. Homeland* (Washington, 2007).

80. Dennis Blair, Director of National Intelligence, "Annual Threat Assessment of the Intelligence Community for the Senate Select Committee on Intelligence," February 12, 2009.

81. Rabasa and others, *Ungoverned Territories*.

82. Howard Kunreuther, Erwann Michel-Kerjan, and Beverly Porter, "Assessing, Managing and Financing Extreme Events: Dealing with Terrorism," Working Paper 10179 (Cambridge, Mass.: National Bureau of Economic Research, 2003).

83. Walter Enders and Todd Sandler, "Economic Consequences of Terrorism in Developed and Developing Countries: An Overview," unpublished paper, 2005 (www.utdallas.edu/~tms063000/website/Econ_Consequences_ms.pdf).

84. Ibid.

85. Mohammed Maitami, Head of the Federation of Yemen Chambers of Commerce, quoted in Paul Schemm, "Rise in Global Food Prices Creates a Crisis in Yemen," *Los Angeles Times*, January 18, 2009.

86. UN Food and Agriculture Organization, "World Hunger Map" (www. fao.org/economic/ess/food-security-statistics/fao-hunger-map/en/); UN News Services, "UN Food Aid Agency Appeals for $500 Million to Offset Soaring Prices," March 24, 2008 (www.wwan.cn/apps/news/story.asp?NewsID=26071 &Cr=wfp&Cr1=prices).

87. Schemm, "Rise in Global Food Prices Creates a Crisis in Yemen."

88. World Bank, "Yemen—Country Water Resources Assistance Strategy," 2005 (www.worldbank.org/).

89. Steven Lee Myers, "Possible Lapses in Security at Yemen Port Investigated," *New York Times*, October 20, 2000.

90. "Yemen's Connection with Al-Qaeda Tied to Domestic Repression" (Eurasia net.org [January 8, 2002]).

91. See *Frontline*, Special Report on Yemen (www.pbs.org/wgbh/pages/frontline/shows/search/journey/yemen.html).

92. President Saleh, quoted in "Soft Approach to Jihadists Starts to Backfire as Poverty Fuels Extremism," (Manchester) *Guardian*, July 30, 2008.

93. USAID, Summary Table, Country/Account Summary (Spigots) FY 2008 Estimate (www.usaid.gov/policy/budget/cbj2009/).

94. Knights, "U.S. Embassy Bombing in Yemen."

95. United Nations Development Program (UNDP), World Bank, and Government of Yemen, "Yemen Poverty Assessment," November 2007 (www.worldbank.org/).

96. UNDP, *Human Development Report 2007/2008* (New York, 2007).

97. CARE International, "CARE in Yemen" (www.careinternational.org. uk/10984/yemen/care-in-yemen.html).

98. Library of Congress, Federal Research Division, "Country Profile: Yemen" (August 2008) (http://memory.loc.gov/frd/cs/profiles/Yemen.pdf).

99. "Yemen to Close 4,000 Religious Schools," *Yemen Times*, February 10, 2005 (www.yemenembassy.org/issues/democracy/index.php).

100. Library of Congress, "Country Profile: Yemen."

101. Duraid Al Baik, "Education Key to Tackling Problem of Saudi Poverty," *Gulfnews*, October 9, 2008 (www.gulfnews.com/news/gulf/saudi_arabia/ 10250638.html).

102. Janine Clark, *Islam, Charity and Activism* (Indiana University Press, 2004).

103. Maurice Greenberg and others, "Terrorist Financing," Report of an Independent Task Force Sponsored by the Council on Foreign Relations, 2002 (www.cfr.org/content/publications/attachments/Terrorist_Financing_TF.pdf).

104. Edmund Hull, U.S. Ambassador to Yemen, interview with *Frontline* (www.pbs.org/wgbh/pages/frontline/shows/search/journey/yemen.html).

105. Clark, *Islam, Charity and Activism.*

106. Jean-Charles Brisard, "Terrorism Financing: Roots and Trends of Saudi Terrorism Financing," report prepared for the President of the Security Council of the United Nations, December 19, 2002.

107. Michael Slackman, "Yemen Battles Itself," *Los Angeles Times*, February 19, 2003.

108. Ibid.

109. Frank Gardner, "Yemen's al-Qaeda Supporters," *BBC News*, August 3, 2002 (http://news.bbc.co.uk/2/low/programmes/from_our_own_correspondent/ 2168543.stm).

110. Mark N. Katz, "Yemen's Connection with Al-Qaeda Tied to Domestic Repression," *Eurasia Insight*, January 8, 2002.

111. UNDP, World Bank, and Government of Yemen, "Yemen Poverty Assessment."

112. Central Intelligence Agency (CIA), "Yemen," *World Factbook* (www. cia.gov/library/publications/the-world-factbook/index.html).

113. At the height of the Iraqi insurgency in 2007, U.S. officials said Saudi charities and patrons were providing "the majority of financing for al Qaeda in Mesopotamia." Richard Oppel, "Foreign Fighters in Iraq Are Tied to Allies of U.S.," *New York Times*, November 22, 2007.

114. Mahler, "The Bush Administration vs. Salim Hamdan."

115. Marshall, *Major Episodes of Political Violence.* See also International Crisis Group, "Yemen: Coping with Terrorism and Violence in a Fragile State," ICG Middle East Report 8 (January 2003); Robert Kaplan,

"A Tale of Two Colonies," *Atlantic Monthly,* April 2003; Yemen program manager for Islamic Relief, interview (www.islamic-relief.com/wherewework/stories/stories.aspx?CountryID=YE).

116. Mahler, "The Bush Administration vs. Salim Hamdan."

117. The project was presented to the World Bank conference "Scaling Up of Poverty Reduction," Shanghai, May 25–27, 2004. It features in World Bank, *Reducing Poverty, Sustaining Growth: Scaling Up Poverty Reduction* (Washington, 2004).

118. World Bank, "Implementation Completion Report on a Credit in the Amount of SDR 56 Million ($75 million) to the Republic of Yemen for a Second Social Fund for Development Project," International Development Association (IDA), IDA-33530 (Washington, 2006).

119. Ghaith Abdul-Ahad, "Somalia: One Week in Hell—Inside the City the World Forgot," (Manchester) *Guardian,* May 29, 2009.

120. World Bank, *Conflict in Somalia: Drivers and Dynamics* (Washington, January 2005).

121. Jeffrey Gettleman, "The Most Dangerous Place in the World," *Foreign Policy* 171 (March/April 2009): 1–5.

122. Oxfam, "Crisis in Somalia/Somaliland" (www.oxfam.org.uk/oxfam_in_action/emergencies/somalia_conflict.html).

123. Combating Terrorism Center, *Al-Qa'ida's (mis)Adventures in the Horn of Africa* (West Point, N.Y.: 2006).

124. Ibid.

125. Ken Menkhaus, "Quasi States, Nation-Building, and Terrorist Safe Havens," *Journal of Conflict Studies* 23 (Fall 2003): 7–23.

126. Shinn, "Al Qaeda in East Africa and the Horn."

127. Blair, "Annual Threat Assessment."

128. Thomas Dempsey, "Counterterrorism in African Failed States," unpublished paper (Carlisle, Pa.: U.S. Army War College, Strategic Studies Institute, 2006).

129. Gettleman, "The Most Dangerous Place in the World."

130. Jeffrey Gettleman, "The Pirates Have Seized the Ship," *GQ,* March 18, 2009.

131. Dempsey, "Counterterrorism in African Failed States."

132. Ibid.

133. Cedric Barnes, "The Rise and Fall of Mogadishu's Islamic Courts," Chatham House Briefing Paper (2007).

134. Shinn, "Al Qaeda in East Africa and the Horn."

135. Shashank Bengali, "Kenyan Islamist Recruits Say They Did It for the Money," McClatchy Tribune News Service, November 19, 2008.

136. Ken Menkhaus, "Somalia after the Ethiopian Occupation," Enough Project Strategy Paper (Washington: Center for American Progress, February 2009).

137. Barnes, "The Rise and Fall of Mogadishu's Islamic Courts"; Shinn, "Al Qaeda in East Africa and the Horn."

138. Menkhaus, "Somalia after the Ethiopian Occupation"; Gettleman, "The Most Dangerous Place in the World."

139. Government Accountability Office, "Somalia: Several Challenges Limit U.S. and International Stabilization, Humanitarian, and Development Efforts" (Government Printing Office, 2008).

140. Ibid.

141. This and other policy recommendations on conflict-sensitive aid are drawn from Priya Gajraj, Shonali Sardesai, and Per Wam, "Conflict in Somalia: Drivers and Dynamics," World Bank Economic and Sector Work (Washington, 2005).

142. Ibid.

143. USAID Budget FY 2007 Actual (www.usaid.gov/policy/budget/cbj2009/).

144. Craig Cohen, "A Perilous Course: U.S. Strategy and Assistance to Pakistan" (Washington: Center for Strategic and International Studies, August 2007).

145. UNDP, *Arab Development Report 2002* and *Arab Development Report 2004.*

146. For further information, see the World Bank's page on Afghanistan's National Solidarity Program (www.worldbank.org/).

CHAPTER FOUR

Poverty, State Weakness, and Civil War

ANDREW LOOMIS

Grace Ikombi was eighteen years old in the early 1990s when he fled his dusty village in Zaire, now the Democratic Republic of the Congo (DRC), for the capital city of Kinshasa. His father was dead after succumbing to malaria, a disease that can be cured with a $2 treatment. His mother had been murdered by Congolese rebels for providing medical care to loyalists of the dictator Mobutu Sese Seko. Ikombi was exhausted and hungry. "I heard that the rebels at least were eating," he shrugged. "So I joined them."[1]

In Abidjan, Côte d'Ivoire, 1,500 miles to the northwest of Kinshasa, stories like Ikombi's are familiar. Morifère Bamba, a member of a rebel group operating out of an Abidjan slum, quit school at the age of twelve. His family was mired in poverty. His mother died and his father could no longer provide for him. So Morfère moved to Abidjan. "The city," he said, "would give me the ability to realize my dream." Yet Morfère found his road to employment blocked by violence on the street. He drifted between criminal gangs before landing in a rebel group. The rebellion offered him an identity as well as sustenance. Indeed, French researcher Ruth Marshall-Fratani observes of Côte d'Ivoire: "The gap between aspirations and possibilities has widened incredibly in the last fifteen years."[2]

Côte d'Ivoire was once one of the most prosperous countries in Africa, relying heavily on agricultural exports to build its economy. To demographers and development experts, it was the "Ivorian Miracle" in a region marked by deep poverty.[3] But as commodity prices dropped in the 1980s and 1990s, state coffers were depleted, investors fled, and conditions began to deteriorate. Corruption and mismanagement—such as kickbacks from cocoa producers and extortion by the police—weakened the government's financial base and eroded public trust in government. The infrastructure fragmented. By the late 1990s, only 55 percent of the adult population was literate and 58 percent had no access to potable water.[4]

Soon, Côte d'Ivoire fell into the same war-ridden cycle of impoverishment and conflict that has enmeshed the DRC. In the fall of 2002, war between rebel insurgents from the poorer northern region and government loyalists in the more prosperous south erupted in Côte d'Ivoire, fueled in part by cultural and political factors. As the state descended into civil war, it was ill-equipped to extinguish an insurgency fed by a volatile cocktail of soaring unemployment rates and a sharp economic downturn.[5]

Across the developing world, poverty undermines state capacity to create jobs, educate people, and provide basic health services. Today, civil conflict is by far the most common form of armed warfare, and its occurrence is overwhelmingly concentrated in poor countries that lack the capacity to govern.[6] In 2005, 90 percent of armed conflicts occurred in low- and lower-middle-income countries.[7] From Sierra Leone and Angola to Tajikistan, Indonesia, and the Philippines, civil wars erupt disproportionately in countries and regions facing endemic poverty, sharp economic decline, or both. Overall, civil wars in the developing world have claimed more than 16 million lives in seventy-three countries and displaced 67 million people since 1945.[8] Scholarship on the causes of civil war reveals a complexity of interacting factors, but the bottom line has become increasingly clear: countries with low income per capita face a substantially higher risk of civil war.[9]

Less clear are the specific circumstances under which poverty increases the risk of war, as the mechanisms vary from country to country. Still, one central trend is that poverty decreases state capacity, weak states create more opportunities for rebellion, and civil wars then lock poor countries into a spiral that further entrenches poverty. Because poverty undermines state capacity, it creates conditions that insurgents can exploit to launch, perpetuate, and restart rebellion. Poverty and state weakness contribute to each phase of conflict: the initial spark before conflict erupts, recruitment during an insurgency, sustained violence during a full-blown civil war, and recurrence after civil war has ended.

Economists invoke this "conflict trap" to explain the puzzle of what Oxford University's Paul Collier calls the "bottom billion": the 1 billion people mired in poverty in developing countries that, in contrast to the rest of the world, have failed to grow in recent decades.[10] The conflict trap also explains why, absent developed country interventions, poor and conflict-ridden countries are unlikely to improve their predicament on their own. Civil war disrupts economic activity, diverts resources from public services, can create massive flows of refugees, increases crime and homicide rates, and promotes the spread of diseases that kill millions of people every year, long after the fighting has stopped.[11]

Humanitarian concerns are not the only reason that Americans should care about the implications of war in distant countries. Wars in those places now have far-reaching implications for U.S., regional, and even global security. Most recent mass atrocities have occurred in countries engulfed in civil war. Furthermore, mounting scholarship confirms that civil war in one country strongly increases the likelihood of violence breaking out in neighboring states.[12] In Central Africa in the mid-1990s, the conflict between Hutus and Tutsi in Rwanda and Burundi helped to ignite a massive civil war in Zaire. Vital U.S. security interests are at stake in several other parts of the developing world where violence has spilled across borders and affected entire regions. In the Horn of Africa, for instance, conflict in Somalia continues unabated despite the presence of African Union peacekeeping forces. Somalia's anarchy has prompted neighboring Ethiopia to intervene militarily and continues to provide international terrorists and pirates with a base of operations.

Global security, including that of Americans, is also compromised when conflict zones incubate transnational threats. Conflict zones in countries from Afghanistan to the Philippines, Sierra Leone, and Somalia have proved to be ideal operating environments for transnational terrorist networks. Al Qaeda gained a foothold in Afghanistan in the 1990s during the brutal civil war that followed the withdrawal of the Soviet Union. Most global drug production takes place in conflict or postconflict countries.[13] The routes traffickers follow from the country of origin to American, Australian, and European markets also go through conflict and postconflict countries. Diseases also spread more quickly in conflict zones, ultimately threatening people in distant countries. States in conflict or bordering on conflict zones in the 1990s had much higher HIV/AIDS rates than peaceful countries.[14] All of these factors convey a strong message to U.S. policymakers: that it is imperative for them to assign far greater priority to breaking the cycle of poverty, state weakness, and violence in developing countries.

CIVIL WARS AND U.S. NATIONAL SECURITY

At its peak of incidence in the 1990s, civil war affected seventy-three countries around the globe, with attendant risks to regional and global security. In response, the United Nations began intervening in conflict and postconflict situations far more frequently. Sixty-three UN peace-keeping operations have been initiated in conflict and postconflict countries since 1948, the large majority after 1990. Today, the organization maintains sixteen missions, most of which are in poor, conflict, and postconflict countries such as Chad, Darfur, the DRC, Côte d'Ivoire, Liberia, Haiti, and Sudan. More than 80,000 foreign troops are on the ground in such countries.

In addition, tens of thousands of active-duty U.S. military personnel are stationed around the world, most deployed in Iraq and Afghanistan. Tens of thousands of U.S. and North Atlantic Treaty Organization (NATO) troops are stationed in Afghanistan in 2009, where they confront a resurgent Taliban and increased terrorist activity. Nearly eight years since the U.S.-led invasion began, the Taliban are regrouping on both sides of the border with Pakistan. Violence now increasingly embroils Pakistan, threatening the country's internal stability and, potentially, the security of its nuclear arsenal. Although neither of these conflicts was caused by poverty, state weakness and low income have exacerbated the wars in both Iraq and Afghanistan. Some U.S. soldiers are stationed in and near strife-ridden impoverished countries, such as those in the Horn of Africa. Furthermore, the increasing frequency of stabilization and reconstruction missions in such countries is absorbing a greater share of U.S. military resources and capability. The Department of Defense recently announced that stability operations are now a core mission of the military, alongside traditional combat and deterrence operations.

In addition to causing a surge in military intervention, the greater incidence of civil conflict has precipitated more numerous humanitarian emergencies, displacements of people, and spikes in global narcotics production and disease epidemics. Many of the world's ongoing complex emergencies are occurring in conflict countries, including the DRC, Haiti, Somalia, Sudan, and Sri Lanka. The dire humanitarian conditions created by civil wars not only threaten the lives of hundreds of thousands of people in the developing world but can also place Americans directly in the line of fire. Between 1997 and 2005, the number of reported killings, kidnappings, and armed attacks resulting in major injuries inflicted on humanitarian workers nearly doubled, with nongovernmental organizations (NGOs) and UN representatives paying the highest price.[15]

Recent research demonstrates that civil wars tend to cluster geographically and spread across borders, as in the African Great Lakes region, in Central Asia, and in the Balkans. Conflict may spread from one country to another because of weak border controls in poor countries. Rebel groups can easily operate across the boundaries of a weak state, gaining access to supplies and weapons in other countries or spreading violent ideologies there. Conflict in one state may also adversely affect the economies of neighboring states, thus putting them at greater risk of conflict. Experts estimate that the average annual growth rate of countries with neighbors at war is 0.5 percentage points less than those with neighbors at peace.[16]

In addition, conflict often creates mass movements of refugees across borders. Currently about 9 million worldwide have fled civil conflict in their home countries.[17] Large numbers of refugee populations can destabilize host countries suddenly burdened with unemployed uprooted individuals who are cut off from their social networks. Fighting between the Congolese army and rebel groups in the eastern region of the Congo forced 1 million people out of their homes—100,000 between August and October 2008 alone. The influx of refugees has further strained the resources of its fragile eastern neighbors, Uganda, Rwanda, and Burundi.

Besides intensifying the trauma of displaced populations and its adverse effects on regional stability, refugee camps can import weapons and divisive ideologies into the host country or serve as staging areas for rebels, since they are often protected by an international presence dedicated to shielding the refugee population. This protection and the general disorder of the camps provide rebels an ideal site to recruit new members, accumulate necessary supplies, and develop operational plans for new attacks. In Congo in 1994, refugees from Rwanda gained enough strength to form a political party that circulated racist propaganda and further reinforced hostilities between the Tutsis in control of the Rwandan government and the Hutus in exile.[18]

As discussed in chapter 3, sustained internal violence creates a security vacuum, soon filled by illicit activities such as terrorist training, and can allow the shipment of nuclear, biological, or chemical materials to ill-intentioned camps. Indeed, most U.S.-designated foreign terrorist organizations use weak and failing states as their primary base of operations to recruit new members, collect arms, and establish safe havens for known terrorists on the run.[19] In Afghanistan and Somalia, for example, terrorist groups such as al Qaeda quickly exploited the lawlessness and limited oversight fostered by war.

Global drug production and trafficking, another scourge of the world's conflict zones, tend to die down when a conflict ends but mushroom when it intensifies. Low-income states have notoriously weak enforcement capability. There is also a reverse pernicious cycle between drug cartels and instability and insurgency. In Afghanistan, opium traffic is brisk. According to UN figures, Afghanistan produced 8,500 tons of opium in 2008 alone, nearly twice the world demand.[20] Opium sales finance the insurgency and undermine the U.S.-led NATO military stabilization mission, as well as export the dangers of narcotics abroad. Cocaine traffic through Central and South America has had a pronounced effect not only in fueling the Colombian war, but also in destabilizing the region at transit points between Colombia and the United States. These criminal chains are heavily dependent on routes through Mexico, where instability and violence also are increasing sharply.

In summary, civil wars directly endanger U.S. lives by creating the ideal environment for global challenges to take root: state capacity is weakened, conflict is therefore prolonged, states then become more vulnerable to war's byproducts, instability intensifies, and ultimately U.S. security is threatened. The human costs of these wars are tragic, and their security implications beyond the zone of conflict only increase the urgency of development in poor, conflict-prone countries.

POVERTY AND CIVIL WAR

Although the number of civil wars in the world has declined since the end of the cold war, more than thirty were still being fought in 2008, which is vastly greater than the number of recent interstate wars. As many as one-third of all countries have experienced internal warfare over the past two decades, and as many as two-thirds of those wars dragged on for at least seven years.[21] Equally disturbing, civil conflicts have proved to be both persistent and enormously costly.

With the end of the cold war, some commentators reasoned that in the absence of U.S.-Soviet rivalry nationalist and separatist forces would swell and sow violence between substate groups. Daniel Patrick Moyni-han, for one, expected ethnic and cultural divisions to fuel most wars in the next decades.[22] Samuel Huntington likewise speculated that the "dominating source of conflict" in the ensuing years would be ethnic differences between people with a distinct "language, history, religion, customs, institutions, and . . . subjective self-identification."[23]

Much data support an alternative conclusion, however: namely, that something other than ethnic hatred is driving domestic wars. A land-mark study on violence between ethnically diverse populations in Africa has found no evidence that ethnic composition or linguistic or religious discrimination are associated with a higher risk of civil war.[24] Consistent with an emerging consensus, the American Political Science Association's Task Force on Difference, Inequality, and Developing Societies has also found that what "makes a big difference" to the potential for large-scale violence is "whether the government is strong and intent on preventing conflict or weak and controlled by leaders who intend to stir up ethnic violence for their political advantage."[25] As the research on ethnicity and conflict continues, more scholars are acknowledging that conflict is a complex phenomenon, attributable to multiple causes. At the same time, consensus is forming that per capita income has a direct, negative relationship to civil conflict risk.

Poor countries are more likely to experience economic shocks that trigger organized violence and more likely to face the prospect of pro-longed or recurrent fighting. A majority of the world's fifty-eight poorest countries have experienced a civil war in recent years.[26] By contrast, countries free of internal violence are "characterized by a per capita income that is more than five times higher than in countries in which wars broke out."[27] Furthermore, 77 percent of all international crises after 1991 involved at least one low-income state.[28] And the "mean per capita GDP in countries affected by civil war at any point from 1960–1999 is less than half that of countries with no civil war experience."[29]

For a country currently in the fiftieth percentile of income, such as Iran, the risk of experiencing civil war within five years is 7–11 percent. For countries in the tenth percentile, such as Uganda, the risk escalates to 15–18 percent. The curvilinear relationship between conflict risk and GDP per capita can be seen in figure 4-1.[30]

An important policy implication flows from this research: "If . . . whatever factors that are genuinely causal are highly correlated with income, then policies which increase income are likely to reduce the

FIGURE 4-1. **Curvilinear Relationship between Conflict Risk and Per Capita GDP**

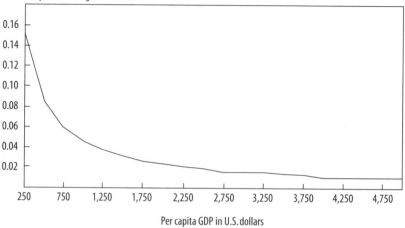

Source: Macartan Humphreys, "Economics and Violent Conflict," Working Paper (Harvard University, 2003), p. 2.

risk of conflict, and countries with low income are likely to be more at risk than those with higher income."[31] Some would add that economic development on its own is insufficient to reduce the global incidence of civil conflict, but that in combination with conflict-prevention measures, "raising levels of economic development will reduce the overall prevalence of political violence in the world."[32] At the same time, aid agencies must take steps to ensure their resources do not serve as further incentives for rebellion, as numerous studies have warned.[33] Even so, the new emerging consensus on poverty and civil war places significant weight on poverty alleviation and economic growth as crucial components of a global conflict prevention and mitigation strategy.[34]

POVERTY, STATE WEAKNESS, AND CIVIL WAR: CONNECTING THE DOTS

Alleviating poverty provides a crucial perspective on long-term strategies to reduce conflict. Efforts to operationalize such strategies must take into account the linkages between poverty and state weakness. Poverty deprives states of the financial resources, administrative capacity, and military might necessary to overwhelm an organized, armed challenge to the central government. State weakness creates conditions that make insurgency more viable, as made clear by empirical evidence.[35] Whether due to poorly trained and equipped government forces or minimal levels of government expertise in running effective counterinsurgency campaigns, states with low per capita GDP invite rebellion.[36]

Poverty contributes to civil wars by providing the incentive for individuals to participate in a rebellion, and by weakening state capacity. The "greed" model, first advanced by Paul Collier and Anke Hoeffler, identifies factors that encourage participation in a rebellion, such as the availability of financial resources to sustain a rebel force or low opportunity costs of forgone earning potential in traditional employment. If the alternatives to rebellion are unattractive—which they are in many poor countries—then more people will be inclined to rebel.[37]

The state weakness model especially is supported by strong evidence that low income per capita is closely linked to an increase in the prospects that civil wars will break out, will persist, and will elude resolution.[38] In practice, the processes that link poverty and rebellion vary substantially across countries and types of civil war.[39] Some of the pathways between poverty and civil war become clearer when one considers poverty's effect on both individual incentive structures and the robustness of state institutions at each stage in the conflict cycle.[40]

Initial Spark

A spark is required to initiate a civil war. Often accompanying the outbreak of civil war is some external shock, which can come in the form of a natural disaster, external violence, or sharp reduction in the price of key commodity exports. Although shocks by themselves are rarely sufficient to spark civil conflict, an external shock can abruptly diminish national income levels and provide the critical link to its outbreak. Abrupt reductions in export commodity prices, to name one example, severely strain national treasuries. Natural disasters can also overburden national resources and imperil the domestic economy, negatively affecting a state's revenue base. A number of studies have uncovered evidence linking external economic shocks with civil war, the pathway being diminished central government revenues and deepening national poverty.[41]

When government revenues shrink, the quality of public services declines, along with public sector incomes. Employees of the state—including teachers, doctors, and soldiers—become unemployed and may resort to selling access to public goods such as education that had previously been provided by the state.[42] As national income levels deteriorate, tax revenue falls, further undermining the capacity of the state to provide critical services such as education, health care, and security. As the state loses its ability to manage the economy and the monopoly on violence, criminal gangs, vigilantes, or private militias are more likely to emerge in this environment of unconstraint. Resource stress can undermine the authority of the regime by placing unrealistically high demands on the state to provide employment, agricultural inputs, or expensive projects designed to placate political opponents.[43]

Economic shocks alone are not a sufficient cause of conflict. A more likely trigger can be found in the inability of low-income countries to provide public goods, sustain employment levels, tamp down illicit economies, and establish security.

Recruitment

Once civil war is under way, poverty increases rebel leaders' success in recruiting new foot soldiers. Rebellion is an attractive option for impoverished individuals with limited education or job opportunities.[44] Youth are particularly vulnerable. Poverty limits their future prospects, and they face greater risks when weak states fail to invest in the institutions of education or sustain high employment levels. Although a surge in their number is not sufficient to deepen a civil war, if they have few employment or educational prospects and no obvious path to economic advancement, the mix becomes volatile. Poverty is the essential link between a large youth population and an effective recruitment strategy. Nearly 60 percent of the world's poor are under the age of twenty-five and thus particularly vulnerable to rebel recruitment. An increasing number of studies point to a statistically significant relationship between high percentages of youth in a country and civil war.[45]

Poverty can help transform an ineffective call to revolution into an effective recruitment tool in two key ways. First, when poverty persists or deepens, rebel groups are more likely to provide people—particularly youth—some marginal economic benefit for joining. Second, when national income levels are depressed and essential state institutions and services have atrophied—including schools, state jobs, and the military—the state is poorly equipped to stave off civil war. Poverty not only increases the likelihood that disaffected populations will take up arms, but it also reduces the state's capacity to stand its ground against a rebellion. Thus rebel greed and state weakness (in particular) turn poverty into a powerful engine of rebel recruitment.

Persistence of Civil War

Although the overall number of domestic conflicts is in decline, civil wars are becoming more intractable. Poverty is a prominent factor explaining why some conflicts resist resolution.[46] Poor states have diminished capacity to end internal violence, and individuals in poor countries have few incentives to end a rebellion, given the absence of alternative economic opportunities.

Poverty also provides outside actors with incentives to prey on a weak state. Poor countries with limited oversight capacity are more likely to harbor illicit markets, for example, which can intensify instability and prolong war. With their high profit margins, illicit economies enable rebels to compete with traffickers and establish a connection to local populations, particularly in labor-intensive illicit markets. Black markets are even more powerfully connected to war because they are difficult to eradicate.[47] Where resources are scarce, both elites and rebels encounter greater illicit rent-seeking opportunities, while the state has fewer resources at its disposal.[48]

In short, poor countries are less likely to end civil wars because they lack effective control over their territory, because external actors have opportunities to meddle in the conflict, and because conflicts tend to impoverish states further and reduce their capacity to develop human and natural resources. Conversely, when rebels are able to loot or exploit natural resources, they have the means to sustain themselves.

Recurrence of Conflict

Civil wars are not only difficult to end but also highly likely to reignite once violence subsides. Of the fifty-eight civil wars that ended between 1945 and 1996, 36 percent started up again. According to some calculations, states that experience a civil war are twice as likely to experience another one.[49] While noneconomic factors help explain this pattern, wars are much more likely to restart in poor countries than in rich ones.[50]

War and poverty are mutually reinforcing: violent internal conflict depletes a state's resources, which in turn makes the state more susceptible to civil war. Of the thirty-four countries least likely to reach the Millennium Development Goals by the 2015 deadline, twenty-two are embroiled in or emerging from civil war.[51] Since civil wars consume resources that otherwise could be used for productive purposes, market economies are kept from functioning efficiently and thus emerge from the conflict poorer and less able to secure the peace. Being poorer, they have fewer employment opportunities for their citizens and are unable to provide public goods. The military and police are often slow to rebuild their capacity after years of fighting and thus are unable to maintain security. This dearth of economic well-being is a key factor in the recurrence of conflict, together with a lack of political openness.[52]

Three points can be made from a policy perspective about the complicated relationship between poverty, state weakness, and conflict. The first point—tragically illustrated by the decade-long war in Sierra Leone—is that once countries are caught in this vicious cycle, action is needed on all three fronts to break it. As long as conflict prevails, states will not have the resources or the capacity to rise out of poverty. Poverty will continue to undermine the state's ability to contend with environmental shocks, entrench the roots of discontent that led to war in the first place, increase the proportion of vulnerable youth, and imperil the state institutions required to sustain peace agreements. Without adequate institutions to govern effectively, sustain the conditions for economic growth, and create confidence in the rule of law, states are highly likely to fall back into conflict.

Second, civil wars have regional and global consequences that cannot be ignored, as the war in Congo makes all too clear with its mutual destabilization of a state and a region. Whether the war's roots were internal or external, there is no debate that—once unleashed—the internal and regional issues have to be addressed in combination. Less well understood are the global dimensions of this conflict: Congo's poverty and weakness fuel the destruction of its rain forests, for example, which in turn contributes to global warming. As discussed in chapter 5, Congo's inability to function effectively as a state deprives it of millions of dollars in potential investments to protect its rain forests.

The third point is that the confluence of poverty, conflict, and collapse of the state leads to a loss of life and exacerbates global threats. Sierra Leone and Congo are proof enough that these tragedies are real, and that the development community must learn from them.

SIERRA LEONE

Like Côte d'Ivoire, Sierra Leone once was widely considered a highly functional state. With its greatly respected university system and British-trained civil service, it was reputed to be the "Athens of West Africa."[53] Between 1950 and 1972, its average growth rate reached 7 percent, one of the highest rates in West Africa.[54]

Yet by the mid-1980s, its economy was starting to slide. Diamond exports, which constituted 70 percent of export earnings through the mid-1980s, fell from 2 million carats in 1970 to 48,000 carats in 1988.[55] The quadrupling of oil prices after 1973 and the collapse of central export commodities such as cocoa, palm kernels, and particularly diamonds contributed to a steep decline in public health.[56] Inflation soared to 40 percent in 1984. In 1991—the year civil war broke out—annual inflation climbed to a staggering 129 percent, robbing people of the ability to pay for basic supplies such as rice and kerosene.[57] The key economic indicator that correlates with the incidence of civil war—per capita income—fell steadily throughout the 1980s, dropping from a high of $380 in 1980 to $140 in 1992.[58]

By 1990 Sierra Leone ranked last on the UN Development Program's Human Development Index, which measures states' performance on economic indicators, literacy, and life expectancy.[59] State hospitals became neglected and devoid of essential medicines, with private health clinics free to charge exorbitant prices. The government also stopped paying teachers. The university system, starved of government funds, collapsed, its top talent fled the country, and the country's youth had fewer opportunities to receive a quality education.[60]

In the wake of the economic collapse and a simultaneous breakdown of democratic institutions, Sierra Leone entered a period of large-scale corruption in which state resources were redirected toward a network of corrupt elites. The ramifications were felt at every level of society, from poorly paid traffic police, who received far more income extorting taxi drivers than from their government salaries, to top officials.[61]

On March 23, 1991, a group of military officers calling themselves the Revolutionary United Front (RUF) launched a military coup from their base in exile in neighboring Liberia. The war that ensued proved among the most brutal of the twentieth century. Tens of thousands lost their lives. More than 2 million people—constituting well over a third of Sierra Leone's population—were displaced. The RUF mutilated 20,000 civilians using machetes and axes to sever body parts. Entire villages were targeted for destruction. Children were recruited into battle by force. Eventually, the conflict affected all regions of the country and severely weakened national political and military institutions.

Contrary to conventional wisdom, Sierra Leone's civil war had little if anything to do with ethnic or religious divisions. Rather, it had almost everything to do with the gradual weakening and impoverishment of the state. Decades of corrupt and violent authoritarian rule helped spark the rebellion, which initially aimed to unseat the political party that had ruled over Sierra Leone for more than twenty years. Many observers have also cast the civil war as a classic struggle for political control over the state apparatus, which it undoubtedly was. However, two of the conflict's most powerful drivers were (1) the state's failure to provide basic services and to lay the conditions for economic growth, and (2) its lack of control over parts of its territory, especially the diamond mines.

From the war's onset in early 1991, RUF leader Foday Sankoh insisted—implausibly—that the insurgency was formed to defend the civilian population. In fact, the RUF took few steps to safeguard the population. More often, civilians suffered grievously at the hands of rebel forces. In one episode, a commander presented himself as the embodiment of "good governance" in Africa while being carried away in a stolen car with the aid of sixteen teenage conscripts.[62] It quickly became apparent that the purpose of the war was not to attain political goals of rebel commanders, but to increase their wealth and access to territory comprising the diamond fields and forests of extremely valuable timber.

With its economy in collapse and government coffers drained, the state was stripped of its ability to build a professional military force to extinguish the rebellion. When the civil war began, the state army consisted of just 3,000 men. Less than a third were trained for combat. The troops were equipped with weapons manufactured in the 1970s and 1980s. Many government soldiers were so poorly paid that they saw economic advantage in defecting from their posts and joining the rebels in plundering the country's resources.

As the war intensified, the strain on government resources became much more acute and further degraded the state's capacity to deliver basic services. By early 1996, 75 percent of school-aged children were not in school, 70 percent of school buildings had been destroyed, and just 16 percent of Sierra Leone's health facilities were functioning.[63] Government employees went for months without a paycheck, and the level of emergency food and medical care provided by aid agencies and churches withered. Deliveries were slowed by sanctions, and much of what did get into the country was stolen by government soldiers and rebels.[64] In 1999, eight years into the war, Sierra Leone was named "the darkest corner of Africa."[65]

One of the mechanisms linking poverty and civil war was the large presence of an alienated youth population with no economic alternatives to taking up arms. At the start of the war, half of the country's 4.5 million people were under the age of nineteen.[66] Poverty, idleness, and high impressionability made Sierra Leone's youth prime targets for rebel recruiters. Furthermore, once the education system collapsed, the youth became disproportionately uneducated and susceptible to joining a rebellion. Indeed, individuals with no formal education were nine times more likely to join the RUF than those who received some postprimary education.[67] Former U.S. ambassador to Sierra Leone John Hirsch notes, "The emergence of the RUF was a reflection of the state's failure to provide education, vocational training, and economic opportunity to a whole generation of youths who grew up seeing no future for themselves."[68]

An additional factor in the rebels' favor was that alluvial diamond deposits in riverbeds or in shallow earth are easily extractable sources of revenue. Because diamonds are also easily transported and have a high per unit value, and transparency and oversight of the diamond industry tends to be minimal, diamonds are highly trafficked in illegal markets.[69] One study has found that after the end of the cold war, civil war became significantly more likely in states having an abundance of extracted diamonds.[70]

In the face of dwindling resources, the government of Sierra Leone was forced to abandon its presence in the diamond-rich border regions, leaving them in the hands of smuggling operations and thus depriving the state of millions of dollars of annual income—which in turn reduced its capacity to extinguish the rebellion.[71] Sierra Leone at one time produced $500 million worth of diamonds a year, but by 2000 its diamond sales had fallen to just $30 million. The resources derived from the secondary production of diamonds helped fund the RUF and perpetuated the insurgency, while spreading instability to neighboring states. At the peak of the war, Liberian rebel leader Charles Taylor was earning a reported $9 million a month, roughly six times the revenue of Sierra Leone.[72]

Less obvious were Sierra Leone's ties with international terrorists and the war's impact on U.S. national security. On August 7, 1998, on the opposite side of the African continent, simultaneous explosions gutted the U.S. embassies in Nairobi, Kenya, and Dar es Salaam, Tanzania. The attack—which put al Qaeda on the map and catapulted Osama bin Laden near the top of the FBI's list of most-wanted terrorists—killed 258 embassy staff and U.S. diplomats and injured more than 5,000 people.

In the immediate aftermath of the tragedy, U.S. officials began to focus on identifying the financial sources that sustained terrorist activities around the world in order to interdict the perpetrators and prevent future attacks. While still contested, evidence has surfaced that financing for the operation came from Sierra Leone through the sale of smuggled diamonds.[73] Al Qaeda allegedly purchased between $30 million and $50 million worth of diamonds from RUF rebels in the months immediately before September 11, 2001.[74]

In addition to al Qaeda, as many as 120,000 Lebanese agents and businessmen with close ties to RUF soldiers were active in Sierra Leone, channeling diamond profits to Hezbollah, the Iranian-backed Shia paramilitary group operating in Lebanon.[75] A European investigator remarked, "Even if only 10 percent went to terrorist organizations, you are talking about millions of dollars in virtually untraceable funds, every year. That is enough to keep a lot of people going."[76]

The eventual end to the war in Sierra Leone required a host of political and security interventions.[77] The Economic Community of West African States (ECOWAS) and the United States exerted intense diplomatic pressure to achieve the Lome Agreement in July 1999, which fell apart within months. In May 2000 the United Kingdom deployed 4,500 troops to Sierra Leone in response to a crisis that developed when the RUF took several hundred UN troops hostage. A new Abuja Cease-Fire Agreement negotiated in November 2000 empowered the United Nations Mission in Sierra Leone (UNAMSIL). UNAMSIL was reconfigured many times, growing from 6,000 to a peak of 17,500 troops.

The Sierra Leone civil war illustrates starkly how poverty and a lack of state capacity foster domestic and regional instability and ultimately threaten U.S. security. Without major diplomatic and security interventions, it is inconceivable that Sierra Leone alone could have broken out of its cycle of conflict, poverty, and state incapacity. The collapse of its economy triggered the failure of the school system, caused employment opportunities to disappear, and eroded oversight of the diamond market, which was then supplanted by illegal channels that depleted the nation's most highly valued natural resource and sowed instability at home and abroad. Remedies to reinforce stability in Sierra Leone should include efforts to improve the economic conditions that make anemic states, unemployed youth, and lootable resources so dangerous.

DEMOCRATIC REPUBLIC OF THE CONGO

If conflict in Sierra Leone became intertwined with networks of global threats, it was but a foreshadowing of what would happen in Congo, where the impact of conflict continues to linger even a decade beyond the period of the most intense fighting. Its wealth of resources and extreme poverty make the DRC a paradox. It is the most resource-rich country in Africa, home to a cover of rain forests, a complex ecosystem of rare plant and animal life, a rich vein of copper and cobalt, 80 percent of the world's reserves of columbite-tantalite (Coltan, used for a wide range of electronic components), and 70 million hectares of unused fertile soil.[78] But 75 percent of Congo's population lives on less than $1 a day, and most have no access to safe drinking water or adequate health care.[79] Much of this territory is out of the reach of government control and open to exploitation. Not surprisingly, this combination of mineral wealth, poverty, and inability to control its territory pushed the country into a series of civil wars.

Most recently, two full-scale wars erupted in the mid-1990s, ultimately resulting in the deaths of an estimated 5 million people, more than in any war since World War II and requiring the eventual deployment of 17,000 UN peacekeepers.[80] The conflict has complex roots, both domestic and international. In 1996 persistent attacks against Rwanda by perpetrators of the Rwandan genocide based in Zaire sparked Rwandan military intervention, initially to separate refugees from the genocidaires and to enable their peaceful repatriation. Thereafter Rwandan involvement escalated, and several neighboring countries joined with Rwanda in supporting the rebel movement, which some months later drove long-time dictator Mobutu Sese Seko out of the country. In 1998 Rwanda again invaded Western Congo, this time to try to topple President Laurent Kabila. This brazen operation provoked at least five other countries to intervene in Congo and sparked what has been called Africa's first world war.

At the same time, Congolese rebel movements were being incited by domestic factors: decades of intense kleptocracy, a lack of basic infrastructure throughout the vast country, intercommunal tensions manipulated by long-time dictator Mobutu Sese Seko and his successors, and dire poverty. In 1995 gross national income (GNI) per capita stood at $130, making the country the second poorest in the world by that measure. Today, the DRC remains violent in places and highly unstable. The risk of renewed conflict is high in part because economic conditions have not improved in any meaningful way: GNI per capita remains the second lowest in the world, having dropped to $120.

While the civil war in Congo is usually described as a phenomenon of interethnic discord between Hutus and Tutsis, it is inextricably inter-twined with an economic crisis that will require economic remedies to reinforce the stability of both Congo and the Rift Valley. In the early 1990s, when rebellion against Mobutu was in its nascent stages, the Congolese economy was in steep decline. By 1996, at the launch of the anti-Mobutu rebellion, real per capita GNI had fallen from a high of $600 in 1980 to less than one-fifth of this value. Annual growth per capita had averaged 1.8 percent a year through the 1980s but then dete-riorated to an average of negative 8.6 percent between 1990 and 1995.[81] Between 1990 and 1999, Congo lost more than 44 percent of its produc-tive capacity, and income levels fell by a total of 74 percent.[82] In 1993 inflation hit a staggering 27,000 percent.[83]

At the same time, many Western governments, including the U.S. Con-gress, began cutting foreign aid, in part because of the decline in Congo's geostrategic significance at the close of the cold war, which brought greater scrutiny of Mobutu's corruption and resistance to reform. Total official development assistance fell from $896 million in 1990 to $195 million five years later. Between internal plundering and reduced foreign aid, Congo grew increasingly unable to fund schools and police, moni-tor criminal activity, and retain the loyalty of key stakeholders, such as the military and powerful elected officials. Congo's citizens faced almost insurmountable challenges in finding jobs or paying for necessities amid a severe currency devaluation. Enrollment in primary education dropped precipitously, from upward of 90 percent through the mid-1980s to less than 50 percent by the late 1990s.[84]

Congo's deepening poverty depleted the state's tax revenue stream and weakened its ability to effectively repel those seeking to profit from the state's weak oversight. Its limited authority beyond Kinshasa made natural assets increasingly vulnerable to opportunistic rebel leaders, underpaid government soldiers and police, and criminals operating in the commerce of valuable extractives. Indeed, all four rebel movements involved in the war against Kabila since 1998 were financed by natural resources—including diamonds, gold, ivory, and timber—and instablity was exacerbated by peripheral states seizing mineral resources. The profit gained from these resources effectively sustained the war through such devices as the taxation of resources by the intervening states and by rebels, as well as looting and expropriation.

Anarchy in eastern Congo facilitated militia operations in thick protected forests, which opened corridors for illicit trade and added fuel to the violence. Networks of people connected with soldiers, police, and rebels exported 11,000 kilograms of ivory from one reserve in 2003 alone. Of the estimated $600 million in diamonds exported from Congo annually, legal exports constituted just 30 percent of the total.[85] Ugandan and Rwandan troops occupied parts of gold-rich eastern Congo, forcing tens of thousands of Congolese into slave-like conditions in the mines in order to extract and steal the country's gold.[86]

Uranium deposits, which exist in substantial amounts in Congo, directly threaten international security. A decrepit but working nuclear reactor with enrichment capabilities is located at the University of Kinshasa. Two uranium rods disappeared in Mobutu's waning months in power, and only one has since been recovered.[87] Constricted salaries and income shortfalls, combined with the state's inability to sufficiently secure this highly valuable commodity on the black market, increase the potential for leakage of a fissile material. Because of Congo's size and resources—minerals and rain forests in particular—its internal disarray has global consequences for the United States and the rest of the international community.

One global challenge that intersects closely with Congo is climate change. The DRC boasts the second largest rain forest in the world. Although the impact of regional activities on global climate is still under debate, scientists have warned that continued deforestation in the DRC and the surrounding region could have harmful effects well beyond the Congo River Basin.[88] An estimated 20 to 30 percent of global greenhouse gases released each year are a result of deforestation. When trees are used for firewood or to make room for agriculture, the carbon dioxide they store is released into the atmosphere. According to the UN Food and Agriculture Organization, about 32 million acres of forests are lost every year. Most of the loss is heavily concentrated in the tropics.[89]

On account of their location, size, and relation to global weather patterns, the degradation of Congo's forests could disturb rainfall patterns beyond the region, especially in West Africa. Deforestation in Congo and throughout the tropics also contributes to warmer temperatures in many higher-latitude regions, including North America. Furthermore, some studies have shown that deforestation in the region could affect the distribution, though not the amount, of global rainfall.

Clearly, deforestation in the DRC has many causes and cannot be traced to a single source. Yet Congo's wars have had a significant impact. For one thing, Congo's refugees and rural residents are less likely to have alternative sources of energy to burning firewood. For another, many observers worry that in the immediate postconflict period, before the state will have a chance to exert control over this large country, the forests will be free for the taking for developers and the timber extraction industry, thus intensifying resource competition. Because Congo remains largely ungoverned, it attracts few investments to preserve the rain forest that could also serve as carbon offsets to developing countries seeking to meet their commitments to global carbon reductions. This challenge and the difficulties it raises for policy are explored in greater depth in chapter 5.

Congo's wars also have multiplied the threat of disease, particularly among those emerging from the remote and war-afflicted Eastern Province. The roster of disease outbreaks in this region in the past two decades reads like science fiction. Virulent new pathogens like Ebola and Marburg fever, diseases mostly controlled elsewhere like polio and monkeypox (closely related to smallpox), potentially pandemic illnesses like influenza and the plague—all have surfaced in the DRC since the 1990s. Clearly, the overwhelming share of this disease burden affects the Congolese people, who are the primary victims of these wars. But the risk to the rest of the world cannot be ignored.

The fact that poverty continues to plague Central Africa—and specifically Congo—should be a warning to U.S. policymakers. The return of violence to Eastern Congo in 2008 was an unwelcome reminder of Central Africa's fragility. The surge in violence displaced 100,000 people in just the first two months of fighting. The violence has since subsided, but Rwanda's continued forays into Congolese territory indicate that the incentive to continue fighting remains. Cross-border political tensions throughout the region have not been resolved, and the economies of neighboring states have not recovered, with the result that the profit motives of outside states remain high and the ability of Congo to forestall intervention dismally low.

As in Sierra Leone and other parts of the developing world, achieving sustainable peace in Central Africa and stemming the global threats that Congo's wars export will depend in part on policymakers' close attention to Congo's economic predicament. It will require carefully targeted development strategies to help reduce the economic incentives that drive and sustain civil war.

POLICY RECOMMENDATIONS

Poor countries with weak central governments that are in conflict, or at risk of conflict, present one of the most difficult challenges to international security. Several decades ago, the United States might have grieved over distant conflicts and provided humanitarian aid when possible, but would have reasoned that by and large such tragedies do not affect American interests. The global linkages explored in this book underscore the perils of this approach. Yet pouring foreign assistance into unstable states with little capacity for or commitment to reform can be a waste of resources. Indeed, effective results have by and large eluded the international community in such environments, and investments in foreign aid have dwindled. The percentage of U.S. bilateral aid allocated to the bottom half of sub-Saharan African countries dropped from 70 percent in 2000 to 49 percent in 2007.[90]

One approach to this problem has been to reward countries that perform well and thus create incentives for countries to fix themselves. In line with this theory, the Millennium Challenge Corporation (MCC) concentrates resources in states on a path to political and economic reform. But the cycle of doom—poverty, state weakness, and conflict—explored in this chapter is rarely broken with incentives. Poor states in conflict seldom have the capacity to break this vicious and reinforcing cycle, and in many cases their despair is fueled by other states and non-governmental actors that they cannot control.

The only way to break the cycle of destruction is to tackle all three of these factors—poverty, state weakness, and conflict—together. That alone is an important insight, but one must also recognize that the task requires sophistication in sequencing, knowledge of local conditions, and capacity to act locally. It will take six kinds of actions to address these challenges.

1. Prevention

Prevention means removing the conditions under which rebel organizations become established and continue fighting. There is no quick way to stimulate economic growth. Conflict and postconflict situations are perhaps the most difficult environments in which to seek policy reform. Nevertheless, in the end, growth will make it more difficult for insurgents to recruit followers and to evade the state. Several preventive strategies stand out from current practice and literature:

—*Peer Reviews*. In virtually every major conflict, government corruption and incompetence have planted the seeds of or exacerbated conflicts. By contrast, African states that have pursued reform grew at about 5 percent annually over the same decade that Congo and Sierra Leone were mired in conflict. These forward-looking states need to share their experience and lead in pressuring corrupt leaders to reform. Ideas on how to expand the peer review mechanisms created under the New Partnership for Africa's Development in 2001 so as to engage a wider range of actors and accelerate and sharpen advice can be found in *Power and Responsibility: Building International Order in an Era of Transnational Threats*, a comprehensive analysis by Bruce Jones, Carlos Pascual, and Steve Stedman.[91]

—*Education*. Aid strategies should increase education and employment prospects for young people in order to reduce the appeal of illicit activities that challenge the integrity of the state. To raise enrollment levels, aid should target school construction and rehabilitation, as well as competitive salaries for teachers. In the early 2000s, for example, Sierra Leone created a National Commission for War-Affected Children, which had some positive rehabilitative effects. In sum, "the specific interests and needs of youth and children must be reflected in the political agenda, economic development, and resource allocation in national and regional budgets."[92]

—*Vulnerability Fund*. Poor and weak states are least able to sustain external shocks. World Bank president Robert Zoellick has proposed a global vulnerability fund to help reduce the likelihood that economic shocks will trigger civil war. Funds would be available to the most at-risk states to help them sustain investments in human and physical infrastructure and to support microfinance initiatives that create jobs.[93] While this fund in itself will not prevent conflict, it can help mitigate the impact of shocks that do trigger conflicts in vulnerable situations, particularly when such threats extend across states.

2. Transparency and Accountability

Increasing transparency and accountability in the extractive industries can help reduce the looting of high-value commodities and overexploitation of natural resources. The Kimberley Process, developed to monitor and verify legal diamond traffic in Sierra Leone, is one such tool. Economic incentives from donor states ensure that state officials adhere to the Kimberly Process. This critical measure will stop aid funds from leaking to al Qaeda and other terrorist groups and will buttress state capacity. The Extractive Industries Transparency Initiative (EITI) takes the Kimberly Process a step further, emphasizing government control over natural resources and reinforcing the public trust.[94] Efforts that make looting more difficult increase the cost of extraction, reduce illegal profits, and ultimately reduce the incentives to rebel. Congo is currently on track to become an EITI member by 2010, and a percentage of U.S. assistance should be contingent on progress in meeting this target date. U.S. aid agencies working in conflict zones should include domestic and multinational corporations in their projects but ask them to comply with protocols that demand transparency and equitable compensation for the extraction of natural resources. These protocols include the UN norms on the Responsibilities of Transnational Corporations and Other Business Enterprises with Regard to Human Rights and the UN Global Compact, which commit participating corporations to a broad set of environmental, labor, and human rights standards. Similarly, states emerging from conflict need to develop the capacity to monitor and adjudicate the use of their own resources. In 2005 Sierra Leone's Truth and Reconciliation Commission advised that the government create a regime to enhance transparency in the mining industry, but the authorities have been slow to adopt the suggestion. Again, foreign aid could encourage expeditious adoption of changes to national laws.[95]

3. A Multilateral and Regional Capacity for Peace Enforcement and Peacekeeping and Civilian Police

Experience in Africa, Haiti, Iraq, and Afghanistan has shown that it is impossible to stimulate economic activity and break out of poverty's traps until security is at a level that allows the population to engage in normal economic activity without fear of being killed, being robbed, or having its investments destroyed. Despite many investments in peace-keeping and peace building, international capacity remains weak, poorly coordinated, and limited in its ability to deliver security and services at a grass-roots level.[96] The UN Peace Building Commission may be a start toward coordination, but the Department of Peacekeeping Operations remains heavily constrained in its ability to mobilize troops quickly. Although the African Union has made great strides in keeping the peace, the scale of its missions in Sudan and Somalia has outstripped capacity. The international community's capacity to deploy civilian police is even more limited, with the result that militaries are often called upon to take on functions for which they are not prepared. One suggested way to boost multilateral and regional capacity is to invest in a comprehensive program for pretrained and standby forces that is organized around a common doctrine and common procedures.[97]

4. Capacity to Deliver Aid at a Decentralized Level

Through its positive effects, decentralized aid can help communities overcome the impacts of conflict. Part of the incentive to sustain peace comes from seeing that peace can bring jobs, services, and security. Official aid agencies tend to channel resources to central governments with a view to increasing their capacity, but aid's impact may not be felt on the ground then, or may be greatly delayed. To complicate matters, regional officials tend to be leery of high officeholders, in part because central governments are often insensitive to local needs. In Afghanistan, for example, funding often fails to move beyond Kabul. In Congo, U.S Agency for International Development (USAID) administrators recently complained that government officials in the capital of Kinshasa reinvested only a small share of the taxes they collected in Ituri Province, where conflict has raged.

Still, decentralization must be handled carefully so it helps communities buy into the concept of a state instead of encouraging separatist tendencies. That was the principle behind the Afghan National Solidarity Program, which made resources available to provinces for projects that fit within a national development strategy, but the levels were too low to have the necessary impact. States must also be able to mobilize technical resources to help local officials develop strategies for attracting investment and coordinating education and health programs with national policies and strategy. Even after eight years in Afghanistan, the United States is still unable to mobilize more than a handful of technical advisers for any given province. By contrast, it can supply 4,000 troops to train the military and police.[98]

One nongovernmental organization that endeavors to help governments deliver results and build capacity at the local level is Mercy Corps. In Kosovo, Mercy Corps sought to address the economic roots of the 1999 civil war by connecting Serb-operated mills producing animal feed with Albanian livestock owners and poultry farms. In Bosnia, another program provides targeted loans to low-income people who have developed business plans but do not have the funds to implement them. Today, fourteen years after the end of the war, more than 59,000 active borrowers are participating in the market economy. And in Kyrgyzstan, Tajikistan, and Uzbekistan, Mercy Corps launched an initiative that includes youth in community decisionmaking and develops youth-focused activities to foster marketable skills through vocational training, master-apprenticeship, and programs for building social and job skills. Each of these innovative programs aims to reduce the economic pressures that undermine stability.

5. Strategies That Build State Capacity

One effective measure in this category consists of establishing a national fund to coordinate the salary levels of government officials, including police officers, military personnel, and other workers in accordance with a regular performance review. The prospects for advancement and higher salaries will motivate people to perform well and make them less inclined to defect from their positions. Competitive state salaries could also prove to be a bulwark against corruption, or at least petty corruption. In Georgia in 2004, for example, the Open Society Institute partnered with United Nations Development Program (UNDP) to create a fund to raise civil servant strategies. The fund is credited with helping to reduce petty corruption, especially among police and customs officers.

Another key to building state capacity lies in the way donors administer their assistance. Some donors, particularly the United States, insist on keeping funds outside of national budgets or in separate accounts in order to reduce the risk of corruption. The result, of course, is an unwieldy array of multiple accounts, often with differing requirements and standards, which drain management capacity and create parallel administrative systems that reduce transparency. Donor behavior is yet another important factor. If multilateral, regional, and bilateral donors, not to mention NGOs, are all seeking direct interaction with policymakers at the same time, government officials will find themselves doing more "coordinating" than fulfilling their functions. Some donors may even hire away the best national staff at higher salaries. A mechanism to combat such problems is for UNDP and the World Bank to design a program based on field pilot projects that would engage host governments, bilateral donors, and the NGO community in formulating self-regulatory guidelines for coordinating donors effectively and tailoring assistance to building rather than detracting from local capacity.[99]

Furthermore, enough cannot be said about the importance of building indigenous capacity to administer the rule of law.[100] A capacity to ensure law and order ultimately determines whether a state is in a position to let international peacekeepers and police withdraw and still avoid a return to violence. Few donors, however, think about the time required to rebuild national police forces and justice systems. A common mistake they make is to train individual units, reinsert them into corrupt bureaucracies, and thereby reinforce a corrupt law enforcement system.

The challenges here are considerable. The international community has no recognized center of excellence for assisting in the establishment of rule of law or for capacity building; nor does it have a repository for deployable capacity. In 2007 fewer than 100 out of about 5,000 civilians deployed worldwide in peace building were employed in governance functions, including the rule of law.[101] The only way to succeed in these areas, and thus accelerate the transition from international to national administration of justice, is to invest in building the international capacity to deliver and sustain assistance in police training, the restructuring of national and local police forces, legal drafting, the training of judges and prosecutors, and the creation of a reliable and humane penitentiary system. At present, there is a disincentive for donors to invest in these areas, since security is not considered official development assistance under OECD guidelines.[102]

6. Former or Potential Combatants Integrated into Society after Conflict

A great deal has been written about the importance of disarmament, demobilization, and reintegration (DDR) programs in returning former combatants to civilian life. Yet one key lesson often overlooked is that the viability of such programs depends on the health of the economies awaiting their return. Send back a group of demobilized and trained fighters to an area with 50 percent unemployment, and a year later 50 percent are still likely to be unemployed. Vulnerable communities need to pursue job creation aggressively, beyond merely finding immediate employment for former combatants.

Given the scope of the challenge, it may at times be appropriate to lure disaffected youth into stabilizing activities via cash incentives and job training. Colombian president Alvaro Uribe followed this precept in a highly effective "reinsertion" program that slashed the ranks of the guerillas within five years by reducing economic incentives to join their bands. In another case, the Sons of Iraq Program modified the incentives of potential recruits. By early 2009, an estimated 91,000 Iraqis had contracted with coalition forces, each receiving the equivalent of $300 (U.S.) a month for providing the country with security services. By April 2008, more than 95,000 members of the group had vowed not to support al Qaeda in Iraq.[103] If donors restrict their aid to transitional programs without pursuing wider development, progress is almost sure to falter. Yet under certain conditions, aid that targets transitional groups can help change the dynamic in postconflict environments.

CONCLUSION

As the late Samuel Huntington observed, "The most important political distinction among countries concerns not their form of government but their degree of government."[104] Poverty alleviation is critical to meeting the challenge of failed states. In an insecure environment, carefully targeted development strategies can improve people's outlook, reduce their desire to seek alternative or illicit revenue, and thus reduce the risk of further conflict.

The connection between poverty, state weakness, and civil war is undeniable. Many challenges associated with civil wars in the developing world have global dimensions. The stakes are too high to avoid the hard task of strengthening weak and failed states and building a capacity for security. This is the only way to break the cycle of violence and give development a chance to work. Ultimately, U.S. security depends upon it.

NOTES

1. Paul Salopek, "Leftover Arms Fuel Continent's Ruinous Wars; Cold War Surplus Wreaks Havoc," *Chicago Tribune*, December 23, 1991.

2. George Packer, "Gangsta War," *New Yorker*, November 3, 2003.

3. Ibid.

4. UNDP, *Human Development Report 2000* (New York, 2000).

5. The combination of intervening variables other than economic factors driving the outbreak of civil war was complex and consequential. Although economic decline was not the only factor affecting stability in Côte d'Ivoire, the focus here is on the critical role it played as a useful antidote to the obsession with sociopolitical forces doing the causal work, which frequently dominates popular accounts of civil war.

6. See, for example, Lotta Harbom and Peter Wallensteen, "Patterns of Major Armed Conflicts, 1998–2007," in *SIPRI Yearbook 2008: Armaments, Disarmament and International Security* (Oxford: Stockholm International Peace Research Institute, 2008).

7. World Bank, *Mini Atlas of Human Security*, Human Security Report Project (Washington, 2008).

8. James D. Fearon and David D. Laitin, "Ethnicity, Insurgency, and Civil War," *American Political Science Review* 97, no. 1 (2003): 75–90.

9. See especially Robert H. Bates, *When Things Fell Apart: State Failure in Late-Century Africa* (Cambridge University Press, 2008); Paul Collier and Anke Hoeffler, "Greed and Grievance in Civil War," *Oxford Economic Papers* 56, no. 4 (2004): 563–95; Paul Collier, Anke Hoeffler, and Dominic Rohner, "Beyond Greed and Grievance: Feasibility and Civil War," *Oxford Economic Papers* 61, no. 1 (2009): 1–27; Fearon and Laitin, "Ethnicity, Insurgency, and Civil War"; Nicholas Sambanis, "Using Case Studies to Expand Economic Models of Civil War," *Perspectives on Politics* 2, no. 2 (2004): 259–79. For a review of the literature covering the relationship between poverty and civil war, see Susan E. Rice, Corinne Graff, and Janet Lewis, "Poverty and Civil War: What Policymakers Need to Know," Global Economy and Development Working Paper (Brookings, 2006).

10. Paul Collier, *The Bottom Billion: Why the Poorest Countries Are Failing and What Can Be Done about It* (Oxford University Press, 2007). In addition to being caught in a conflict trap, says Collier, many poor countries are vulnerable to a "natural resource trap," are "landlocked with bad neighbors," and are trapped in "bad governance in a small country."

11. See, for instance, Hazem Ghobarah, Paul Huth, and Bruce Russett, "The Postwar Effects of Civil Conflict," unpublished paper (www.princeton.edu/rpds/seminars/pdfs/russett_civilconflict.pdf).

12. Kristian Skrede Gleditsch, "Transnational Dimensions of Civil War," *Journal of Peace Research* 44, no. 3 (2007): 293–309. See also Nicholas Sambanis, "A Review of Recent Advances and Future Directions in the Literature on Civil War," *Defense and Peace Economics* 13, no. 6 (2002): 215–43; and Ted Robert Gurr, "Why Minorities Rebel: A Global Analysis of Communal Mobilization and Conflict since 1945," *International Political Science Review* 14, no. 2 (1993): 161–291.

13. Paul Collier and others, *Breaking the Conflict Trap: Civil War and Development Policy*, Policy Research Report (Washington: World Bank, 2003).

14. Ghobarah and others, "The Postwar Effects of Civil Conflict."

15. Abby Stoddard, Adele Harmer, and Katherine Haver, "Providing Aid in Insecure Environments: Trends in Policy and Operations" (London: Humanitarian Policy Group, 2006), p. 1.

16. Collier and others, *Breaking the Conflict Trap*, p. 35.

17. United Nations High Commissioner for Refugees (UNHCR), "State of the World's Refugees, 2006" (www.unhcr.org/cgi-bin/texis/vtx/template?page=publ&src=static/sowr2006/toceng.htm [April 20, 2008]).

18. Sarah Kenyon Lischer, *Dangerous Sanctuaries: Refugee Camps, Civil War, and the Dilemmas of Humanitarian Aid* (Cornell University Press, 2005), pp. 78–80.

19. Monty Marshall, "Global Trends in Violent Conflict," in *Peace and Conflict 2005*, edited by Monty Marshall and Ted Robert Gurr (College Park, Md.: University of Maryland, Center for International Development and Conflict Management, 2005). See also Stewart Patrick, "'Failed' States and Global Security: Empirical Questions and Policy Dilemmas," *International Studies Review* 9, no. 4 (2007): 652.

20. Kirk Kraeutler, "U.N. Reports That Taliban Are Stockpiling Afghan Opium to Ensure Income Source," *New York Times*, November 28, 2008.

21. Marshall, "Global Trends in Violent Conflict," p. 13. The data utilized in the report were compiled from the Correlates of War Project, an academic study launched by David Singer in 1963 and designed to present a comprehensive history of warfare.

22. Daniel P. Moynihan, *Pandaemonium: Ethnicity in International Politics* (Oxford University Press, 1993).

23. Samuel P. Huntington, "The Clash of Civilizations?" *Foreign Affairs* 72, no. 3 (1993): 22–28.

24. Fearon and Laitin, "Ethnicity, Insurgency, and Civil War." Other scholars have uncovered new evidence that ethnic differences are not a powerful explanation for the incidence of war. See Yahya Sadowski, *The Myth of Global Chaos* (Brookings, 1998), pp. 145–69.

25. Task Force on Difference, Inequality, and Developing Societies, "The Persistent Problem: Inequality, Difference, and the Challenge of Development" (Washington: American Political Science Association, 2008), p. 44. See also James D. Fearon and David D. Laitin, "Explaining Interethnic Cooperation," *American Political Science Review* 90, no. 4 (1996): 715–35; James D. Fearon and David D. Laitin, "Review: Violence and the Social Construction of Ethnic Identity," *International Organization* 54, no. 4 (2000): 845–77; Ashutosh Varshney, *Ethnic Conflict and Civic Life: Hindus and Muslims in India* (Yale University Press, 2002).

26. Collier, *The Bottom Billion*, pp. 17, 27.

27. Collier and others, "Beyond Greed and Grievance," pp. 19–20.

28. J. Joseph Hewitt, Jonathan Wilkenfeld, and Ted Robert Gurr, "Peace and Conflict 2008: Executive Summary" (College Park, Md.: University of Maryland, Center for International Development and Conflict Management, 2008).

29. Sambanis, "Using Case Studies to Expand Economic Models of Civil War," p. 259.

30. Macartan Humphreys, "Economics and Violent Conflict," Working Paper (Harvard University, 2003), p. 2. See World Bank list of economies (July 2008) (http://siteresources.worldbank.org/DATASTATISTICS/Resources/CLASS.XLS).

31. Collier and others, "Beyond Greed and Grievance," p. 10.

32. Nicholas Sambanis, "Poverty and the Organization of Political Violence: A Review and Some Conjectures," unpublished paper (Yale University, July 2004), p. 50.

33. See, for instance, Herschel Grossman, "Foreign Aid and Insurrection," *Defense Economics* 3, no. 4 (1992): 275–88.

34. Furthermore, as the World Bank notes, the only type of aid that is fungible and therefore susceptible to capture by rebel groups is food or humanitarian aid. See World Bank, "Aid, Policy and Peace: Reducing the Risks of Civil Conflict," Conflict Prevention and Reconstruction Unit, Dissemination Note 9 (Washington, February 2003).

35. Fearon and Laitin, "Ethnicity, Insurgency, and Civil War," p. 83.

36. James Fearon, "Economic Development, Insurgency, and Civil War," in *Institutions and Economic Performance*, edited by Elhanan Helpman (Harvard University Press, 2008), p. 296. Douglas Woodwell makes a similar argument that the strength of the British army dampened the escalation of violence in Northern Ireland between 1969 and 1994. See Douglas Woodwell, "The 'Troubles' of Northern Ireland: Civil Conflict in an Economically Well-Developed State," in *Understanding Civil War: Evidence and Analysis*, edited by Paul Collier and Nicholas Sambanis (Washington: World Bank, 2005). See also Bates, *When Things Fell Apart*. Ekaterina Stepanova notes: "Weak or dysfunctional state capacity appears to be the main condition for the fragmentation of armed violence." See Ekaterina Stepanova, "Trends in Armed Conflicts," in *SIPRI Yearbook 2008*, p. 44.

37. Paul Collier, "Rebellion as a Quasi-Criminal Activity," *Journal of Conflict Resolution* 44, no. 6 (2000): 839–53; Collier and Hoeffler, "Greed and Grievance in Civil War."

38. See Collier and others, "Beyond Greed and Grievance."

39. Sambanis, "Using Case Studies to Expand Economic Models of Civil War," p. 260.

40. Sambanis suggests that the employment of a series of small-N case studies is an effective approach to gain insight into these causal mechanisms, and "a secondary line of inquiry" should be opened "to illuminate the pathways

through which independent variables influence the dependent variable (civil war)." Nicholas Sambanis, "Conclusion: Using Case Studies to Refine and Expand the Theory of Civil War," in *Understanding Civil War*, edited by Collier and Sambanis, p. 329.

41. Markus Brückner and Antonio Ciccone, "Growth, Democracy, and Civil War," Discussion Paper DP6568 (Washington: Center for Economic and Policy Research, 2008); Oeindrila Dube and Juan Vargas, "Are All Resources Cursed? Coffee, Oil and Armed Conflict in Colombia" (Cambridge, Mass: Weatherhead Center for International Affairs, 2006); Edward Miguel, Shanker Satyanath, and Ernest Sergenti, "Economic Shocks and Civil Conflict: An Instrumental Variables Approach," *Journal of Political Economy* 112, no. 4 (2004): 725–53.

42. Bates, *When Things Fell Apart*, pp. 104–05.

43. Colin H. Kahl, "Demography, Environment, and Civil Strife," in *Too Poor for Peace? Global Poverty, Conflict, and Security in the 21st Century*, edited by Lael Brainard and Derek H. Chollet (Brookings, 2007), pp. 62–63.

44. There is some debate in the literature as to whether the relationship between poverty and recruitment success is a direct one. Mechanisms other than the desire for economic profit can enhance recruitment efforts, such as conscription, abduction, or a desire for revenge. See Stathis N. Kalyvas, *The Logic of Violence in Civil War* (Cambridge University Press, 2006), pp. 96–99.

45. Lael Brainard, Derek H. Chollet, and Vinca LaFleur, "The Tangled Web: The Poverty-Insecurity Nexus," in *Too Poor for Peace?* edited by Brainard and Chollet, p. 11. See Collier and others, "Beyond Greed and Grievance"; Henrik Urdal, "People vs. Malthus: Population Pressure, Environmental Degradation, and Armed Conflict Revisited," *Journal of Peace Research* 42, no. 4 (2005): 417–34. For a discussion of the relationship between youth bulges and civil war, see Rice and others, "Poverty and Civil War," pp. 10–11.

46. Paul Collier, Anke Hoeffler, and Måns Söderbom, "On the Duration of Civil War," *Journal of Peace Research* 41, no. 3 (2004): 253–73; James D. Fearon, "Why Do Some Civil Wars Last So Much Longer than Others?" *Journal of Peace Research* 41, no. 3 (2004): 275–301; Fearon and Laitin, "Ethnicity, Insurgency, and Civil War," p. 77. Paul Collier has noted that the average civil war lasts ten times longer than average international conflict.

47. Vanda Felbab-Brown, "Globalization and Narcoterrorism," in *State of Corruption, State of Chaos: The Terror of Political Malfeasance*, edited by Michaelene Cox (Lanham, Md.: Lexington Books, 2008), pp. 15–31.

48. For an extended discussion of resource depletion as a contributing factor to civil war, see Thomas Homer-Dixon, "Straw Man in the Wind," *National Interest*, no. 93 (2008).

49. Barbara F. Walter, "Does Conflict Beget Conflict? Explaining Recurring Civil War," *Journal of Peace Research* 41, no. 3 (2004): 371. In other research, Paul Collier and Anke Hoeffler found that 44 percent of civil wars in their

sample restarted. See Paul Collier and Anke Hoeffler, "Military Expenditure in Post-Conflict Societies," *Economics of Governance* 7, no. 1 (2006): 89–107.

50. Kalyvas, *The Logic of Violence in Civil War.*

51. Jeffrey D. Sachs, *Investing in Development: A Practical Plan to Achieve the Millennium Development Goals* (New York: UN Millennium Project, 2005).

52. Walter, "Does Conflict Beget Conflict?" p. 372.

53. John L. Hirsch, "Sierra Leone: Diamonds and the Struggle for Democracy," International Peace Academy Occasional Paper (Boulder, Colo.: Lynne Rienner, 2001), p. 13.

54. A. B. Zack-Williams, "Sierra Leone: Crisis and Despair," *Review of African Political Economy* 49 (1990): 23.

55. Ibid., pp. 24, 25.

56. Ibid., p. 24.

57. Economic figures extracted from World Bank data (http://econ.worldbank.org/WBSITE/EXTERNAL/EXTDEC/0,,menuPK:476823~pagePK:64165236~piPK:64165141~theSitePK:469372,00.html).

58. Measured in 2006 U.S. dollars.

59. UNDP, *Human Development Report 2000* (New York, 2008), p. 16.

60. Zack-Williams, "Sierra Leone: Crisis and Despair," pp. 27–28.

61. Ibid., p. 32. The 2005 report of Sierra Leone's Truth and Reconciliation Commission directly attributed the war to decades of corrupt rule (www.unhcr.org/refworld/country,,HRW,,SLE,456d621e2,47a87c1241,0.html).

62. Paul Richards, "Rebellion in Liberia and Sierra Leone: A Crisis of Youth?" in *Conflict in Africa*, edited by Oliver Furley (New York: I. B. Tauris, 1995), p. 150.

63. Lansana Gberie, *A Dirty War in West Africa: The RUF and the Destruction of Sierra Leone* (Indiana University Press, 2005), p. 6.

64. "Sierra Leone: Disaster Waits," *The Economist,* January 31, 1998.

65. "The Darkest Corner of Africa," *The Economist,* January 9, 1999.

66. "Witness to Truth: Report of the Truth and Reconciliation Commission of Sierra Leone" (2004) (http://trcsierraleone.org/drwebsite/publish/v3b-c4shtml).

67. Macartan Humphreys and Jeremy M. Weinstein, "Who Fights? The Determinants of Participation in Civil War," *American Journal of Political Science* 52, no. 2 (2008): 447. In an extensive set of interviews with youth combatants in Sierra Leone, Krijn Peters and Paul Richards found that child soldiers repeatedly invoked the limited economic opportunities and excess of disposable time as factors that enhanced the attractiveness of membership in the RUF. Krijn Peters and Paul Richards, "'Why We Fight': Voices of Youth Combatants in Sierra Leone," *Africa* 68, no. 2 (1998): 183–210. See also William Sampson Klock Reno, *Corruption and State Politics in Sierra Leone*, African Studies Series (Cambridge University Press, 1995); Paul Richards, *Fighting for the Rain Forest: War, Youth & Resources in Sierra Leone*, African Issues (Portsmouth, N.H.: Heinemann, 1996).

68. John L. Hirsch, "War in Sierra Leone," *Survival* 43, no. 3 (2001): 150.

69. "Terrorist Financing: U.S. Agencies Should Systematically Assess Terrorists' Use of Alternative Financing Mechanisms" (U.S. General Accounting Office [GAO], November 2003), pp. 20–21.

70. Lujala Päivi, Nils Petter Gleditsch, and Elizabeth Gilmore, "A Diamond Curse? Civil War and a Lootable Resource," *Journal of Conflict Resolution* 49, no. 4 (2005): 538–62.

71. Zack-Williams, "Sierra Leone: Crisis and Despair," p. 25.

72. Reno William, "Clandestine Economies, Violence and States in Africa," *Journal of International Affairs* 53, no. 2 (2000): 433–59.

73. According to the GAO, in the 1990s al Qaeda established a direct conduit between diamonds smuggled out of Sierra Leone by rebel soldiers and operations in East Africa setting up diamond mining and trading companies in Kenya and Tanzania. Court transcripts from the 2001 trial of al Qaeda operatives in the United States revealed that diamonds had been a critical component of the terrorist organization's financial structure. See GAO, "Terrorist Financing," p. 21; Global Witness, "For a Few Dollars More: How al Qaeda Moved into the Diamond Trade" (April 2003), p. 7; Doug Farah, "Al Qaeda Cash Tied to Diamond Trade; Sale of Gems from Sierra Leone Rebels Raised Millions," *Washington Post*, November 2, 2001.

74. GAO, "Terrorist Financing," p. 21; Global Witness, "For a Few Dollars More," p. 8. See also Douglas Farah's April 2, 2004, testimony before the House Africa Subcommittee, referenced in Jim Fisher-Thompson, "Congress Told of Terrorist Links to Diamond Trade in West Africa," *Washington File* (U.S. State Department, April 9, 2004).

75. GAO, "Terrorist Financing," p. 5.

76. Farah, "Al Qaeda Cash Tied to Diamond Trade."

77. For a comprehensive case study of the end to the civil war in Sierra Leone, see William Durch, ed., *Twenty-First-Century Peace Operations* (Washington: U.S. Institute of Peace Press, 2006).

78. UN Mission in the Democratic Republic of the Congo, "Why the D.R.C. Matters?" (www.un.org/Depts/dpko/missions/monuc/drc.pdf [February 2009]).

79. "UN Report Points to 'Alarming' Levels of Poverty in D.R.C.," (Johannesburg) *Mail & Guardian*, December 17, 2008.

80. Congo was known as Zaire until Mobutu Sese Seko was overthrown in 1997.

81. World Bank, *Key Development Data and Statistics* (http://web.world bank.org/WBSITE/EXTERNAL/DATASTATISTICS/0,,contentMDK:20535285~menuPK:1192694~pagePK:64133150~piPK:64133175~theSitePK:239419,00.html).

82. Pierre Englebert, "Life Support or Assisted Suicide? Dilemmas of U.S. Policy toward the Democratic Republic of Congo," in *Short of the Goal: U.S.*

Policy and Poorly Performing States, edited by Nancy Birdsall, Milan Vaishnav, and Robert L. Ayres (Washington: Center for Global Development, 2006), pp. 54–55.

83. World Bank, *Key Development Data and Statistics*.

84. Englebert, "Life Support or Assisted Suicide?" p. 56.

85. Douglas Farah, "Digging up Congo's Dirty Gems; Officials Say Diamond Trade Funds Radical Islamic Groups," *Washington Post*, December 30, 2001.

86. Human Rights Watch, "The Curse of Gold" (New York, 2005), p. 3.

87. Englebert, "Life Support or Assisted Suicide?" p. 72.

88. World Bank, DRC fact page (http://web.worldbank.org/WBSITE/EXTERNAL/COUNTRIES/AFRICAEXT/CONGODEMOCRATICEXTN/0,,contentMDK:20779255~menuPK:2114031~pagePK:141137~piPK:141127~theSitePK:349466,00.html#1).

89. Food and Agriculture Organization, Newsroom (www.fao.org/newsroom/en/news/2006/1000385/index.html).

90. This figure does not account for U.S. contributions to international organizations such as UNICEF and the UNDP or other channels of indirect foreign assistance. Steve Radelet, "What's Behind the Recent Declines in U.S. Foreign Assistance?" CGD Notes (Washington: Center for Global Development, 2008); Stewart Patrick and Kaysie Brown, "Fragile States and U.S. Foreign Assistance: Show Me the Money," Working Paper 96 (Washington: Center for Global Development, 2006).

91. Bruce Jones, Carlos Pascual, and Stephen John Stedman, *Power and Responsibility: Building International Order in an Era of Transnational Threats* (Brookings, 2009), pp. 263–64.

92. Ismail O. D. Rashid, "West Africa's Post-Cold War Security Challenges," in *West Africa's Security Challenges: Building Peace in a Troubled Region*, edited by Adekeye Adebajo and Ismail O. D. Rashid (Boulder, Colo.: Lynne Rienner, 2004), p. 389.

93. Robert Zoellick, "A Stimulus Package for the World," *New York Times*, January 22, 2009.

94. Paul Collier and Anke Hoeffler, "The Challenge of Reducing the Global Incidence of Civil War," *Copenhagen Consensus 2004* (2004), pp. 21–22.

95. UNHCR, "World Report 2008—Sierra Leone" (www.unhcr.org/refworld/country,,HRW,,SLE,456d621e2,47a87c1241,0.html).

96. See Jones and others, *Power and Responsibility*, chap. 7.

97. See ibid., pp. 195–203.

98. Gerry J. Gilmore, "Trainers 'Critical' to Obama's New Afghan-Pakistan Plan, Mullen Says," American Forces Press Service, March 27, 2009.

99. See Jones and others, *Power and Responsibility*, p. 262.

100. For a useful course syllabus with multiple references to readings on issues ranging from legal drafting to judicial reform and law enforcement, see

Louis Aucoin, "Rule of Law in Post Conflict Societies" (http://fletcher.tufts.edu/humansecurity/pdf04/ILO%20L252%20Rule%20of%20Law%20in%20Post%20Conflict%20Societies.pdf).

101. Jones and others, *Power and Responsibility*, p. 191.

102. Ibid., p. 265.

103. Greg Bruno, "Finding a Place for the Sons of Iraq," Backgrounder (Council on Foreign Relations, January 9, 2009) (www.cfr.org/publication/16088/).

104. Samuel P. Huntington, *Political Order in Changing Societies* (Yale University Press, 1968), p. 1.

CHAPTER FIVE

Feeding Insecurity? Poverty, Weak States, and Climate Change

JOSHUA BUSBY

Since the severe droughts of the 1980s, the nomadic herders and more settled agriculturalists of Darfur have been in conflict over grazing rights. Despite periodic tension and confrontations in earlier years, the two had previously shared the semiarid region's resources and, at least until legal reforms in 1970, had local mechanisms for resolving disputes.[1] In a more anodyne telling of the region's history, pastoralists, on their periodic dry season peregrinations, had been able to graze their camels and cattle on the hills around the farmers' lands. The farmers allowed the herders to use their wells and shared the chaff and husks left over from the harvests. When the rains persistently failed in the 1980s, resources dwindled, a problem accelerated by overgrazing and farming practices. Farmers started fencing off their lands to keep the nomads out, so herders, including migrants from Chad, pushed further south in search of other grazing lands, bringing them into conflict with other settled agriculturalists.[2] These tensions gave rise to the first Darfur wars of 1987–89 and then 1994–98. By 2003 the acrimony between the parties, now involving a variety of ethnic groups, escalated into intense fighting. The Sudanese government weighed in on the side of the herders, arming them and providing air support for their depredations against the farmers, thereby contributing to a gross abuse of human rights against civilians.[3]

In June 2007 UN secretary-general Ban Ki-moon fingered climate change "amid the diverse social and political causes" as the ecological spark that ignited the Darfur conflict.[4] Some Sudan experts strongly disagreed, arguing that "the most important culprit for violence in Darfur is government, which not only failed to utilize local and central institutions to address the problems of environmental stress . . . , but actually worsened the situation through its militarized, crisis management interventions whenever political disputes have arisen."[5] If famine and drought were primarily to blame, some added, "why have scores of environmental catastrophes failed to set off armed conflict elsewhere?"[6] Others worried that invoking climate change as a potential cause for the conflict would let the government off the hook. Still others found the connections between climate change and conflict "highly problematic as they suggest a near deterministic relation between the environment and armed conflict, thereby relieving the main actors of their own responsibility."[7]

This debate underscores a number of challenges for those that draw connections between environmental change and security. What purpose is served by making such claims? Does it potentially help the people of Darfur? What is meant by the term "security"? Security for whom? The people of Darfur? The people of the United States?

The relationship between environmental quality, poverty, and security is necessarily messy, with feedback mechanisms that are still only hazily understood. The "environment" alone covers a diversity of phenomena, and even narrowing the focus to climate change still encompasses a broad issue. This chapter lays bare the complexity of extrapolating from the likely physical effects of climate change to its impact on social and economic systems. The scientific evidence suggests climate change will likely have a disproportionate effect on poor countries with weak governance, particularly in Africa and Asia.[8] Moreover, poverty and weak state capacity will in turn impede efforts to address environmental challenges in some of the places that need such help the most, including the Horn of Africa, parts of South Asia, and specific countries like Haiti and the Democratic Republic of the Congo (DRC).

At this point, the consequences of climate and environmental change for regional and international security are less clear. Although evidence of the links between climate change and a variety of security outcomes (and there are likely to be a number of them) is mounting, there is a temptation to claim more certainty about the connections than is yet warranted. Even so, some appreciation of the uncertainties will actually help policymakers forge working majorities rather than impede action. With politically charged issues like climate change, overstating the threat for policy gain could be self-defeating, undermining the very agenda that advocates of more robust policies are championing. At the same time, it is important to consider the interaction between resource scarcity and other contributors to conflict (such as ethnic tensions and poverty), particularly since conflict may be difficult to resolve without addressing those environmental stressors.

WHY "SECURITIZE" CLIMATE CHANGE?

The main purpose of a volume like this one is to inform and improve policymaking. If, as its contributors argue, poverty and state weakness are interrelated, poor states with weak governance will be less able to deal with threats such as climate change that can have wide impacts on resources, food, and migration. In order to address problems like climate change, policymakers must therefore take into account the constraints imposed by poverty and weak governance.

A broader purpose here is to persuade interested publics in the developed world that the threats in poor countries affect their own security, and thus that poverty alleviation should be an important element of a U.S. national security strategy. In other words, this volume speaks not just to the parochial security concerns of poor countries but also to wider interests of influential and rich countries like the United States that have the capacity to provide foreign assistance.

Wealthy countries, largely responsible for the greenhouse gas concentrations that cause global warming, have been asked to provide billions of dollars in financing to help poor countries adapt to climate change by improving their coastal defenses against storm surges, investing in drought-resistant crop varieties, developing early warning systems and evacuation plans in the event of weather disasters, and so on. Those investments would ensure that the worst effects of climate change, including the security consequences identified in this chapter, do not come to pass or are less severe than anticipated. Modest investments of this nature would also likely avert the need for more expensive disaster response and crisis management strategies later on, such as the mobilization of foreign militaries for humanitarian relief and possibly conflict termination and peacekeeping. Since the mobilization of those funds, particularly in the United States, is likely to be part of a broader policy of climate mitigation, the fate of foreign assistance for poor countries may be bound up with how climate change is approached in general. Despite the attraction of "securitizing" climate change—that is, naming climate change a security

FIGURE 5-1. Number of State-Based Armed Conflicts by Type, 1946–2006

Number of conflicts

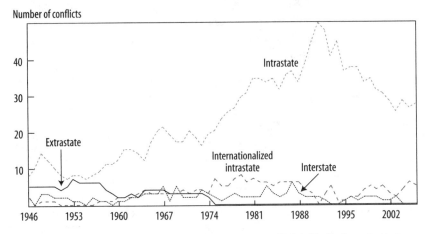

Source: Human Security Project, "Human Security Report 2006" (University of British Columbia, Human Security Centre, 2006). Data for 2006 with corrections to 2003 and 2005 interstate conflicts from Halvard Buhaug, Nils Petter Gleditsch, and Ole Magnus Theisen, "Implications of Climate Change for Armed Conflict," SDCC Working Paper (Washington: World Bank, February 25, 2008).

issue—it entails some risks. In particular, proponents must not overemphasize the links between climate change and conflict and thus reify the partisan divides that have frozen climate policy in the past.

In the past several years, a stream of reports from think tanks, nongovernmental organizations (NGOs), and governments has suggested that climate change could be a "threat multiplier," particularly in the developing world. Countries with a history of instability, weak state capacity, and sectarian divides are expected to be increasingly vulnerable to extreme weather, droughts, floods, storms, declining agricultural output, and water scarcity.[9]

As a number of observers have warned, one drawback of viewing climate change as a security issue is that it becomes the kind of problem that is entitled and perhaps requires emergency, potentially militarized, attention, which may not be appropriate and may end up diverting resources to less efficient purposes. Successfully evoking national security necessarily activates the policy apparatus whose core mission is to prepare to fight and win wars, skill sets that may have limited utility for a global public good that demands transformations in energy systems and investments in adaptive measures.[10] Critics worry that security concerns might merely serve as political theater: "Serious thinking about climate change must recognize that the 'hard' security threats that are supposedly lurking are mostly a ruse. They are good for the threat industry—which needs danger for survival—and they are good for the greens who find it easier to build a coalition for policy when hawks are supportive."[11]

A clear conception of what constitutes "security" is essential to avoid focusing exclusively on the presence or absence of conflict or the opposite danger of widening our view of security so much that it encompasses any threats to human welfare.[12] An overly restrictive focus on climate and armed conflict may leave one analyzing a dwindling set of cases as state-based armed conflicts become rare. There have been no new cases of interstate conflict since 2003 (see figure 5-1), while intrastate conflicts or civil war have declined from the high watermark of the early post–cold war years.[13]

This holds for Africa, the world's most conflict-ridden continent. The number of conflicts in sub-Saharan Africa, for example, declined from sixteen in 1999 to seven in 2006. Moreover, the number of non-state conflicts in the region—that is, between warring non-state rebel groups—dropped from twenty-eight in 2002 to twelve in 2006.[14] Intra-state conflict is concentrated in the "shatter belt," which includes two bands in the Horn of Africa and the Great Lakes region, and an area from the Caucasus to the Philippines (figure 5-2).[15]

Of course, these trends may not last, especially if the connections with climate change are valid, and indeed may already be starting to tick up again. Furthermore, climate change has other security implications that may be equally if not more severe than conflict, such as its contribution to the increasing destructive potential of natural disasters. Disasters may swamp civilian authorities' capacity to respond, even if they fail to give rise to violent conflict.[16]

In terms of the narrow climate-conflict nexus, thus far there is some, but limited, evidence to support the more far-reaching claims about the connections between climate change and violence, state failure, or both. In this context, advocates and scholars risk undermining the persuasive impact of their arguments by overstating the claimed security consequences of climate change and the certainty with which they make their claims. Extreme partisanship has paralyzed the policy debate on climate change in the United States for more than a dozen years. When it comes to shifting public and elite perceptions on this issue, bipartisan support in the United States will be essential. Efforts that overstate the degree of confidence about the security connections will play into rising fears that

FIGURE 5-2. Intrastate Armed Conflicts, 2007

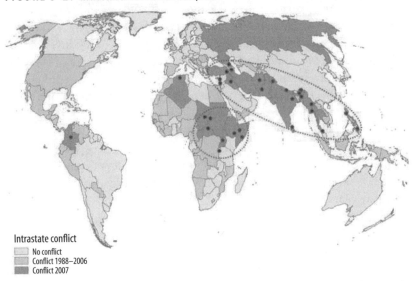

Intrastate conflict
- No conflict
- Conflict 1988–2006
- Conflict 2007

Source: Halvard Buhaug and others, "Implications of Climate Change for Armed Conflict" (Washington: World Bank, 2008).

the problem has been oversold. In March 2009 Gallup reported that 41 percent, the highest proportion ever, believe the threat of climate change has been exaggerated (figure 5-3).[17]

Equally worrying, many Americans view the underlying scientific connections between greenhouse gas emissions and climate change through a partisan filter. Although a 2006 Pew Center poll found considerable agreement on the solid evidence of global warming among a majority of Democrats (81 percent), Republicans (58 percent), and Independents (71 percent), only 24 percent of Republicans believed the evidence showed human activity to be the cause, compared with 54 percent of Democrats and 47 percent of Independents.[18] Another poll in March 2008 showed the partisan gap on climate change had grown to more than thirty percentage points, up from an indistinguishable difference in 1998 (figure 5-4).[19]

Members of Congress are even more divided than the public on this issue. In February 2007, in a poll of some 113 members of Congress, only 13 percent of Republicans (down from 23 percent in April 2006) said it had been proved beyond a reasonable doubt that man-made causes were responsible for warming compared with 95 percent of Democrats.[20]

Aside from long-term mitigation programs to reduce greenhouse gas emissions and decarbonize the economy, investments in adaptation are

FIGURE 5-3. Public Opinion on Climate Change Exaggeration

Percentage indicating the seriousness of global warming

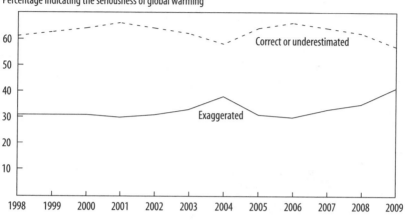

Source: Lydia Saad, "Increased Number Think Global Warming Is Exaggerated," Gallup Poll, March 11, 2009.

the most important initiatives governments can take to head off the worst consequences of climate change, including the security concerns discussed in this chapter. For poor countries, most of those resources will have to come from external sources. As of May 2009, however, the United States had contributed zero dollars to the Global Environment Facility's various adaptation funds and zero dollars to a World Bank–administered trust fund for disaster reduction. The cap-and-trade bill wending its way through the U.S. Congress in 2009 includes provisions that would generate revenue. The measure that passed the House of Representatives in June 2009 sets aside 1 percent of the yearly allowances for the period 2012–21 for helping poor countries adapt, with increases to 2 percent scheduled for 2022–26 and to 4 percent for 2027–50.[21] With carbon allowances in 2016 estimated to be worth between $80 billion and $108 billion, the funds for international adaptation could reach $800 million to $1 billion in that year alone. Another 5 percent of allowances for 2012–25 are set aside for international forest conservation, valued at an estimated $4 billion to $5.4 billion in 2016.[22]

Climate change policy is at a critical juncture. Even with a sixty-vote majority in the U.S. Senate, the Democratic Party may not yet have the unity of interests and perspective on climate change to get a domestic cap-and-trade bill passed, revenue from which could conceivably generate reasonably large resources for both domestic and international adaptation

FIGURE 5-4. Partisan Gaps in Public Opinion on Climate Change

Percentage saying the effects of global warming have already begun[a]

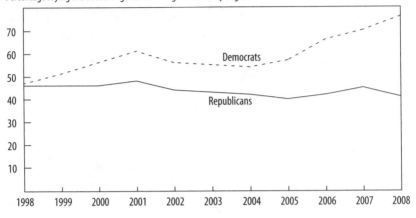

Source: Riley E. Dunlap, "Partisan Gap on Global Warming Grows," Gallup Poll, May 29, 2008.
a. Results for political independents not shown.

programs, as well as for the conservation of tropical forests. Efforts that are as clear about what is not known as what is known are more likely to gain support. For those who have yet to fully accept the causal arguments linking greenhouse gases to climate change, particularly Republicans, exaggeration could be distinctly unattractive. While this may strike some readers as an unseemly interjection of politics into policy, the messaging on this issue is extremely important. The ability of development and health advocates to forge a bipartisan U.S. coalition on debt relief and HIV/AIDS in the late 1990s and early 2000s has served those constituencies well. Climate change advocates will need similar support.[23] With this in mind, it is time now to examine evidence for various connections between climate change and violent conflict, the hypothesized security link that has dominated both the scholarly and policy communities.

The Evidence

Like the early discussion of environmental security in the 1990s, the recent spike in attention has focused largely on the connections between environmental change and conflict. For policymakers, this emphasis misses the point made earlier, that conflicts are rare and perhaps becoming rarer. Exclusively focusing on conflict might lead to an impoverished view of security.

Disasters, made more likely and more severe by climate change, affect security. Natural disasters can be as destructive as warfare, with major implications for modern militaries, which have increasingly been tapped to provide humanitarian relief and rescue services. At the very least, the diversion of military assets for humanitarian purposes has opportunity costs in terms of other activities those soldiers could have been engaged in. Of course, disasters may indeed make conflict more likely, but even where this is not the case, failed disaster management can pose broader legitimacy and credibility challenges for governments, as was the U.S. experience in the aftermath of Hurricane Katrina.

In discussing the connections between climate change and conflict and climate change/disasters and the opportunity cost of military deployments, both dynamics emphasize the security consequences that emanate from climate change. One can invert this logic and think about insecurity and state weakness as having an impact on a country's ability to protect its environment. This section discusses these three concerns in turn: conflict, disasters, and environmental protection under insecurity.

Uniting all three issues is an appreciation of relative vulnerability. Owing to their geography, some countries are more exposed to risks from climate change than others. However, vulnerability depends only in part on environmental factors. Rich, well-governed countries are less likely to suffer the consequences of climate change as they have greater resources, capacity, and resilience to respond than do weak, failing, and failed states. For example, the Index of State Weakness and the map for climate vulnerability developed by Columbia University's Center for International Earth Science Information Network (CIESIN) both indicate that the poorest countries, particularly in sub-Saharan Africa and South and Southeast Asia, are especially vulnerable (see the index in chapter 2).[24]

CIESIN's metrics of sensitivity in this instance included socioeconomic attributes but not security factors such as a country's past history of conflict or broader insecurity in its neighborhood.[25] In a subsequent study in 2008, CIESIN looked at three attributes of political risk: (1) whether a country was located in a dangerous neighborhood, (2) if it had a history of crisis, and (3) its level of capacity. These were combined with three measures of environmental vulnerability based on future climate projections: (1) the size and percentage of the population located near coastal areas, (2) countries with low adaptive capacity at different ranges of projected temperature increases, and (3) countries facing water

TABLE 5-1. Countries Most Vulnerable to Climate and Political Risks

Coastal population exposure[a]			
Total population exposed	Percentage of population exposed	Aggregate temperature changes[b]	Water scarcity[c]
China (74), Philippines (58), India (67), Indonesia (77)	Philippines (58), Egypt (78), Indonesia (77)	South Africa (110), Nepal (22), Morocco (96), Bangladesh (48), Tunisia (120), Paraguay (75), Yemen (30), Sudan (6), Côte d'Ivoire (10)	Mozambique (39), Côte d'Ivoire (10), Nigeria (28), Iraq (4), Guatemala (60), Zimbabwe (8), Ethiopia (19), Somalia (1), China (74), Syria (57), Algeria (59)

Source: Drawn from the Index of State Weakness (see chapter 2). Figures in parentheses indicate the country ranking on the index. Climate risk based on 2030 projections, and political risk based on historical data on three indicators of instability: dangerous neighborhood (1992–2005), crisis history (1990–2005), and low capacity from the World Bank Government Effectiveness indicators (dates not specified).

a. Population exposed based on countries with two or more of these instability risk factors sorted by population, that is, the number of people projected to be living within 1 meter of the low-elevation coastal zone (LECZ) in 2030. Percentage of population refers to the highest percentage of projected population in 2030 within 1 meter of the LECZ.

b. Based on countries with two or more of the risk factors.

c. Based on countries with two or more instability factors, sorted by change in percentage of population in water scarcity 2000–30.

scarcity (see table 5-1, which also shows country rankings on the Index of State Weakness in parentheses).

Countries with high risk factors for instability and coastal vulnerability were located by and large in Asia (these included China, India, the Philippines, and Indonesia), while many of those with low adaptive capacity and subject to aggregate temperature increases were located in North Africa (notably Morocco, Tunisia, and Sudan). Many of the countries subject to water scarcity and political risk were located in Africa (notably Ethiopia, Mozambique, and Nigeria). Hence countries in sub-Saharan Africa appear to be among the most vulnerable to climate change and among the lowest performers on the Index of State Weakness.

Missing from this discussion of climate and political risk thus far is a final concern: strategic value. Is anarchy or state failure anywhere a problem everywhere?[26] Are countries that simultaneously carry the burden of political and climate risk important for the national security of others? Some countries are more strategically important than others—as allies, sources of raw materials, conduits for transit, potential adversaries, or sources of damaging blowback or spillovers.[27] The effects of climate change in these areas would likely be of considerable interest to policymakers in the United States and other donor countries.

The effects of climate change in China or Pakistan, for example, or even in Haiti (given its proximity to the United States), are going to be more significant than effects in Burkina Faso. That said, events have a way of surprising people. Who would have thought that pirates off the coast of Somalia would have been an issue of any significance some years ago? Nevertheless, part of the challenge in anticipating the security consequences of climate change and the appropriate anticipatory action must be to identify where climate risk, political risk, and strategic importance come together. A first step will be to review the evidence on the connections between climate and conflict, climate and disasters, and environmental protection amid insecurity and weak state capacity.

Climate Change and Conflict

The predominant concern in the emerging literature on climate and security is how climate change, as a "threat multiplier" or "stressor," will, with its variety of effects, make violent conflict more likely. Many of the relevant issues are revealed in contentious exchanges between environmental security scholar Thomas Homer-Dixon, Sudan scholar Alex de Waal, and climate and energy specialist David Victor. According to de Waal, "In the case of Darfur, it's pointless to ask about, or to argue over, the relative importance of climate change as a cause of the violence." For Homer-Dixon, however, the crisis in Darfur cannot be adequately explained without including "climate change as a causal factor."[28]

Ultimately, the debate here comes down to assessments of relative causal weight. Critics of Homer-Dixon's position argue that environmental factors have little independent value in explaining the cause of conflict. But in Homer-Dixon's view, it is difficult to separate causal dynamics that are inherently intertwined, as in the case of the complex, indirect consequences of resource scarcity for intrastate security: "Resource stress always *interacts* in complex conjunction with a host of other factors— ecological, institutional, economic and political—to cause mass violence." Note that the causation tends to be indirect; fighting is not about the natural resources directly, but scarcity and resource pressures lead to "forms of social dislocation—including widening gaps between rich and poor, increased rent-seeking by elites, weakening of states and deeper ethnic cleavages—that, in turn, make violence more likely." Furthermore, recognizing the trends in conflict, Homer-Dixon argues that "this violence is almost always *sub-national*; it takes the form of insurgency, rebellion, gangsterism and urban criminality, not overt interstate war."[29]

Perhaps assessments of causal weight may be beside the point. If the crisis in Darfur is caused at least in part by resource scarcity, then the question becomes whether resolving the conflicts over grazing rights and access to water is necessary to end the broader conflict. If the answer is yes, then environmental concerns must be addressed in the solution. In short, resource scarcity, particularly sudden shifts in resource availability, can add to other factors that cause tension and conflict in a society. Where climate change will exacerbate such scarcities, failure to address the impact of volatile rains, recurrent droughts, extreme weather events, and other effects of climate change could undermine broader policies of conflict prevention and resolution.

The exchange between de Waal and Homer-Dixon points to the limits of qualitative case studies of conflict and the difficulty of assessing the relative importance of some causes when outcomes depend on multiple factors. One of the enduring criticisms of the literature on environmental security from the 1990s was that it relied on anecdotal evidence with unclear generalizability. This inspired the move to quantitative studies of conflict with large datasets that offered more potential for providing broadly generalizable findings (despite the difficulty of getting at precise causal mechanisms in individual cases). But the data were so poor that it was not possible to establish clear links between environmental change and conflict. When the State Failure Task Force (now the Political Instability Task Force) found no connection between environmental variables and state failure in 1998, part of the problem was the lack of data for environmental indicators. Data on water quality, for example, were available for only thirty-eight countries. In view of these limitations, the task force's next two reports omitted environmental variables.[30]

However, recent scholarship has made considerable progress both in finding better data (particularly on subnational indicators of conflict and environmental vulnerability) and specifying causal relationships. Even so, there is little unanimity on the contribution of climate change to conflict. Part of the problem is the fact that climate change is a novel problem. Most effects of climate change will occur in the future, for which the past may not be a good guide. As a consequence, looking backward to historical data to understand the connections between environmental degradation and conflict may not be all that useful.[31]

Nonetheless, scholars have sought historical analogues of the physical effects of climate change on conflict, by examining factors such as rainfall variability/availability, land degradation, migration/refugee movements, and disasters. Although an exhaustive discussion of the findings to date is beyond the scope of this chapter, a cursory review indicates the potential security consequences of climate change that one could test empirically.[32]

If, for example, climate change is likely to lead to more variable precipitation, one can test, as Marc Levy and his colleagues have done, whether rainfall volatility has historically been correlated with a higher incidence of violent conflict. Using this approach, Levy and his colleagues found variable rainfall made the onset of violent conflict more likely.[33] The specific mechanism is still unclear, but it may be that harsh economic conditions drive people to fight over remaining scarce resources or may tempt them to join rebel movements.[34] Day laborers and farmers may be among those most affected by the loss of income that follows crop failures, as short-term swings in rainfall may leave less time for adaptation. Alternatively, powerful groups may take advantage of the latent tension when resources are scarce and weigh in on the side of one faction, as the Sudanese government did in Darfur.[35] The three causal dynamics can be diagrammed in simplified form as follows:

Scarcity

Climate effects ⟶ Competition over scarce resources ⟶ Fighting over scarce resources

Scarcity, mediated by rebel group offer

Climate effects ⟶ Competition ⟶ Offer to join the rebels ⟶ Fighting

Exploitation

Climate effects ⟶ Competition ⟶ Powerful actor takes sides/sows division ⟶ Fighting

This representation presupposes a number of antecedent conditions, as these kinds of climate effects would generally have security consequences in countries already beset by other problems, including poverty and weak governance. Despite the promising work on water scarcity and conflict, other studies have found weaker support for water-related variables and conflict. Work with subnational data suggests that water scarcity (as well as land degradation) may have weak or insignificant effects on conflict; such studies find that political and economic factors are more important in the onset of violent conflict.[36]

Low overall water availability appeared to be insignificant in the Levy study as well, making variation, flux, and disruption the more likely mechanism to induce conflict. However, many persist in connecting climate change to water scarcity and conflict. Jeffrey Sachs, for example, implied that the Taliban were better able to recruit in Afghanistan because of water scarcity: "Many conflicts are caused or inflamed by water scarcity. The conflicts from Chad to Darfur, Sudan, to the Ogaden Desert in Ethiopia, to Somalia and its pirates, and across to Yemen, Iraq, Pakistan, and Afghanistan, lie in a great arc of arid lands where water scarcity is leading to failed crops, dying livestock, extreme poverty, and desperation."[37]

Yet the historical record for direct conflict over scarce water resources, particularly at the interstate level, is almost nonexistent. As researchers have pointed out: "So far, . . . no international water dispute has escalated to the level of war. Indeed, . . . the last international war over water, in Sumeria, occurred 5,000 years ago."[38] The evidence for intrastate conflicts suggests it is not scarcity per se but variable rains that have more evidentiary links to conflict.

Climate variability is important because deviation from the normal or expected upends patterned behavior and gives people little time to anticipate, plan, and prepare, forcing them to scramble for measures that can protect their livelihoods and families.[39] In Darfur, for example, rainfall declined appreciably between 1920 and 1970, but there was no long-term downward trend from 1970 on.[40] However, rainfall was quite volatile in this period, with significant year-to-year fluctuations (figure 5-5).[41]

Therefore the scarcity diagram can now be recast:

Variability

Rainfall variability ⟶ Emergency protection ⟶ Conflict over sudden change ⟶ Fighting

Any discussion of water scarcity and conflict should ultimately focus on causal mechanisms for which the evidence is most compelling. For example, linking Taliban recruitment success to water scarcity assumes a general water scarcity–conflict link, for which the evidence to date is less persuasive than the evidence about rainfall volatility and conflict.[42] For all the reasons noted earlier, such conceptual stretching of a complex subject, which often occurs in the translation of academic to policy-relevant prose, may prove less rather than more effective.

Migration is another mechanism often invoked as a potential cause of climate-induced conflict. Through discrete events like hurricanes, climate change may spur large numbers of people to move to more hospitable places, between or within countries. Here it is essential to disaggregate the reasons people move, whether the migration is permanent or temporary, induced by sudden distress, or a product of seasonal patterns or contract work.[43] Intense storms, like those that have led Bangladeshis to cross over into India, give rise to distress movements. More gradual

FIGURE 5-5. El Fasher Annual Rainfall, 1917–2005

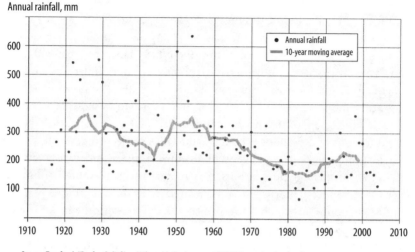

Source: Tearfund, "Darfur: Relief in a Vulnerable Environment," 2007 (www.tearfund.org).

processes such as persistent drought or slowly rising sea levels may spur permanent migration, as expected for a number of low-lying island nations in the South Pacific.

Like the Hutu who fled in the aftermath of the 1994 Rwandan genocide to the Congo, refugees may trigger conflict, possibly by eliciting a cross-border response from their former country (if they were out of favor at home). They may also clash with locals over scarce resources, the disagreements exacerbated by a number of fault lines, such as differences over ethnicity, race, religion, nationality, or a history of past conflict.[44] Alternatively, clashes with locals might land migrants into trouble with the host national or regional government and thereby elicit a response from their own home or regional government on their behalf. These three possibilities can be diagrammed as follows:

Migrants pursued by home government

Climate effects ⟶ Migration ⟶ Home government/region goes after migrants ⟶ Conflict

Migrants and scarcity

Climate effects ⟶ Migration ⟶ Competition with locals over scarce resorces ⟶ Conflict

⬆

Fault lines

Migrants + Scarcity + Interstate dispute

Climate effects ⟶ Migration ⟶ Competition ⟶ Host repression ⟶ Home intervention

Some studies have found that countries experiencing an influx of refugees from neighboring states are significantly more likely to experience civil wars.[45] Unlike political refugees, however, climate refugees may not be as prone to organized violence, as they may perceive their dislocation as an act of God so may not blame their new hosts for inadequately addressing their needs. Whether environmental migration turns violent depends on how local governments handle the inflow of new arrivals.[46] Migratory movements may also be less likely to lead to violence because of their largely local and temporary nature.[47] Of course, for low-lying island nations and perhaps even dry land areas subject to desertification, that assumes migrants can eventually return home. Climate change, in addition to displacing populations, may make some places uninhabitable. If so, the conflict patterns often associated with massive, more permanent migrations—in which refugees become fed up with the lack of new opportunities or host populations are unable to cope with the refugees, for example—could become much more likely. At present, no one really knows how many people will be displaced by climate change in the coming years. The most widely cited figure is 200 million people by 2050, derived through "heroic extrapolations," according to its authors.[48]

As suggested earlier, the *climate change → migration → conflict* link often involves natural disasters.[49] As with variability, the supposition is that so-called "swift onset disasters," because of their dislocative effects, ultimately give people reasons to take up arms or engage in criminality out of desperation. Given that disasters provide local populations with teachable moments about how much their governments care for them, governments that fail to respond adequately may find their legitimacy challenged and the dissatisfied populations easily recruited by opposition or rebel movements. This, coupled with the physical destruction wreaked by disasters, can lead to local anarchy and looting. Such challenges to the state's monopoly of force, though perhaps temporary, can give rise to broader criminal activity and violence.[50] It took 70,000 soldiers to restore order from the temporary lawlessness in New Orleans after Hurricane Katrina. If that can happen in the United States, one can imagine the relative vulnerabilities of poor and weak states.

Some early studies have suggested disasters might help diminish civil conflicts by producing a rallying effect, inspiring former antagonists to resolve common problems together, but a more recent view is that disasters can foster local competition for resources.[51] Only in rare circumstances, as occurred after the 2004 Asian tsunami, will groups involved in conflict be so weak or so profoundly affected by a disaster that they will be less likely to fight on. Otherwise, disasters may well foster competition for basic resources—food, water, shelter, relief—and make conflict more likely. One study found earthquakes made violent conflicts more likely, particularly in poor countries with a history of conflict. Earthquakes also increased the likelihood of rebellions and, to a lesser extent, civil wars, again especially in poor countries with a recent history of conflict. It is thought that these effects can be generalized to other kinds of natural disasters.[52]

Another study also found that disasters enhanced the risk of violent conflict in countries with high levels of inequality, mixed regimes (partial democratization), and slow economic growth. Disasters may increase grievances and incentives to grab scarce resources and may undermine a state's capacity to respond. That study found that a "rapid-onset" natural disaster like an earthquake or hurricane was 50 percent more likely to generate violent civil conflict than other kinds of slower-moving disasters.[53]

Here, the causal diagrams include other important elements, particularly weak state capacity and poverty:

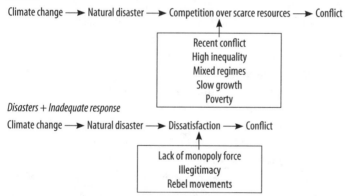

Disasters

Climate change ⟶ Natural disaster ⟶ Competition over scarce resources ⟶ Conflict

> Recent conflict
> High inequality
> Mixed regimes
> Slow growth
> Poverty

Disasters + Inadequate response

Climate change ⟶ Natural disaster ⟶ Dissatisfaction ⟶ Conflict

> Lack of monopoly force
> Illegitimacy
> Rebel movements

Needless to say, much more work needs to be done to assess how environmental and sociopolitical sources of vulnerability conjoin and to identify the precise mechanisms by which conflict has come about historically—and could emerge in the future.

Weak State Capacity, Climate Change, and Disasters

The climate-conflict connection has received outsized attention in policy circles, but the more likely short-term and pervasive consequence of climate change will be increases in the severity and number of extreme weather events, such as floods, hurricanes, storms, droughts, extremely hot days, and heavy precipitation. The specific contribution of climate change to the severity and number of particular kinds of disasters is still being debated within the scientific community, but the general expectation is that climate change will exacerbate weather extremes.[54] The aggregate patterns of disasters reveal three trends. First, the number of reported natural disasters has gone up (which analysts note may be a function of better data rather than changes in weather patterns as a result of climate change). Second, mortality figures related to disasters have come down. Disaster preparedness has made most disasters much less lethal. Third, because populations are increasing, particularly along densely populated coasts and in urban areas, the total affected population has increased sharply (see figure 5-6).[55] Poor countries in the developing world, with their capacity constraints, are far more vulnerable to natural disasters than advanced industrialized countries. The human impact on poor countries is almost always more severe. Moreover, while they have less valuable property to lose, disasters have a more significant economic impact on poor countries.

With the rising number of reported disasters and number of people affected, modern militaries are increasingly deployed to deal with natural disasters as local fire, water, and rescue services are overwhelmed by the consequences of extreme weather events. Rich countries have had to deploy their troops both domestically and internationally in response to natural disasters. Among wealthy countries, the most notable domestic deployment was the U.S. response after Hurricane Katrina in 2005, when the peak mobilization exceeded 70,000, soldiers—including 22,000 on active duty and more than 50,000 members of the National Guard, or about 10 percent of the total guard strength.[56] Greece and Australia are two other advanced industrialized countries that have called on their soldiers to fight forest fires in recent years. The military is becoming a vital instrument of disaster management and response.

Internationally, the United States and other Western militaries have been increasingly deployed to respond to humanitarian disasters. Since the 1990s, a number of extreme weather events—acute and persistent droughts, floods, and hurricanes—have elicited calls for such relief. As a result, disaster assistance has become a more normal capability of the U.S. military since the deployment of nearly 30,000 to Somalia in

FIGURE 5-6. Natural Disaster Deaths and People Affected, 1900–2008

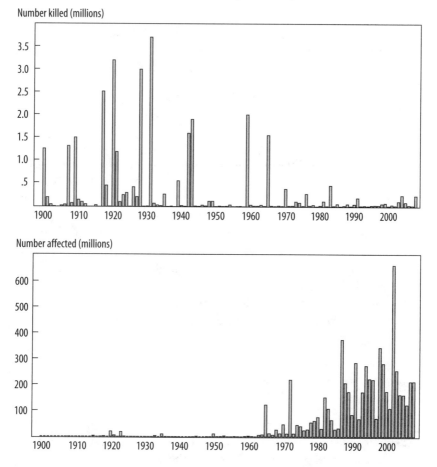

Source: Center for Research on the Epidemiology of Disasters, "EM-DAT Database" (www.emdat.be/ExplanatoryNotes/glossary.html).

Operation Restore Hope in December 1992. The U.S. military was dispatched to Central America in 1998 in the wake of Hurricane Mitch, to Haiti in 2004 after torrential rains and mudslides, later that year to Asia following the tsunami, and to Pakistan in 2005 after its massive earthquake. U.S. forces were also at the ready to provide aid after Cyclone Nargis struck Myanmar in 2008, but the country's military dictatorship allowed only the Air Force to provide assistance. These are but a

TABLE 5-2. Countries Most Vulnerable to Disasters, 1968–2007[a]

Droughts	Floods	Windstorms
Burkina Faso (44), Mozambique (39), Rwanda (24), Somalia (1), Tanzania (55)	Afghanistan (2), Bangladesh (48), Malawi (46), Mozambique (39), Nepal (22), Nigeria (28), Somalia (1), Sudan (6), Tanzania (55)	Bangladesh (48), Madagascar (49), Mozambique (39)

a. Figures in parentheses indicate country ranking on the Index of State Weakness.

few examples of a wider normalization of disaster relief as part of the activities of the U.S. and other militaries.

Indeed, postdisaster relief operations may be more likely to occupy defense assets than wars over resource scarcity.[57] Such military mobilization for domestic or international humanitarian relief presents some opportunity costs in terms of limited manpower and infrastructure. If the incidence or severity of climate disasters were to increase as scientists expect, then the trade-offs between national defense and humanitarian relief could become more stark. If the countries affected were strategically important, the trade-off would be more about competing national security directives. The following diagram summarizes the dynamic in such cases:

Disasters + Humanitarian intervention

Climate change ⟶ Natural disaster ⟶ Large-scale suffering ⟶ Relief ⟶ Diversion of military assets/Humanitarian intervention

The modeling of future climate effects can help identify areas at greatest risk of climate disasters. Past incidence of disasters might also be a reasonably good guide to the distribution of future disasters (at least in the short run), if not to their frequency and magnitude. On the basis of data from countries with a high population, a low GDP, and a history of a high number of disasters, researchers have found that a number of countries in Africa and Asia are particularly vulnerable to floods, droughts, and windstorms (table 5-2) (this metric of disaster risk is not entirely separable from the Index of State Weakness).[58] Similar patterns emerge when the same data are analyzed by a different methodology identifying the top five vulnerable countries according to the numbers killed, populations left homeless, and the total number affected (table 5-3).[59]

While these past records of historic disasters tell something about the relative vulnerability of different countries, the precise effects of natural

TABLE 5-3. Top Countries by Climate Disaster Vulnerability, 1980–2002

Category of vulnerability	Top five
Mortality	Ethiopia, Bangladesh, Sudan, Mozambique, India
Mortality per thousand	Mozambique, Sudan, Ethiopia, Honduras, Bangladesh
Homeless	Bangladesh, China, Pakistan, Philippines, Vietnam
Homeless per thousand	Tonga, Bangladesh, Laos, Samoa, Sri Lanka
Affected	China, India, Bangladesh, Ethiopia, Iran
Affected per thousand	Botswana, Antigua and Barbados, Bangladesh, Zimbabwe, Malawi

disasters on particular places remain a subject of great debate. Scientists have sought to model complex weather systems, and yet their ability to specify the likely consequences for particular places at the subnational level is patchy at best. Even if there is near unanimity on the overall direction and anthropogenic source of much of the climate change seen in recent years, scientists continue to vigorously debate pieces of the overall puzzle, including whether climate change will exacerbate the severity and number of hurricanes. Nonetheless, the overall direction is clear; poor countries with weak governance in the developing world, particularly in sub-Saharan Africa and the densely populated countries of South Asia, are also especially vulnerable to natural disasters.[60]

Insecurity, Poverty, and Environmental Protection

Thus far, the focus here has been on the consequences of climate change for security concerns, including conflict and disaster response. However, violence and insecurity, coupled with bad governance and endemic poverty, are also likely to have an impact on environmental quality and mediate between a state's ability to respond to its own problems and contribute to global or regional public goods. As noted earlier, intrastate violence is largely confined to a handful of countries in the developing world, particularly in sub-Saharan Africa, parts of Asia, and the Middle East. The environmental risks of conflict include the land-use implications of unexploded ordnance, the contamination of groundwater and the air from damage to infrastructure, and the direct destruction of habitats. A whole range of harmful effects—from deaths, birth defects, and defoliation caused by Agent Orange in Vietnam to the outbreaks of disease from the accumulation of bodies in Rwanda's rivers after the 1994 genocide to the deliberate sabotage of oil wells during the Gulf War—make it clear that war leaves an environmental footprint.

TABLE 5-4. Environmental Performance and Peace Indices, 2008

Country	Environmental performance ranking (150 countries)	Global peace ranking (140 countries)
Niger	150	129
Angola	149	110
Sierra Leone	148	n.a.
Mauritania	147	120
Mali	146	99
Burkina Faso	145	81
Chad	144	135
Democratic Republic of the Congo	143	128
Yemen	142	106
Guinea-Bissau	141	n.a.
Djibouti	140	n.a.
Guinea	139	n.a.
Solomon Islands	138	n.a.
Cambodia	137	91
Iraq	136	140
Mozambique	135	50
Madagascar	134	43
Burundi	133	n.a.
Rwanda	132	76
Zambia	131	53
Sudan	130	139
Central African Republic	129	134
Benin	128	n.a.
Nigeria	127	129
Bangladesh	126	86

n.a. Not available.

Equally important, countries experiencing domestic instability are less able to protect their own biological resources. The twenty worst performers on the 2008 Environmental Performance Index[61] are among today's most conflict-ridden states, according to the Global Peace Index (GPI) (see table 5-4).[62] Even a number of countries that currently have a lower rank on the GPI (that is, are more peaceful) have experienced wrenching conflict in the past twenty years, including Rwanda, Mozambique, and Cambodia.

Many of the countries most affected by conflict also possess natural assets of global significance, such as biodiversity sites and carbon sinks created by forests, which remove carbon dioxide from the atmosphere and temporarily store carbon in their living matter. One study found that "over 90% of the major armed conflicts between 1950 and 2000 occurred within countries containing biodiversity hotspots, and more than 80% took place directly within hotspot areas."[63] Commonly concentrated in major tropical forest reserves, such hot spots could play an important role in reducing greenhouse gases. For a variety of reasons discussed in the next section, however, countries suffering from conflict and inadequate governance will have considerable difficulty contributing to this vital global public good.

CASE EXAMPLES

This section focuses on the impact of disasters on Haiti and the difficulty in protecting the DRC's natural resources, given the Congo's past history of violence, its weak state capacity, endemic poverty, and continued instability.

Haiti

Haiti's misfortunes are all too familiar. The country has lacked stable government for much of its history and as a result has long suffered crippling poverty, persistent political instability, and violence. Though it shares an island with the Dominican Republic, the two countries have developed along very different trajectories. While by no means a paragon of governance, the Dominican Republic was ninety-first on the Index of State Weakness of 141 countries, whereas Haiti, at number 12, was the Western Hemisphere's least strong state. Other indicators of quality of life suggest a growing disjuncture between these neighbors. Between 1980 and 2004 the ratio of the Dominican Republic's GDP per capita in purchasing power parity to that of Haiti increased from 2.1 to 5.1 (see figure 5-7).[64]

What accounts for this widening gap in achievement? To be sure, Haiti's colonial origins and tortured history have played a role, as has the fractured nature of its society. Sadly, the venality and incompetence of Haitian leaders continued into the post-Duvalier era. Haiti's poverty and political weakness have in turn contributed to its environmental vulnerability and been a consequence of its degraded environment.

In the Environmental Performance Index, Haiti had the lowest environmental performance of any country in the Americas in 2008.[65] The

FIGURE 5-7. GDP per Capita in Purchasing Power Parity, Dominican Republic and Haiti, 1980–2006

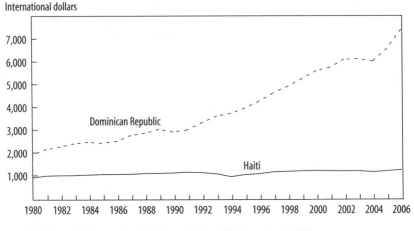

Source: International Monetary Fund, *World Economic Outlook* (Washington, October 2008).

dramatic difference in Haiti's forest cover compared with that of its neighbor (captured by satellite and aerial photos) encapsulates Haiti's susceptibility to extreme weather events such as floods and landslides. By 2005 Haiti's forest cover was down to 3.81 percent, compared with the Dominican Republic's 28.44 percent.[66]

The combination of a dysfunctional government and poverty has created a vicious cycle in which peasant communities in search of fuelwood put their own lives in jeopardy through land-use practices that strip the hillsides bare of tree cover. The resulting erosion has made it difficult for rural communities to sustain their livelihoods and pushed Haiti's annual rural-to-urban migration in excess of 75,000, swelling the mass of shantytowns in the unstable capital city of Port-au-Prince, which is already home to 2.5 million, or one-quarter of the country's population.[67] The large, unemployed and underemployed urban population has, in turn, made Haiti more susceptible to political instability. Haitians are also much more vulnerable to the Caribbean's yearly storms than their wealthier Dominican counterparts. According to a 2004 report of the United Nations Development Program (UNDP), natural disasters are 100 times more lethal in Haiti than in the Dominican Republic.[68]

The world has repeatedly witnessed this vulnerability over the past decade. In February 2004 an armed rebellion successfully deposed

President Jean-Bertrand Aristide. A UN peacekeeping force, led at first by 1,000 U.S. marines, was authorized to restore order on behalf of the interim government. In the midst of this political chaos, devastating floods killed nearly 3,000 people between May and September of that year. Already on the island as peacekeepers, the American soldiers—by then some 1,900 of them—were able to stave off even worse effects by airlifting food and drinking water and evacuating the injured from submerged towns.[69] A UN stabilization force of more than 7,000 soldiers and 2,000 police has remained in Haiti since June 2004.[70]

In April 2009 the International Crisis Group reported that "between 2001 and March 2007, natural disasters resulted in 18,441 deaths, 4,708 injuries and 132,000 homeless." Hence "reversing a decades-long trend of environmental destruction is essential to Haiti's development, social and economic stability and, ultimately, security." On an island with a population just shy of 10 million inhabitants, some 6.4 million persons were affected, with damages estimated at $6.4 billion. Between August and September 2008, a succession of four storms and hurricanes affected an additional 800,000, left nearly 800 dead, and caused damages of nearly $900 million.[71] For a country that is already poorest in the hemisphere, such economic losses represent a significant diversion of resources from other unmet social needs.

With climate change, the effects of extreme weather events on Haiti are likely to make a difficult situation much worse, though the models for the effects of climate change in the Caribbean have yet to provide a sense of what might happen in particular geographic areas. These models vary widely in the trends and direction of future precipitation.[72]

The future frequency, as well as the intensity, of hurricanes is one of the most salient concerns for Haiti. While much of the scientific community agrees that climate change will trigger more numerous and intense and extreme weather events, whether these trends are yet observable and attributable to climate change is still being debated. The Fourth Assessment of the Intergovernmental Panel on Climate Change issued in 2007 found no clear global trend in the *frequency* of tropical cyclones. However, the number of tropical storms in the North Atlantic (which is relevant for Haiti) from 1850 to 1990 was about ten a year, five of which were hurricanes. From 1998 to 2007, the average number was about fifteen a year, with eight hurricanes. Although better reporting of data may in part account for this trend, scientists appear more confident that the specific North Atlantic link between climate change and hurricane frequency is related to human activity. As for hurricane *intensity*, the scientific community is more confident that the severity of hurricanes, if not their number, has increased, though this too is still actively debated. A number of peer-reviewed studies suggest the strongest hurricanes have increased in number over the past two or three decades.[73]

What are the implications of Haiti's vulnerability to natural disasters for the United States? To begin with, the U.S. military is called upon periodically to provide humanitarian relief, as it did in 2004 after devastating floods and again after the intense hurricane season of 2008. The political violence that periodically has plagued Haiti has also been an impetus for U.S. and UN military interventions to restore order. To the extent that environmental conditions in Haiti are indirectly or directly contributing to Haiti's political instability and violence, climate change could increase the need for such deployments.

In addition, Haiti's proximity to the United States makes it a natural concern because negative spillovers—such as its growing role as a conduit for drugs—might affect American interests. More salient for U.S. policy, however, is the extent to which desperate Haitians have an incentive to migrate to the United States. Natural disasters and environmental degradation prompt rural-to-urban migration not only within Haiti also but between Haiti and the United States. In the first weeks after Hurricane Georges struck Haiti in 1998, the number of interdictions from the U.S. Coast Guard spiked sharply, even in comparison with other potential causes of Haitian migration.[74]

An influx of refugees would be particularly problematic for the United States, both in terms of interdiction and possible strategic blackmail. Haiti, like Cuba, has long used the threat of migration to extract concessions from the United States, knowing that the U.S. public tends to react negatively to sudden influxes of large numbers of migrants, particularly from Haiti. In 1980 Fidel Castro forced the United States to accept more than 100,000 Cubans after he encouraged tens of thousands to migrate to Florida during the Mariel boatlift. And, in 1994, Jean-Bertrand Aristide, in exchange for U.S. intervention to restore him to power, dissuaded thousands of Haitians from emigrating to the United States.[75] In the absence of U.S. action to address climate change or support risk reduction, countries in the region could be tempted to use the threat of migration again. Whether the migration of Haitians would on its own constitute a national security threat to the United States is unclear. On the one hand, the desperation that drives Haitians to seek a better life in the United States is understandable. On the other hand, sudden flows of migrants would create challenges for local law enforcement, the military, and Coast Guard, who would likely be called upon to detain refugees at sea and establish holding facilities as President Bill Clinton did in the mid-1990s when he used Guantánamo Bay to house nearly 50,000 Haitian and Cuban refugees. Incidents such as this could elevate the migration issue to become a more significant fault line in international politics.

The Democratic Republic of the Congo

The Democratic Republic of the Congo, with the third worst score on the Index of State Weakness and seventh worst score on the Environmental Performance Index, stands as a stark reference case for the analyses in this volume.[76] Conflict has compounded the DRC's failings in these areas, making it difficult to protect the environment.

The former Zaire's slide into chaos began long before its long-time kleptocratic president Mobutu Sese Seko was deposed and died in 1997.[77] The international community has attempted to come to grips with violence in the DRC with a UN peacekeeping force in place since 1999. That force is the UN's largest peacekeeping deployment, with more than 16,500 soldiers, an additional 1,000 police, and several thousand other civilians and military observers.[78]

The DRC could be a major beneficiary of avoided deforestation schemes, given the extent of the tropical forests in the Congo Basin. Nearly 20 percent of the world's greenhouse gases are absorbed by tropical forests.[79] With deforestation and land clearing responsible for nearly a fifth of the world's annual greenhouse gas emissions, advocates of efforts to reduce greenhouse gas emissions have sought schemes to slow down the rate of deforestation. These schemes are known as avoided deforestation or reduced emissions from deforestation and forest degradation (REDD).

REDD schemes offer an opportunity to reduce greenhouse gas emissions at low cost. For major emitting industrial countries like the United States, avoided deforestation could be a much more cost-effective way to address climate change than retrofitting industrial facilities.[80] For this reason, the draft climate bill circulating in the U.S. Congress in 2009 sets aside 5 percent of the allowances to support international forest carbon conservation efforts.

A $500 million World Bank pilot program and a number of private efforts are also being developed to compensate heavily forested countries for keeping their forests intact and preventing deforestation in the first place. According to a 2007 study by the Woods Hole Research Center, the DRC stands to gain as much as $120 million to $400 million a year in income to rural households through REDD schemes and also a 50 percent reduction in greenhouse gas emissions. For a country that received $800 million in foreign assistance and had a per capita income of $125 in 2005, this would be a significant source of income.[81]

A forthcoming study by Resources for the Future has mapped the biological potential of different places on the planet for their ability to reduce such emissions through avoided deforestation. Without controlling for or overlaying indicators of government capacity, the research team found that the Congo River Basin, with its vast tracts of unaltered forest, offers the best biological potential for low-cost avoided emissions on the planet. The DRC alone has 1.1 million square kilometers of dense tropical forests, an area twice the size of France. As the country "with the most profit potential in carbon markets," it could increase its annual GDP by 20 percent between 2012 and 2020.[82]

Despite this profit potential for generating forest carbon, other risk factors—including readiness, ease of doing business, and governance—still make the Congo Basin "a region with among the highest investment risk in the world."[83] Given the fragility of the DRC's government, rich history and recent past of violent conflict, and incapacity to establish domain over its territory, the DRC is not in an optimal position to take advantage of the avoided deforestation potential, at least in the short run.

Such schemes require particular sorts of government capacity, notably the ability to collect information and conduct surveillance, both to establish the baseline for forest cover and to monitor changes over time. Ultimately they would have significant economic value, enabling emitters of greenhouse gases in rich countries to meet their obligations by supporting avoided deforestation activities in the developing world. Those investments will only be meaningful, however, if the recipient governments have monitoring capability.

Some functions along these lines can be performed by satellite technology, but they must be backed by a capacity to deter illegal deforestation. In addition, countries must be able to distribute the revenue generated from the scheme. Otherwise, the schemes cannot be guaranteed to meet their goals. If governments do not have the capacity to distribute funds equitably, forest carbon credits could become something of a resource curse, putting traditional rural forest-dwelling communities at a disadvantage.[84] The revenues would be valuable enough for contracts to become contestable items, worthy of political control and possibly a source of conflict in and of themselves. Indeed, badly designed, the program could encourage a sort of "green blackmail," whereby countries would initiate deforestation programs merely to extort payments from donors to stop them from continuing that deforestation. Given these concerns, only countries possessing a modicum of stability and governance capacity can reassure investors that their programs will provide adequate monitoring, distribute income equitably, and deter undesirable behavior. The DRC government is unlikely to generate this kind of confidence for investors interested in taking advantage of its great REDD potential. Despite these various concerns, the World Bank included the DRC in its list of countries potentially eligible for REDD projects in 2008. As of March 2009, the bank was preparing a plan for the DRC, which might set the stage for the government's actual readiness but could prove to reveal as much about the country's fundamental barriers to participation as anything else.[85]

The DRC's forestry and conservation policies have been nearly as volatile as its security situation in recent years. In eastern Congo near the Ugandan border, media reports suggest that fighting and poverty have put increased pressure on the resources, animals, and fishing in and around Lake Edward: in desperation, people have deforested for fuelwood, overhunted hippo and elephant populations, and overfished lakes.[86] In other parts of the country, rebels have driven park rangers out of the Virunga Mountains gorilla reserve. A census revealed that gorilla populations had increased during the fighting—perhaps because the region was too violent for poachers.[87] As for its forestry policy, the DRC has issued concessions to foreign firms for timber on a number of occasions, but in the face of outside pressure, canceled them.[88] It is unclear whether the country possesses enough stability to permit large logging operations to function. That said, it would be a tragedy if the price of peace in the DRC were a swift uptick in logging.

For the United States, instability and weak governance in heavily forested countries like the DRC means fewer sites and sources of low-cost emissions reductions. If the DRC and other countries remain less able to contribute to the global public good of emissions reductions of greenhouse gases, the United States will have to do more through expensive and politically difficult domestic policy measures. There is, and will likely continue to be, a large disjuncture between the kinds of domestic climate policies that are politically possible in the United States and what scientists believe are necessary to avoid the worst consequences of climate change. The hardest part for the United States has simply been getting started. Successful international REDD programs could buy the United States some time while its policies adjust. Where this option is foreclosed or limited, the country will likely be increasingly blamed for being the world's largest historic emitter of greenhouse gases. Inaction on climate change limits the negotiating room for American diplomats in a variety of settings and provides opponents of the United States convenient excuses to blame America. Therefore, it has an additional incentive, among others, to limit and reduce these negative reputational consequences. If a reservoir of good will around the world is important for U.S. national security, then actions on climate change are likely to become increasingly important. With REDD schemes offering some of the best potential for emissions reductions, the conditions in heavily forested countries like the DRC become more relevant to U.S. strategic interests than they might appear to be at first blush.

CONCLUSIONS AND POLICY IMPLICATIONS

Because climate change is a highly polarized and politically contested subject in the United States, efforts to oversell its security implications could backfire. A more evenhanded review of the state of knowledge on climate-security connections, such as provided in this chapter, could defuse some of the hyperbole and point policymakers in the right direction. Although violent conflict obviously remains an important topic for them to consider, other security issues arising with climate change, such as those in the wake of natural disasters, demand their attention. Disaster response, particularly to poor countries with weak governance, is already becoming a normal part of military deployments and will probably become an even more important security concern. It must also be recognized that conflict and unstable governance make environmental protection difficult, and that environmental variables are not merely a cause and conflict an outcome. Indeed, conflict contributes to poor environmental quality. This chapter has explored these dynamics throughout the developing world, notably in Darfur (in the discussion of the connections between climate and conflict), Haiti (between climate change, disasters, and negative spillovers), and the DRC (between conflict and environmental quality).

TABLE 5-5. Poor Country Adaptation Needs by 2015

	Estimated cost, 2015	
Need	Percent of OECD GDP	Billions of 2005 U.S. $
Climate-proofing development investment	0.1	44
Adapting poverty reduction to climate change	0.1	40
Strengthening disaster response	—	2
Total	0.2	86

The security connections with climate change bear more study.[89] An important avenue to explore further is the circumstances under which climate consequences come together with state capacity, poverty, and other variables to give rise to violence. To this end, various states should be assessed as to their relative vulnerability to the risks of climate change. Since these risks are largely local ones, identifying these risks at the subnational level will be increasingly important. However, such assessments need to include indicators of political risk, since vulnerability is only partly a function of geography. Where such risks transcend borders, however, analyses need to consider broader regional vulnerability.

Enough is already known about the relative vulnerability of large and densely populated coastal areas, drought-prone regions reliant on rain-fed agriculture, and other at-risk sites for countries to begin investing in adaptive measures and risk reduction. Such programs are often justified on the grounds of cost-effectiveness in any case. To the extent that the causal connections between climate change and conflict ultimately have some validity, investments in adaptation and risk reduction (from coastal defenses to better building codes, early warning systems, and evacuation strategies) will also improve the prospects for peace and help to avoid violence.

Internationally, however, there are scant funds for adaptation or the reduction of disaster risk. Poor countries' needs for adaptation could run to billions of dollars: the UNDP's 2007/2008 Human Development Report estimated that pro-poor adaptation programs would require $86 billion a year by 2015.[90] As of 2008, resources available for this were only in the hundreds of millions (table 5-5).

The World Bank's Global Environment Facility (GEF) administers three adaptation-related funds for developing countries: the Special Climate Change Fund (SCCF), the Least Developed Country Fund (LDCF), and the Adaptation Trust Fund. As of early 2009, pledges to GEF adaptation programs totaled slightly more than $300 million, but actual disbursements were only a small fraction of that amount.[91] Though the United States is a donor to the GEF, it has not contributed to existing adaptation funds, nor has it, as a non-party to the Kyoto Protocol, contributed to the new Adaptation Trust Fund. Even the Global Facility for Disaster Reduction and Recovery (GFDRR), a new fund established in 2006 by the World Bank and UN International Strategy for Disaster Reduction (ISDR), had received only modest contributions of $79 million by 2008, which included $16.8 million of the bank's own resources. Again, the United States, as of this writing, has not contributed anything.[92]

Should a cap-and-trade bill with provisions for adaptation finance pass the U.S. Congress, the resources for international adaptation would increase considerably, although they would fall well short of what advocates believe will be necessary to insulate poor countries from the worst consequences of climate change. In any event, the international transfer of funds of more than $80 billion a year for adaptation alone, as envisioned by the UNDP, is unlikely and could suffer from the kinds of distortions and inadequacies that have plagued traditional foreign assistance programs, even if funds were made available. As the United States debates the broader bill on climate change, it should give some additional thought to the modalities by which such adaptation funds will be delivered. UN-administered programs may be politically challenged in the United States, and the GEF, as a World Bank instrument, has weak legitimacy in developing countries and possibly capacity constraints of its own. The House 2009 version of the cap-and-trade bill empowers the secretary of state, in consultation with the U.S. Agency for International Development (USAID), the Treasury, and the Environmental Protection Agency, to distribute the funds for international adaptation, with at least 40 percent (and no more than 60 percent) delivered multilaterally.[93] Bilateral programming has certainly worked well for the United States in delivering antiretroviral AIDS therapy, but it is unclear that this is an appropriate model for climate adaptation or that USAID or another bilateral U.S. entity is institutionally capable of delivering the size and nature of adaptation funds the cap-and-trade program would provide.

One large challenge for the international community will be to help poor countries burdened by postconflict problems and weak governance to expand their capacity, not only for adaptation but also for improving public health, reducing greenhouse gas emissions, and conserving forests. Given the mixed track record of foreign assistance thus far, this may be a tall order in poor countries despite the good intentions of donors, unless they can devise more effective mechanisms for assistance, both bilateral and multilateral.

If the measures discussed here—research, adaptation, and capacity building—are supported and are successful, the resulting contributions could diminish the security consequences of climate change in the developing world, strengthen environmental protection, and better provide global public goods. The impact on living standards and state capacity would, in turn, improve the prospects for a peaceful resolution of present conflicts and avoidance of disputes in the future.

NOTES

1. United Nations Environment Program (UNEF), "Sudan: Post-Conflict Environmental Assessment" (2007), chap. 3. One of the leading exponents of environmental degradation and drought as a contributing factor in the conflict in Darfur has been Mohamed Suliman. See, for example, Mohamed Suliman, "Ethnicity from Perception to Cause of Violent Conflicts: The Case of the Fur and Nuba Conflicts in Western Sudan" (London: Institute for African Alternatives, July 1997).

2. Stephan Faris, "The Real Roots of Darfur," *Atlantic Monthly*, April 2007, pp. 67–71. Faris bases his narrative on Darfur in part on the work of Alex de Waal, who, though disputing the causal story, confirms much of the historical arc. Both de Waal and M. W. Daly state the occurrence of severe drought in 1983 set the stage for the famine of 1984–85 and conflict of 1987–89. See M. W. Daly, *Darfur's Sorrow: A History of Destruction and Genocide* (Cambridge University Press, 2007); Alex de Waal, *Is Climate Change the Culprit for Darfur?* (New York: Social Science Research Council [SSRC], June 25, 2007) (http://blogs.ssrc.org/darfur/2007/06/25/is-climate-change-the-culprit-for-darfur/).

3. In advocacy circles, the differences between the farmers and the herders are often described in racial terms as differences between Africans and Arabs, with government-backed Arabs committing atrocities against the Africans. However, the reality of ethnicity in Darfur is far more complex. Ethnicity was at one time more fluid and based on vocation rather than recognizable physical differences. A number of tribes make up the rebels in Darfur, not all of which can neatly be described as "African." All are Sunnis and Arabic speakers. As Mahmood Mandami writes, Western campaigners' "characterisation of the violence as 'Arab' against 'African' obscured both the fact that the violence was not one-sided and the contest over the meaning of 'Arab' and 'African': a contest that was critical precisely because it was ultimately about who belonged and who did not in the political community called Sudan." Mahmood Mamdani, "The Politics

of Naming: Genocide, Civil War, Insurgency," *London Review of Books,* 2007. For a similar view, see Mohamed Suliman, "Ethnicity from Perception to Cause of Violent Conflicts."

4. Ban Ki-Moon, "A Climate Culprit in Darfur," *Washington Post,* June 16, 2007. For a similar view, see Jeffrey Sachs, "Ecology and Political Upheaval," *Scientific American* 295, no. 1 (2006): 37; "Poverty and Environmental Stress Fuel Darfur Crisis," *Nature* 449 (September 2007): 24; "Land, Water, and Conflict," *Newsweek.* July 7–14, 2008. Most scientists would shy away from attributing a single incident to human-induced climate change, claiming only that climate change would make events like this one more likely.

5. De Waal, *Is Climate Change the Culprit for Darfur?* See also Declan Butler, "Darfur's Climate Roots Challenged," *Nature* 447 (June 2007):1038.

6. Idean Salehyan, "The New Myth about Climate Change," *Foreign Policy* (August 2007) (www.foreignpolicy.com/story/cms.php?story_id=3922). For an elaboration of this argument, see Idean Salehyan, "From Climate Change to Conflict?: No Consensus Yet," *Journal of Peace Research* 45, no. 3 (2008): 315–32.

7. Halvard Buhaug, Nils Petter Gleditsch, and Ole Magnus Theisen, "Implications of Climate Change for Armed Conflict," SDCC Working Paper (Washington: World Bank, February 25, 2008) (http://siteresources.worldbank.org/ INTRANETSOCIALDEVELOPMENT/Resources/SDCCWorkingPaper_ Conflict.pdf).

8. See Intergovernmental Panel on Climate Change (IPCC), *Fourth Assessment Report—Climate Change 2007: Impacts, Adaptation and Vulnerability* (Geneva, April 13, 2007); *Fourth Assessment Report—Climate Change 2007: The Physical Science Basis* (February 5, 2007); *Fourth Assessment Report—Regional Climate Projections* (Contribution of Working Group I to the Fourth Assessment Report, 2007).

9. Center for Naval Analyses, "National Security and the Threat of Climate Change" (Alexandria, Va., 2007). For a more complete review of this literature, see Josh Busby, "The Climate Security Connection: What It Means for the Poor," in *Climate Change and Global Poverty: A Billion Lives in the Balance?* edited by Lael Brainard, Abigail Jones, and Nigel Purvis (Brookings, 2009).

10. Daniel Deudney, "The Case against Linking Environmental Degradation and National Security," *Millennium* 19, no. 3 (1990): 461–76. See also Ole Waever, "Securitization and Desecuritization," in *On Security*, edited by R. D. Lipschutz (Columbia University Press, 1995). For additional discussion and citations, see Josh Busby, "Who Cares about the Weather? Climate Change and U.S. National Security," *Security Studies* 17, no. 3 (2008): 468–504. For similar discussions applied to disease, see Stefan Elbe, "Should HIV/AIDS Be Securitized: The Ethical Dilemmas of Linking HIV/AIDS and Security," *International Studies Quarterly* 50, no. 1 (2006): 119–44; Jeremy Youde, "Who's Afraid of

a Chicken? Securitization and Avian Flu," *Democracy and Security* 4, no. 2 (2008): 148–69.

11. David Victor, "What Resource Wars?" *National Interest,* November/ December 2007. See also Stephen M. Walt, "The Renaissance of Security Studies," *International Studies Quarterly* 35, no. 2 (1991): 211–39.

12. For my discussion of the narrow focus of climate and conflict and critique of the human security literature, see Busby, "Who Cares about the Weather?" and "The Climate Security Connection."

13. Such conflicts may become rare, in part because of the expansion of peacekeeping activities in the post–cold war era that have enabled a number of long-running conflicts to be settled. Armed conflicts are recorded when there are at least 25 battle deaths; when battle deaths exceed 1,000, the conflict is called a war. Interstate conflicts refer to conflicts between states; intrastate conflicts, including civil wars, reflect conflicts between a government and a non-state group. Extrastate conflicts, mostly colonial in nature, are between a state and an armed group outside the state's territory. Internationalized intrastate conflicts occur when the government, or an armed group opposing it, receives military support from one or more foreign states. See Human Security Project, "Human Security Report 2006" (University of British Columbia, Human Security Centre, 2006). Data for 2006 with corrections to 2003 and 2005 intrastate conflicts are from Buhaug and others, "Implications of Climate Change for Armed Conflict."

14. Human Security Project, "Human Security Report 2008" (University of British Columbia, Human Security Centre, 2008).

15. Buhaug and others, "Implications of Climate Change for Armed Conflict." Map from UCDP, PRIO, "UCDP/PRIO Armed Conflict Dataset v4-2008" (www.prio.no/CSCW/Datasets/Armed-Conflict/UCDP-PRIO/).

16. Josh Busby, "Climate Change and National Security: An Agenda for Action" (Council on Foreign Relations, 2007); Nigel Purvis and Josh Busby, *The Security Implications of Climate Change for the UN System* (Washington: Woodrow Wilson Center, 2004); Busby, "Who Cares about the Weather?"; Busby "The Climate Security Connection."

17. Lydia Saad, "Increased Number Think Global Warming Is 'Exaggerated,'" Gallup Poll, March 11, 2009.

18. Pew Research Center for the People and the Press, *Little Consensus on Global Warming*, July 12, 2006.

19. Riley E. Dunlap, "Partisan Gap on Global Warming Grows" Gallup Poll, May 29, 2008.

20. National Journal, *Congressional Insiders Poll* (February 3, 2007).

21. For adaptation allowances, see H. Res. 2454, sec. 782, subsec. n. For forest allowances, see section 781 (www.opencongress.org/bill/111-h2454/text).

22. Peter Behr, "Carbon Allowances—The Glue in House Energy Package," *Greenwire*, May 26, 2009.

23. Joshua Busby, "'Bono Made Jesse Helms Cry': Debt Relief, Jubilee 2000, and Moral Action in International Politics," *International Studies Quarterly* 51, no. 2 (2007): 247–75.

24. Gary Yohe and others, *A Synthetic Assessment of the Global Distribution of Vulnerability to Climate Change from the IPCC Perspective that Reflects Exposure and Adaptive Capacity* (Columbia University Center for International Earth Science Information Network [CIESIN], April 2006), especially the map, Global Distribution of Vulnerability to Climate Change, at http://sedac.ciesin. columbia.edu/mva/ccv/maps/MAP_4_3.pdf. See also Susan E. Rice and Stewart Patrick, "Index of State Weakness in the Developing World," Brookings Global Economy and Development Report (2007).

25. CIESIN constructed a variable measuring a country's adaptive capacity and its sensitivity. Adaptive capacity includes ratios of human resources dependency and literacy rates, economic capacity (market GDP per capita) and income distribution, and environmental capacity (population density, sulfur dioxide emissions, percentage of unmanaged land). Sensitivity includes settlement/infrastructure, food security, ecosystems, human health, and water resources. See Yohe and others, *A Synthetic Assessment of the Global Distribution of Vulnerability to Climate Change from the IPCC Perspective that Reflects Exposure and Adaptive Capacity.*

26. For a potentially expansive view of U.S. interests, see the remarks of General John Abizaid (Ret.) at the University of Texas in December 2008: "As the world gets smaller and becomes more global, can we put up with places out there that are falling apart to the point where they affect the rest of us? In the past, we could" (www.robertstrausscenter.org/events/view/72 [beginning at 1:15:53]).

27. For an expanded treatment of this theme, see Busby, "Who Cares about the Weather?"

28. Thomas Homer-Dixon, "Cause and Effect" (SSRC, August 2, 2007) (http:// blogs.ssrc.org/darfur/2007/08/02/cause-and-effect/).

29. Thomas Homer-Dixon, "Straw Man in the Wind," *National Interest,* January 2, 2008. For a similar summary of the earlier literature, see Thomas Homer-Dixon, *Environment, Scarcity, and Violence* (Princeton University Press, 1999).

30. On the work of the State Failure Task Force, see Daniel C. Esty and others, "State Failure Task Force Report: Phase II Findings" (Science Applications International, 1998). See also Busby, "Who Cares about the Weather?" For a similar discussion, see Buhaug and others, "Implications of Climate Change for Armed Conflict."

31. Busby, "Who Cares about the Weather?" For a similar point, see Buhaug and others, "Implications of Climate Change for Armed Conflict."

32. For a summary of the literature, see Buhaug and others, "Implications of Climate Change for Armed Conflict." See also Busby, "Who Cares about the

Weather?"; Salehyan, "From Climate Change to Conflict?"; Ragnild Nordås and Nils Petter Gleditsch, "Climate Change and Conflict," *Political Geography* 26, no. 6 (2007): 627–38. For its part, the IPCC has begun to mention the links between climate and security, but as Nordås and Gleditsch note, the references to scholarly peer-reviewed publications are scant. See Nordås and Gleditsch, "IPCC and the Climate-Conflict Nexus," paper presented at International Studies Association Meeting, New York, February 15–18, 2009.

33. Marc A. Levy and others, *Freshwater Availability Anomalies and Outbreak of Internal War: Results from a Global Spatial Time Series Analysis*, Human Security and Climate Change Conference, Oslo, Norway, 2005. For a similar premise and results, see Cullen S. Hendrix and Sarah M. Glaser, "Trends and Triggers: Climate Change and Civil Conflict in Sub-Saharan Africa," *Political Geography* 26, no. 6 (2007): 695–715.

34. For a discussion of these mechanisms, see Jon Barnett and W. Neil Adger, "Climate Change, Human Security and Violent Conflict," *Political Geography* 26, no. 6 (2007): 639–55. See also Buhaug and others, "Implications of Climate Change for Armed Conflict."

35. Colin Kahl calls this strategic use of scarcity the "exploitation hypothesis," in contrast to the "deprivation hypothesis," which presumes that conflict is induced by scarcity itself. See Colin H. Kahl, *States, Scarcity, and Civil Strife in the Developing World* (Princeton University Press, 2006).

36. Clionadh Raleigh and Henrik Urdal, "Climate Change, Environmental Degradation and Armed Conflict," *Political Geography* 26, no. 6 (2007): 674–94. Weak or no support for water scarcity or other environmental variables such as deforestation as a contributor to civil war or armed conflict has also been found by Ole Magnus Theisen, "Blood and Soil? Resource Scarcity and Internal Armed Conflict Revisited," *Journal of Peace Research* 45, no. 6 (2008): 801–18.

37. Jeffrey Sachs, "Water Wars," *Project Syndicate*, April 2009.

38. Buhaug and others, "Implications of Climate Change for Armed Conflict." For a similar conclusion, see German Advisory Council on Global Change (WBGU), *Climate Change as a Security Risk: Summary for Policymakers* (Berlin, June 26, 2007).

39. Buhaug and others, "Implications of Climate Change for Armed Conflict."

40. Given that other countries in the region experienced a break in rain patterns thirty years ago but did not subsequently experience conflict, this thirty-year trend may not explain the triggers for conflict in 2003, according to Michael Kevane and Leslie Gray, "Darfur: Rainfall and Conflict," Environmental Research Letters, 2008 (www.iop.org/EJ/article/1748-9326/3/3/034006/erl8_3_034006.html#erl281852s4).

41. Tearfund, "Darfur: Relief in a Vulnerable Environment," 2007 (www.tearfund.org/webdocs/website/Campaigning/Policy%20and%20research/Relief%20in%20a%20vulnerable%20envirionment%20final.pdf).

42. Sachs, in previous editorials, was more careful to reference the important work of his Columbia colleagues on rainfall variability and conflict. See, for example Jeffrey Sachs, "Land, Water, and Conflict," *Newsweek*, July 7–14, 2008 (www.newsweek.com/id/143700?tid=relatedcl).

43. Clionadh Raleigh and Lisa Jordan, "Climate Change, Migration and Conflict," paper presented at American Political Science Association meeting, Boston, August 28–31, 2008.

44. For a discussion of these dynamics, see Rafael Reuveny, "Climate Change–Induced Migration and Violent Conflict," *Political Geography* 26, no. 6 (2007): 656–73.

45. Idean Salehyan and Kristian Skrede Gleditsch, "Refugees and the Spread of Civil War," *International Organization* 60, no. 2 (2006): 335–66.

46. On climate change–induced migration as a plausible cause of interstate conflict, see Nils Petter Gleditsch, Ragnhild Nordås, and Idean Salehyan, *Climate Change and Conflict: The Migration Link* (New York: International Peace Academy, May 25, 2007).

47. Raleigh and Jordan, "Climate Change, Migration and Conflict."

48. Oli Brown, "The Numbers Game," *Forced Migration Review*, November 2008; Norman Myers, "Environmental Refugees: An Emergent Security Issue," Thirteenth Economic Forum, Prague, May 22, 2005, pp. 23–27. For an extended discussion, see also Nordås and Gleditsch, "IPCC and the Climate-Conflict Nexus."

49. Datasets that track natural disasters use a very specific definition, referring not only to the physical attributes of the storm or flood, but to the type of response that is appropriate. The Centre for Research on the Epidemiology of Disasters (CRED) defines a natural disaster as a "situation or event, which overwhelms local capacity, necessitating a request to national or international level for external assistance; an unforeseen and often sudden event that causes great damage, destruction, and human suffering." A disaster is entered into its database if at least 10 people are reported killed, 100 people reported affected, a state of emergency has been declared, or a call for international assistance has been issued. See CRED, "EM-DAT Database" (www.emdat.be/ExplanatoryNotes/glossary.html).

50. See my discussion in Busby, "Who Cares about the Weather?"

51. For an exploration of these questions, see www.disasterdiplomacy.org.

52. Dawn Brancati, "Political Aftershocks: The Impact of Earthquakes on Intrastate Conflict," *Journal of Conflict Resolution* 51, no. 5 (2007): 715–43.

53. Philip Nel and Marjolein Righarts, "Natural Disasters and the Risk of Violent Civil Conflict," *International Studies Quarterly* 52, no. 1 (2008): 159–85.

54. Working Group II's contribution to the IPCC's Fourth Assessment wrote: "Confidence has increased that some weather events and extremes will become more frequent, more widespread and/or more intense during the 21st century." IPCC, *Fourth Assessment Report—Climate Change 2007: Impacts, Adaptation*

and Vulnerability. The scientific evidence in support of the specific claims about hurricanes is discussed in this chapter's section on Haiti.

55. "Affected" refers to people requiring immediate assistance during a period of emergency. It also includes displaced or evacuated people. See CRED, "EM-DAT Database." For a discussion of the greater vulnerability to disasters in urban areas and the links between disasters and poverty, see United Nations, "2009 Global Assessment Report on Disaster Risk Reduction: Risk and Poverty in a Changing Climate" (2009).

56. Michael Waterhouse and JoAnne O'Bryant, "National Guard Personnel and Deployments: Fact Sheet," Report RS22633 (Congressional Research Service, January 10, 2007).

57. See Busby "The Climate Security Connection," "Who Cares about the Weather?" and "Climate Change and National Security"; Purvis and Busby, *The Security Implications of Climate Change for the UN System.*

58. Raleigh and Jordan, "Climate Change, Migration and Conflict."

59. Bradley C. Parks and J. Timmons Roberts, *A Climate of Injustice: Global Inequality, North-South Politics, and Climate Policy* (Cambridge, Mass.: MIT Press, 2006).

60. For more extended discussions of climate change and disasters, see Busby, "Who Cares about the Weather?"and "The Climate Security Connection."

61. Yale University, "Environmental Performance Index 2008" (http://epi.yale.edu/Americas). The project website describes the scale as follows: "The quantitative metrics underlying the 2008 EPI encompass 25 indicators chosen through: a broad-based review of the environmental science literature; in-depth consultation with a group of scientific advisors in each policy category; the evidence from the Millennium Ecosystem Assessment, the Intergovernmental Panel on Climate Change, the Global Environmental Outlook-4, and other assessments; environmental policy debates surrounding multilateral environmental agreements; and expert judgment. Each indicator builds on a foundation either in environmental health or ecological science."

62. Institute for Economics and Peace, "Executive Summary," 2008 (www.visionofhumanity.org/gpi/about-gpi/overview.php). According to the Global Peace Index (GPI) website, the dataset ranks the relative states of peace of different countries: "The index is composed of 24 qualitative and quantitative indicators from highly respected sources, which combine internal and external factors ranging from a nation's level of military expenditure to its relations with neighbouring countries and the level of respect for human rights. These indicators were selected by an international panel of academics, business people, philanthropists and peace institutions. The GPI is collated and calculated by the Economist Intelligence Unit."

63. Thor Hanson and others, "Warfare in Biodiversity Hotspots," *Conservation Biology,* February 19, 2009, pp. 1–9.

64. International Monetary Fund, *World Economic Outlook* (Washington, October 2008) (www.imf.org/external/pubs/ft/weo/2008/02/index.htm).

65. Yale University, "Environmental Performance Index 2008." Haiti's score was 60.7 on a 100-point scale. By contrast, the Dominican Republic had a score of 83. The average for the Americas was 78.

66. Rhett Butler, "Haiti," Mongabay.com, 2006 (http://rainforests.mongabay.com/deforestation/2000/Haiti.htm); Rhett Butler, "Dominican Republic," Mongabay.com, 2006 (http://rainforests.mongabay.com/deforestation/2000/Dominican_Republic.htm).

67. International Crisis Group, "Haiti: Saving the Environment, Preventing Instability and Conflict," April 28, 2009.

68. Julia Taft, "Storm-Tossed Lessons," *New York Times,* October 3, 2004.

69. Francie Grace, "Haiti Handover As Floods Devour," *CBS News*, May 31, 2004.

70. United Nations, "2009 Global Assessment Report on Disaster Risk Reduction: Risk and Poverty in a Changing Climate" (2009).

71. International Crisis Group, "Haiti: Saving the Environment, Preventing Instability and Conflict."

72. N. Mimura and others, "Small Islands. Climate Change 2007: Impacts, Adaptation and Vulnerability," in *Contribution of Working Group II to the Fourth Assessment Report of the Intergovernmental Panel on Climate Change,* edited by M. L. Parry and others (Cambridge University Press, 2007).

73. Pew Center on Global Climate Change, "Hurricanes and Climate Change FAQs," undated (www.pewclimate.org/hurricanes.cfm). For an accessible account of these debates, see Chris Mooney, *Storm World: Hurricanes, Politics, and the Battle over Global Warming* (New York: Harcourt, 2007). See also my discussion in Busby, "Who Cares about the Weather?"

74. Stephen Shellman, "Political Persecution or Economic Deprivation? A Time-Series Analysis of Haitian Exodus, 1990–2004," *Conflict Management and Peace Science* 24, no. 2 (2007): 121–37.

75. Kelly M. Greenhill, "Extortive Engineered Migration: Asymmetric Weapon of the Weak," *Conflict, Security and Development* 2, no. 3 (2002): 105–16.

76. Rice and Patrick, "Index of State Weakness in the Developing World."

77. For a review of Congo's slide into poor governance, see Pierre Englebert, "Life Support or Assisted Suicide? Dilemmas of U.S. Policy toward the Democratic Republic of Congo," in *Short of the Goal: U.S. Policy and Poorly Performing States,* edited by N. Birdsall, M. Vaishnav, and R. L. Ayres (Washington: Center for Global Development, 2006).

78. United Nations, "2009 Global Assessment Report on Disaster Risk Reduction."

79. Rhett Butler, "Rainforests Absorb 20% of Emissions Annually," Mongabay.com, February 19, 2009 (http://news.mongabay.com/2009/0218-forest_carbon.html).

80. See my discussion in Busby, "Climate Change and National Security."

81. To achieve those savings, the mean price of carbon would need to be between $19 and $65 per ton. See Rhett Butler, "Returns from Carbon Offsets Could Beat Palm Oil in Congo DRC," Mongabay.com, December 4, 2007 (http://news.mongabay.com/2007/1204-congo_whrc.html); and Nadine Laporte and others, "Reducing CO2 Emissions from Deforestation and Degradation In the Democratic Republic of Congo: A First Look" (Woods Hole Research Center, December 3–14, 2007) (http://whrc.org/BaliReports/assets/Africa_Bali_Booklet.pdf).

82. Resources for the Future (RFF), "Forest Carbon Index: Technical Report" (Washington, 2009, forthcoming).

83. The index adjusts the forest carbon supply potential for three risk factors: readiness, ease of doing business, and governance. RFF created the Index of Readiness, while the other indicators were drawn from World Bank data. Readiness involves remote-sensing capacity and environmental market experience. Ease of doing business measures regulations affecting ten stages of a business's life: starting a business, dealing with licenses, employing workers, registering property, getting credit, protecting investors, paying taxes, trading across borders, enforcing contracts, and closing a business. Governance has six dimensions: voice and accountability, political stability, government effectiveness, regulatory quality, rule of law, and control of corruption.

84. For a review of these concerns, see Tom Griffiths, "Seeing 'RED': 'Avoided Deforestation' and the Rights of Indigenous Peoples and Local Communities," Forest Peoples Programme, June 2007.

85. World Bank, "World Bank Engagement in the DRC's Forest Sector," n.d. (http://web.worldbank.org/WBSITE/EXTERNAL/COUNTRIES/AFRICAEXT/EXTAFRSUMESSD/EXTFORINAFR/0,,contentMDK:22110942~pagePK:1489 56~piPK:216618~theSitePK:2493451,00.html?cid=3001).

86. Delphine Schrank, "As Go the Hippos...," *The Atlantic*, June 2009 (www.theatlantic.com/doc/200906/congo-ecology).

87. Stefan Lovgren, "Spectacular Gorilla Growth in Congo, Despite War," *National Geographic*, January 27, 2009.

88. Rhett Butler, "Congo Cancels Logging Contracts Covering 13M Hectares," Mongabay.com, January 21, 2009 (http://news.mongabay.com/2009/0121-congo.html).

89. The U.S. Department of Defense recognized this as well, as part of a new 2008–09 initiative in support of social science. A University of Texas–led research team, including this author, was awarded a multimillion dollar grant to study climate change and security in Africa.

90. UNDP, *Human Development Report 2007/2008* (New York, 2007).

91. As of May 2009, for example, the LDCF had pledges totaling $176.5 million and the SCCF had pledges of $121 million. Another $50 million was available for the Strategic Priority on Adaptation under the GEF Trust Fund. See

Global Environmental Facility, "Status Report on the Special Climate Change Fund," May 26, 2009 (www.gefweb.org/uploadedFiles/Documents/LDCFSCCF_Council_Documents/LDCFSCCF6_June_2009/LDCF.SCCF.6.Inf.2.pdf). The December 2007 climate negotiations in Bali made the GEF the trustee of the Adaptation Trust Fund, with funding derived from a portion of the proceeds from Clean Development Mechanism (CDM) projects. Two percent of the Certified Emission Reduction (CER) from the CDM is dedicated to the Adaptation Fund. As of February 2009, the Trust Fund had received donations of $3.548 million and a loan of $700,000 from the LDCF. See Global Environmental Facility, "Status Report on the Administrative Trust Fund Resources" (Washington, February 25, 2009). The value of those credits was estimated to be worth between $80 million and $300 million a year from 2008 to 2012. See UN Framework Convention on Climate Change, "UN Breakthrough on Climate Change Reached in Bali" (Bonn, December 15, 2007).

92. GFDRR, "Global Facility for Disaster Reduction and Recovery: Donor Pledges and Contributions," June 8, 2009.

93. See H. Res. 2454, sec. 494 (www.opencongress.org/bill/111-h2454/text).

CHAPTER SIX

State Weakness and Infectious Diseases

MIRIAM ESTRIN and CARL MALM

The year is 1959. Within twelve months, the Belgian Congo will declare its independence and be wracked by a series of political uprisings. Private mercenaries will flood the country to protect mining interests. Six years later, a CIA-led coup will bring to power a brutal dictator named Joseph Désiré Mobutu, who will reign over the country throughout three decades of poor governance and corruption. By 1996 Congo will be entrenched in a devastating civil war that will kill millions. But all of that is still to come.

The major event in the Belgian Congo in 1959 was neither an earth-shattering revolution nor the rise of a corrupt leader, but a blood test. A Bantu man presented himself at a clinic in the capital city of Léopoldville with conditions indicating sickle cell disease. To identify the disease, doctors ordered a fateful test that many years later would reveal the first known case of HIV.[1]

The possibility that a blood test in a distant colonial capital might matter on the streets of New York and San Francisco, and ultimately all across America, could not have been fathomed by medical scientists or security officials. The methods for international disease surveillance critical to halting emerging epidemics had not been established. Such surveillance could have exposed a virus that lurked undetected for decades. It could have controlled a disease that continues to kill Americans, Africans, and people from every continent at alarming rates. Ultimately, millions of lives might have been saved.

At the time the Congolese man contracted HIV/AIDS, Congo's health conditions were abysmal. In 1960 life expectancy stood at a meager forty-one years, compared with seventy years in the United States.[2] A long-standing history of neglect had hollowed out the health system. During the reign of Belgium's King Leopold II from 1885 to 1908, violence and disease killed millions of Congolese.[3] By the time of Congo's independence in 1960, bad governance and poverty had left the majority of the population with little or no access to health care.

At the time of the Bantu man's blood test, Congo and its travails mattered little to most of the world. In retrospect, strong health care systems might have better fought AIDS as it unfolded. While the precise origin of AIDS is not known, this disease, which has killed a half-million Americans, clearly originated outside U.S. borders and decades before anyone in the United States recognized the threat. By then it was too late to save hundreds of thousands of American lives, much less tens of millions of African lives. None are experiences the United States or the international community can afford to repeat.

Yet that is the risk when the United States fails to help poor and weak states develop the capacity to fight diseases of concern to U.S. national security. Of course, poverty is not solely responsible for all disease outbreaks, all diseases in poor countries are not a national security concern to the United States, and all diseases that threaten the nation will not come from the poorest or weakest countries. However, poor countries are more likely to have infectious diseases emerge within their borders and are less able to control them. An increasing volume of global travel and trade makes diseases in poor countries more likely to reach the United States. Thus, diseases that emerge and fester in poor, weak states can threaten Americans.

This chapter is concerned with the spread of infectious diseases from poor or weak states to the United States—and the resulting public health emergency that could threaten American lives. Eradicating poverty and disease is not merely a worthwhile end in its own right. In today's interdependent world, policies that help poor countries to prevent, monitor, and control diseases within their borders can ultimately protect Americans.

INFECTIOUS DISEASES AND U.S. NATIONAL SECURITY

Some infectious diseases—for example, HIV/AIDS, drug-resistant tuberculosis, and pandemic flu—are clear national security threats to the

United States. They have the potential to make people sick, hurt the American economy, kill millions of Americans, incapacitate troops, undermine allies, and be used by terrorists to spawn chaos. These are deadly diseases that have the ability to spread rapidly and widely. AIDS alone killed 580,000 Americans through 2007.[4]

Infectious diseases already kill about 170,000 Americans annually.[5] While the aggregate number of deaths from infectious diseases in the United States has decreased over the long term, this trend has not been constant. In the 1980s death rates from infectious disease took an *upward* swing, due to factors such as HIV/AIDS and antibiotic resistance, but they then declined again in 1996.[6] Because infectious diseases are constantly evolving, a new strain could emerge at any time or an existing disease could become more lethal. Since 1973 scientists have identified more than thirty new infectious diseases.[7] This rapid pace—one emerging infectious disease a year—is unparalleled in history.[8] Moreover, their threat arises not only from pathogens spreading naturally, but also from terrorists releasing infectious agents in order to intentionally spread deadly diseases, as the anthrax attacks in the United States showed.

While the homeland is America's primary national security concern, deployed American soldiers are under even more immediate threat, and disease can take a high toll during some operations.[9] Soldiers infected abroad may also carry disease back to the United States. The 1968 flu pandemic, for example, entered the United States via American soldiers returning from Vietnam and killed 34,000 people back home, most of them civilians.[10]

Disease outbreaks also carry economic costs. In 2003 the severe acute respiratory syndrome (SARS) virus cost the global economy about $30 billion in production losses.[11] Emergency response measures may include restrictions on normal travel and trade, which curtails economic activity in both large and small economies.

In today's interconnected world, an infectious disease anywhere can spread everywhere, especially given the density of airline traffic. Air passengers numbered 2.1 billion in 2006, a figure expected to increase by 3 to 5 percent a year over twenty years.[12] In 2007, 903 million international tourists traveled worldwide, up from 25 million in 1950, and today's tourists travel to more destinations in the developing world.[13] Increases in the international trade of live animals provide even more opportunities for pathogens to stow away in food cargo.[14] Given the volume of exchange, it is unrealistic to think that all diseases can be halted at every country's borders.

The rate of trade has also increased sharply, facilitating the spread of disease. In 1580 it took just over a year for an influenza pandemic to spread from Asia to all of the populated continents.[15] In 2003 SARS traveled to thirty-two countries—and over 5,000 miles—in just three months before it was contained.[16] An influenza pandemic could travel from Hong Kong to the United States in as little as eighteen days.[17] As the swine flu outbreak of April 2009 shows, such occurrences can cause distress in even the strongest nations.

While it is impossible to know where the next disease threat will arise, poor countries and poor regions within emerging economies are likely hot spots.[18] The swine flu outbreak in April 2009 showed that not all outbreaks will come from the poorest or weakest states. But low-latitude developing nations, particularly those in South Asia, Southeast Asia, and Africa, are said to be likely sources.[19] These countries have little capacity to detect and control known diseases, much less monitor the emergence of unknown forms. And the capacity and funds for surveillance and response are concentrated in the rich countries of the developed world, precisely the places where these diseases are least likely to emerge.[20]

INFECTIOUS DISEASES AND THE DEVELOPING WORLD

An unfavorable and worsening mix of factors—demographics, poor governance, conflict, and climate change—means that infectious diseases often overburden countries in the developing world. Some of these factors are not connected with poverty: the concentration of poultry and pig populations in China, for example, is a key contributor to avian flu outbreaks. But conditions of poverty often do matter. Population growth and urbanization pack more people into teeming slums and already over-crowded homes, facilitating the spread of disease. In rural areas, population growth has forced people to move into wilderness areas where they come into increased contact with animals that may harbor new sources of infection. Indeed, 60 percent of emerging diseases are zoonoses, or diseases that are transferred from animals to humans.[21] During violent conflict, which is disproportionately concentrated in the world's poorest regions, warring parties deplete food sources and demolish health

infrastructure, making a famished and fleeing population more susceptible to diseases and more likely to spread them.[22] Global warming and
changes in climate will also spread diseases to new areas and increase
the global burden.[23] The worst consequences will ensue in low-income
countries, where an increase in extreme weather events and diseases like
malaria is expected to affect more people and overstress already weak
health systems.[24] The risks are heightened in regions in which failures of
political will, ineffective governance, and the poor response of political
leaders allow diseases to spread unabated.

Poor countries generally do not have the resources or infrastructure
to control infectious diseases. Of the 13.3 million deaths the diseases
cause worldwide each year, most occur in the poorest parts of the world
and are the result of only a small subset of diseases.[25] Pneumonia, for
example, kills approximately 2 million children in the developing world
annually, but only 1,000 children in the industrialized world.[26] Diarrheal
disease, which can be mitigated with a simple oral rehydration mix of
clean water, sugar, and salt, kills nearly 3 million a year in the developing world but presents little threat to the developed world.[27]

Although diseases associated with poverty do not necessarily affect
Americans directly, country-level poverty facilitates the spread of disease. High rates of disease in poor countries sap meager government
revenues, weaken state capacity, and trap countries in vicious cycles of
reduced income, declining productivity, and lower economic growth.
Health systems that cannot contend with diseases of poverty in the present will be less likely to deal with other diseases that threaten the United
States in the future.

State health systems in poor countries are by and large inadequate.
The World Health Organization (WHO) estimates that health expenditures of $35 to $50 per person a year are required to provide basic
life-saving services. Yet sixty-four states fail to meet the annual $50 per
capita expenditure, and thirty of these fail to provide at the $20 level.[28]
Physicians and hospital beds are in shorter supply in low-income countries than in high-income countries.[29] Without accessible roads, a sick
person living in a remote area may never reach a hospital. Without effective regulation, pills sold at a pharmacy may not disclose the ingredients
on the label; indeed, 10 to 30 percent of remedies sold in developing
countries are adulterated or contain no active ingredients at all.[30] Even
worse, taking incomplete doses could cause strains of the disease being

treated to become drug resistant, which could deplete the world's supply of medicine. Without an effective surveillance system, states cannot detect dangerous diseases and notify the international community.

In sum, a poor person living in a poor and weak state is less likely to survive an illness than someone living in a developed state. Moreover, poor and weak states typically lack the capacity to stop diseases from traveling across borders. Individual and national poverty allow diseases to emerge and spread, and add to the challenge of tackling disease threats of concern to U.S. national security. Response strategies must emphasize the prevention of new infections, global surveillance that relies on national data from the developing world, and the capacity to control diseases at their point of origin.

Disease Prevention

Ideally, governments should prevent diseases before they take hold and spread. Properly planned disease prevention can be cost-effective and saves lives. Vaccination, for example, is often less expensive than disease control. The $100 million in global funds amassed *in total* to eradicate smallpox is estimated to have saved the world $1.35 billion *a year*, a cost-benefit ratio of 1:450.[31] Prevention efforts that alleviate impoverished living conditions or provide toilets and clean water can fight a host of infectious diseases. Prevention is essential to sustaining an effective response to disease. Lessons from fighting HIV/AIDS show that "if countries do not succeed in stemming the tide of new infections, the need for treatment will continue to increase and outpace their ability to develop the capacity to meet it."[32] Investments in immunizations, targeted poverty alleviation, and education in healthy practices offer cost-effective ways to prevent diseases from emerging and spreading to populations far beyond their point of origin.

Global Surveillance that Relies on National Data

Prevention alone cannot stop all diseases, however. To react effectively to disease epidemics, officials in both developed and developing countries must have early and accurate information about the scope of the problem. Effective global surveillance starts at the local level, with laboratories equipped with sufficient resources, communication tools, and technicians to collect data, interpret the results, and pass the information along to those in charge of disease response.[33] Local public budgets bear the costs for such systems, which poor countries cannot afford and weak states ruled by authoritarian governments fail to pay. In addition to bolstering their prevention capacity, then, the United States should help developing countries build effective surveillance systems to detect disease outbreaks. All countries benefit from international surveillance networks, but the strength of such systems depends on the strength of each country's capabilities.

Health experts have recognized the importance of cooperating on control efforts as far back as the 1851 International Sanitary Conference of Paris, convened to fight the spread of cholera. Today's core international agreement on public health is founded on the World Health Organization's International Sanitary Regulations, adopted in 1951 and updated in 1969 as the International Health Regulations (IHR).[34] Under these early regulations, monitoring was only required at a country's borders and the WHO could only take reports of disease outbreaks from the state. Just six diseases had to be reported, and there were no penalties if a state failed to do so.[35]

In 2005, 194 countries agreed that it was important to expand the IHR to improve the legal framework for coordinating surveillance and response. The revisions broadened the number of notifiable diseases from six specific diseases to all public health events that "may constitute a public health emergency of international concern."[36] Nongovernmental sources were also allowed to report outbreaks, which gives states less room to conceal them. In addition, the new IHR required signatories to design and implement programs that meet "core capacity requirements for surveillance and response."[37] The IHR now obliges countries under international law to survey and report disease outbreaks. This assumes that each state has the capacity to identify such events, yet the WHO allocates no funds to meet these requirements.[38] Thus, although the legal framework for global health is in place, capacity to comply with that framework is lacking in the world's poorest and weakest states.

Some shortcuts are possible, and developing countries can sometimes rely on outside networks for support, including the WHO's Global Outbreak Alert and Response Network (GOARN), military networks like the U.S. Defense Department's Global Emerging Infections Surveillance and Response System (GEIS), and informal networks that monitor disease data on Internet websites. But gaps remain. Support from GEIS, for example, extends only to countries in bilateral relations with the United States and thus leaves some areas of the world unmonitored.

Despite these improvements to the global health architecture, the world is still not prepared for disease outbreaks. Surveillance can only be effective if it extends to all of the places where diseases may emerge. This includes the teaming slums and rural villages of the developing world—which may not be hospitable to policy implementation. To date, efforts to bolster U.S. disease surveillance domestically have done little to address the simultaneous need for surveillance in countries where political will is low or resources limited. Without an early-warning system in place everywhere, diseases will be more likely to break out and spread undetected.

Containing Disease

If the global surveillance system fails, countries must be able to fight diseases within their borders. The 2005 update of the IHR legally binds countries to improve their capacity for response. But these measures will likely remain unimplemented so long as resources are not available to help developing countries build the capacity for complex disease response. In the absence of local capacity, outside teams can step in to fight outbreaks. After outbreaks of Ebola plagued several African states, the WHO, the U.S. Centers for Disease Control and Prevention, and nongovernmental organizations (NGOs) intervened to fight the deadly hemorrhagic fever. While such responses are crucial in emergencies, in the long term they can hurt developing countries if local health systems are replaced rather than complemented or bolstered by international actors.

To control disease, local agencies must be capable of tackling and halting emerging health outbreaks at their source. The United States can assist with investments in basic health infrastructure, which can improve all three of the imperatives at the heart of this discussion: disease prevention, surveillance, and control. Such investments will be critical to prevent diseases like avian flu from becoming devastating global pandemics. The United States will face significant challenges in building health capacity in poor countries that lack the political will to fight infectious diseases. Such environments could thwart long-term health interventions "if the donors put large sums into such countries, only to see the efforts wasted and the donor taxpayers lose confidence."[39] In these toughest challenges, can policymakers make a difference? Case studies of avian influenza and HIV/AIDS, some of the world's gravest health threats, may help provide an answer.

CASE STUDY: AVIAN INFLUENZA AND PANDEMIC FLU
EMERGING FROM POOR AND WEAK STATES

Volcanic plateaus and verdant mountains dot the border of the Karo highlands in northern Sumatra, Indonesia. Lush with waterfalls and hot springs, the landscape also holds more than 200 tiny farming villages. In one of these villages lived Puji Ginting, a woman of thirty-seven who worked in a nearby village selling fruit and chilies in the marketplace. In late April 2006, Ginting fell ill. A few days later her family came together to celebrate an annual harvest festival with a feast of chicken from the marketplace or perhaps from her own backyard.[40] The meal passed uneventfully. Then tragedy struck: within two weeks, Ginting and six of her relatives—her sons, her brother, her sister, her nephew, and her one-year-old niece—were dead.

Samples later revealed they had contracted highly pathogenic avian influenza, making it the largest group of deaths related to this disease on record.[41] When reports of the outbreak broke, epidemiologists rushed to the scene to control the virus and collect samples. These samples would be essential for understanding its genetic makeup, developing a flu vaccine based on this genetic information, and potentially saving millions of lives. Avian influenza would not necessarily have remained confined to Ginting's family nor to her village nor the hundreds of villages surrounding it. This small cluster of illnesses might have sparked a deadly pandemic across the globe.

The possibility—even the inevitability—of a pandemic flu virus reaching the United States presents a significant security threat, with potential economic and human consequences. According to recent projections, a pandemic could cause millions of deaths around the world, with 1.7 million in the United States alone.[42] Experts estimate as many as 42 million outpatient visits and 734,000 hospitalizations in the United States.[43] Hospitals would be overwhelmed and "the surge capacity in health systems will likely be insufficient to cope . . . even in industrialized countries."[44] With their far weaker health institutions, developing countries would find staff professionals and hospitals "easily overwhelmed."[45]

Fortunately, the virus that struck Ginting and her family was contained. If the incident had occurred a mere eight months later, epidemiologists might not have been so fortunate. In late December 2006, Indonesia decided to stop sharing its virus samples. By resisting cooperation with the global health community, its government amplified the epidemiological threat. As a result, avian influenza preparedness must now include diplomatic negotiations over virus samples, adding to the complex scientific challenges in vaccine development and institutional challenges in building health capacity in poor and weak states.

THE CONTEXT: POVERTY, CORRUPTION, AND RISK

In rural areas of Indonesia—where most of the backyard poultry is raised and avian influenza known to strike—34 percent of the population lives below the poverty line.[46] The country's 1.4 billion chickens are raised on poultry farms and in 30 million households.[47] The poultry sector employs more than 10 million Indonesians.[48] When avian flu breaks out, many farmers are loath to participate in the all-important early-warning system and instead hide signs of illness, rushing their birds to market before the disease is detected, their birds are culled en masse, and poultry is rejected by buyers. Under normal market conditions, many of these farmers could earn more money from a sale in the marketplace than from compensation after a government-ordered cull.[49] Any farmer who can sell a sick chicken without penalty for more than the culling rate has an incentive to seek profit over public health.

State management of avian flu is hampered by Indonesia's system of decentralized government. Three years after the 1998 disintegration of the authoritarian Suharto regime, Indonesia began an experiment in decentralization that transferred more than 16,000 public service facilities to regional control.[50] In the ensuing confusion over responsibilities for reporting health outbreaks, communications networks and health information systems broke down. Health recommendations issued at the national level were left to local officials to fund and implement.[51] As a result, notes one WHO epidemiologist, the power of central government authorities "only extends to the walls of their office. The advice must reach nearly 450 districts, where local officials then decide whether to take action."[52] When local officials failed to give proper attention and funding to the health sector, it caused a "near collapse of surveillance systems, one of the backbones of disease control."[53]

The international community has not ignored the threat of avian flu in Indonesia but has been cautious about providing aid that could be wasted or misused. Indonesia ranks 126 out of 180 countries on Transparency International's Corruption Perceptions Index.[54] This indicator of widespread corruption makes it easy to see why international donors are hesitant to send funds for pandemic preparedness. Effective disease response requires communities to work together with local and national governments, a daunting challenge if trust in public officials is low.

Virus Sharing and Global Health

Indonesia's decision in 2006 to withhold samples of the avian influenza virus set global pandemic preparedness back considerably. Indonesia's concern, argued Health Minister Siti Fadilah Supari, was that drug companies would use virus samples obtained for free to develop, patent, and profit from the resulting vaccines. Being too poor to buy the vaccines, Indonesia would fail to benefit from the very samples it had shared at no cost. Supari has claimed a supportive alliance of health ministers from 112 other nations, including India and Brazil, who worry that only people in rich countries would be protected in a pandemic.[55] As a representative from Thailand told the WHO, if a pandemic hits, "they survive and we die."[56]

The samples that Indonesia withholds are critical for risk assessment and vaccine development. The WHO uses virus samples to make seed strains for candidate vaccines; the WHO then shares these seed strains with any pharmaceutical manufacturer that requests them. All the same, 70 percent of vaccine production capacity resides in North America and Europe, with much of the rest in Australia, Japan, and China.[57] Developing countries simply do not have the capacity required to develop significant quantities of vaccine. They can provide the virus samples to the international community and then hope to buy the vaccines developed from those samples.

Even then, global capacity is limited. A pandemic virus could spread faster than the months it takes scientists to develop a vaccine for that unique strain, drug companies to manufacture it, governments to disseminate it, and health workers to administer it. The current stockpile of vaccines falls far below the number of doses needed to protect the global population. Only 350 million doses of vaccine can be produced at current capacity, and 500 million doses at optimal capacity.[58] Even a WHO plan to switch to a vaccine that could yield 2.3 billion doses of pandemic vaccine would still fall tragically short—by billions—of the number of vaccines needed during a pandemic for a global population of 6.7 billion.[59]

At least three interrelated problems could further reduce access to vaccines in developing countries. First, there is no international agreement on procedures for distributing vaccines after an outbreak, which means that countries that are the locus of an outbreak may not necessarily be the first to get the vaccine needed to contain it. Second, better-organized and wealthier governments in high-income countries will contract with pharmaceutical companies to purchase vaccines before production, thus capturing most of the limited supply before it is even available. Third, developing countries like Indonesia are left in the precarious position of bidding for the remaining—and even more limited—supply of vaccine during a crisis, with all the added encumbrances and complications of delivery and distribution.

The current vaccine development system leaves both developed and developing countries in a potentially precarious position. On one hand, if a pandemic strain emerges from a developing country that holds virus samples hostage, as Indonesia did, then vaccine production will be inhibited and all populations will face a graver threat. On the other hand, if poor nations surrender the virus samples without guaranteed access to needed vaccines, this creates another form of moral hazard. Clearly, need, production capacity, and access can only be properly aligned through a transnational agreement on public policy and commercial practice.

From Indonesia to Global Implications

Pandemic influenza emerging from states like Indonesia is unlikely to be confined to one country or even to one region. Pandemic influenza could emerge in a weak state, incubate in a weak public health system, prey on the poorest people in that system, and then spread through travel or trade to the United States. Given its potential for killing on a grand scale, avian flu is possibly the greatest single infectious disease threat to U.S. citizens. An estimated 71 million people could die around the world. Economic losses could reach $3 trillion.[60] Today's global interconnectedness could help spread a flu pandemic faster than any before.[61] Not every influenza outbreak guarantees a doomsday scenario, but neither is the threat pure hyperbole. If a highly lethal virus that spreads easily between humans emerges—and many scientists believe that one will—it could spark a new pandemic that would be "the event of our lifetime."[62] Regular seasonal influenza already travels around the globe each year, killing 500,000 people, 36,000 of whom are Americans.[63] A strain can jump continents in just days.[64] For most people, most of the time, the disease is unpleasant, but not deadly. But every ten to fifty years a new strain emerges to which few people are immune.[65] Such strains can then explode in a population, killing a far greater number than normal seasonal influenza. During the twentieth century, global influenza pandemics occurred in 1918, 1957, and 1968. Of these, the most famous is the 1918 pandemic, which killed 50 million to 100 million people in less than six months.[66] The last pandemic occurred forty years ago.

The virus that has been under watch is H5N1 avian influenza, but as the April 2009 H1N1 swine flu outbreaks show, a lethal outbreak could come from an unexpected viral strain. These two viruses are not the same: H5N1 is an animal virus endemic in bird populations of Indonesia and other countries that does not spread easily between humans; H1N1 is a newly discovered virus that does spread easily from person to person.[67] Whatever the strain, a lethal virus that spreads easily among humans is of concern to a global population with no immunity.

Beyond the human tragedy, a pandemic could have significant economic impacts. According to one model, a moderate pandemic could reduce global output by 2 percent and a severe influenza pandemic by 4.8 percent.[68] Low-income countries, with greater population density and greater disease risk from poverty, would be hit harder than high-income countries.[69] In a severe pandemic, losses to gross domestic product (GDP) in East Asia could reach 8.7 percent.[70] The greatest economic losses from pandemic influenza would not occur from lives or work-hours lost, but from attempts to avoid infection.[71] As the disease spread, about 60 percent of economic losses would accrue from the cessation of travel on crowded airplanes and in tightly packed subway cars, from eating at home instead of in busy restaurants, and from avoiding germs at movie theaters or at popular tourist destinations.[72] Worker deficits in areas such as transportation or law enforcement could mean a temporary breakdown of social order. Even if some countries were prepared for the first strike of avian influenza, history teaches that a second wave usually spreads across the globe within a year.[73]

Models quantifying the human and economic consequences of pandemic influenza are, of course, constrained by many uncertainties. They cannot guarantee outcomes, but they can project plausible scenarios useful for determining the necessary resources for preparedness.[74] Recent models do suggest that a "large investment of resources" will be necessary.[75] In these unpredictable situations, country leaders should not be complacent, nor should they contribute to the hysteria. Instead, they must be prepared to contend with emerging disease threats appropriately.

U.S. and International Policy

In light of the urgent need for a coordinated, international response capacity that extends across the world, the current state of global influenza preparedness is discouraging. Despite widespread awareness that this ticking time bomb is due to explode, a senior avian influenza expert at the United Nations estimates that collectively, global preparedness to fight the deadly pandemic is only at 40 percent.[76] One reason is that the global recession has cut hundreds of millions of dollars in funding and thousands of workers—even from state and local health agencies responsible for disease outbreaks in the United States.[77] Furthermore, collective efforts have not adequately addressed the needs of poor and weak states in meeting necessary levels of preparedness.

Although the U.S. government has allocated funding to address the threat of avian flu and pandemic influenza, it has targeted insufficient amounts at poor countries with weak public health systems. President Barack Obama's budget for fiscal 2010 allocated $584 million to U.S. agencies and centers for pandemic preparedness, which required another $1.5 billion in fiscal 2009 for supplemental appropriations to respond to H1N1 outbreaks and prepare for a pandemic in the United States.[78] President George W. Bush requested $7.1 billion in the 2006 Pandemic Influenza Act, but $251 million—or just 3.5 percent—was budgeted toward efforts to detect and contain outbreaks overseas.[79] A January 2006 international pledging conference established the Avian and Human Influenza Facility, which provided $77 million in grants to more than forty developing countries in support of pandemic preparedness, but these funds are still too limited to support state capacity building.[80]

An estimated $4 billion is needed *annually* to fight the global flu threat.[81] Since the first outbreaks of avian influenza in 2003, countries have pledged a total of $2.7 billion for international aid to fight the virus, leaving a two- to three-year funding gap of $1.2 billion to $1.5 billion that threatens the sustainability of the cumulative investment.[82] Policymakers worry that donors are suffering from "flu fatigue," as they tire of pledging money.[83] Their perceptions of the threat have risen and fallen over time, and there has been a lull in attention to pandemic flu in the past few years as fewer outbreaks have occurred. But the tradeoffs are clear: invest $4 billion annually for pandemic preparedness or expect a $3 trillion crisis that could kill millions.[84]

In the event of an avian influenza outbreak, communities, governments, the private sector, nongovernmental groups, and the international community must come together to support efforts of prevention, surveillance, and response. Health systems in the developing world could be overwhelmed by pandemic.[85] To prepare for this and other health challenges, developing countries must build broad health capacity that can quickly handle any emerging disease threat. To bolster global health security, the United States and the international community must help developing countries build such a capacity. The United States must also pressure governments to cooperate on virus sharing while addressing their legitimate concerns about equity.

These challenges become only more acute, of course, when poor and weak governments lack the political will to build capacity or undertake reforms that allow them to develop functioning and sustainable health systems. Then the challenge is to build institutional capacity without the support of the state. But is it possible to circumvent recalcitrant governments? The experience in combating HIV/AIDS—thus far the largest attempt to address the impacts of an infectious disease—sheds some light on both the prospects for controlling the effects of the disease and the limitations in overcoming it.

CASE STUDY: CIRCUMVENTING GOVERNMENTS IN THE INTERNATIONAL RESPONSE TO HIV/AIDS

In April 2000 President Thabo Mbeki of South Africa sent a five-page letter to world leaders stating his view that the HIV virus does not cause AIDS. It was a shocking pronouncement from the leader of a country in which 5.7 million people are living with HIV—more than the number in any other country in sub-Saharan Africa.[86] Mbeki refused to accept free donations of antiretroviral drugs and grants from global health initiatives; instead his national health minister urged AIDS victims to treat the disease with garlic, lemon juice, and beetroot.[87] The United States and the international community strongly condemned South Africa's assertions, which helped pressure the government to eventually change its position in 2004. But by then the crisis had intensified. As a direct result of the South African government's negligence, an estimated 330,000 people died.[88] Initially, international actors had to circumvent the government to address the threat: "We did an enormous amount of good in the early days in South Africa," said Randall L. Tobias, the first U.S. global AIDS coordinator, "not because of the Health Ministry, but in spite of the Health Ministry."[89]

AIDS currently affects 33 million people around the world.[90] The disease, said Secretary of State Colin Powell in 2003, "is more devastating that any terrorist attack, any conflict or any weapon of mass destruction. . . . AIDS shatters families, tears the fabric of societies, and undermines governments. AIDS can destroy countries and destabilize entire regions."[91] In addition, AIDS can wipe out large swaths of the workforce and help put the cycle of productivity into decline. To deal effectively with the AIDS crisis, countries must have the capacity and the will to fight it.

Given the magnitude of the AIDS crisis, the economic and security concerns, and worries about the spread of disease to countries around the world, the biggest challenge is what to do when states, especially weak states, ignore the disease within their borders. The international response has been to circumvent weak governments to fight the disease. The Global Fund to Fight AIDS, Tuberculosis, and Malaria, the United Nations Joint Program on HIV/AIDS (UNAIDS), and the U.S. President's Emergency Plan for AIDS Relief (PEPFAR) are three major efforts that have pooled tremendous funding to fight this disease. The United States alone has invested billions of dollars in PEPFAR, the largest health initiative in history to fight a single disease. Perhaps no other international effort on global health provides a better platform for evaluating the costs and benefits of circumventing governments and decentralizing operations when states are weak or lack the political will to fight a disease.

Interim Data: A Mixed Picture

Overall, the experience with HIV reveals that when national governments are uncooperative, working around them by decentralizing operations and engaging local communities can be effective in the short term. But without broader health capacity, the effort will ultimately be unsustainable in weak states.

The range of studies that evaluate the effects of HIV/AIDS-related programs is limited. Two studies, one by the Institute of Medicine and another by scientists at Stanford University, offer a first look at the success of PEPFAR, the largest of these programs. The Institute of Medicine, established under the National Academy of Sciences to provide policymakers with nonbiased advice on health, was mandated under the act that established PEPFAR to evaluate the program after three years.[92] The study by Stanford scientists, published in 2009 in the *Annals of Internal Medicine*, was the first of its kind to isolate the effects of PEPFAR's programs in focus countries on HIV-related deaths and HIV prevalence in sub-Saharan Africa.[93] Beyond these two landmark studies, NGOs, health workers, and researchers working on the ground in countries fighting HIV offer varied insights on the success of decentralized HIV programs.

These studies show several advantages to using outside groups to work around governments. Most important, it can save lives. In the only quantitative evaluation of PEPFAR's programs, researchers found that death rates from AIDS declined by more than 10 percent in focus countries, averting more than 1 million deaths.[94] PEPFAR proved that health services can be effective and rapidly scaled up in poor countries and difficult environments.[95] Second, donors contracting work to NGOs and the private sector can bring greater efficiency and accountability to delivering services in corrupt countries.[96] Third, actors perceived as neutral parties, often humanitarian NGOs and the United Nations, bring legitimacy and independence and can act in countries wary of other outside actors.[97] They can gain access to neglected populations, show ministers evidence of success, work in partnership with local groups and ministers, and help pressure national governments to make health a priority.[98]

Outside groups carry some disadvantages as well. Most significant, working around governments by establishing parallel structures can erode state capacity to deliver health services and cause national health systems to crumble. Well-funded NGOs can lure government health workers to their specialized programs with high salaries, further depleting the government of human resources to deal with other health issues.[99] In addition, many of these outside efforts are channeled through vertical, disease-specific programs funded over the short term, with success defined by meeting quantitative goals. But progress toward general capacity building is not easily quantified and is tied to indicators of capacity rather than the number of people treated, numbers of condoms distributed, or other similar categories. When these groups fail to coordinate their efforts, they encourage "multiple, semi-autonomous, overlapping projects clustered in some regions of the country." And when the work is completed, "personnel and equipment are often dispersed, creating no lasting impact on infrastructural development."[100] To avoid these problems, donors must harmonize their activities and balance the short-term need to act urgently in crisis settings with the long-term need to build health system capacity.[101]

Key Lessons of Circumventing Weak States

The experiences of the international community in bypassing governments to prevent, monitor, and treat HIV/AIDS present several key lessons:

Threat assessments are a high priority because they help outside groups determine the proper response and allocation of resources. In states experiencing emergency outbreaks on a large scale, immediate intervention is urgent, and groups must often bypass the government. Where the threat is less dire, outside groups have more time to work to build sustainable health systems.[102]

More funding from programs that target single diseases should be used to build state capacity. Health services can be delivered via two basic models: horizontal delivery and vertical delivery. Horizontal delivery programs are usually channeled through public health systems and focus on comprehensive basic care, whereas vertical programs target single diseases, such as HIV/AIDS, and can be delivered outside the public health system.[103] Since vertical, disease-specific programs attract more attention and funding than horizontal programs, it would be imprudent to shut them down.[104] Practitioners should still trumpet the horizontal approach, but they should also work to tie funds from the popular vertical programs to capacity building. The U.S. Congress is beginning to learn this lesson. When it reauthorized PEPFAR in 2008 and tripled its budget to $48 billion through 2013, it allocated more funding to building health systems in the focus countries.

Reliable, empirical data are crucial to determining which models are most effective. To understand which programs work and which do not, one must rigorously evaluate models for intervention. This is especially important when billions of dollars are being expended on a program, as in the case of PEPFAR. Hard data, published in peer-review publications, will help determine which programs to scale up and introduce to other countries and which to discard. Accurate data will also be essential to map crisis areas and recognize patterns of risk.[105] A credible system for evaluating programs can promote cost-effective solutions, build donor confidence, and prove the benefits of intervention to difficult governments.[106]

Policy must balance the challenge of treating patients immediately with the need to prevent future infections to fight the HIV/AIDS crisis over the long term. In the first authorization of PEPFAR, 55 percent of the funding was allocated for treatment and 20 percent for prevention.[107] Because antiretroviral treatments have averted deaths from HIV/AIDS and prolonged life, funding under the PEPFAR reauthorization—which totals $48 billion over five years—will be insufficient for treatment unless the incidence of HIV in Africa is significantly lowered.[108] Furthermore, prevention efforts are shown to bring substantial payoffs: one model that evaluated the cost-effectiveness of highly active antiretroviral therapy and prevention found a payoff of twenty-eight life-years for every life-year gained on the HIV/AIDS treatment.[109] In local communities, media campaigns and education in schools, in peer-counseling programs, and in the workplace can help promote safe practices.[110] But prevention alone is insufficient. Over the long term, it is vital to strike "the right balance between treatment and prevention with insufficient resources for the burden of the epidemic is a major challenge for comprehensive care programs, such as PEPFAR."[111]

International efforts should build indigenous support from local leaders and community members. When national governments are unco-operative, decentralized operations, working directly with local governments and communities, can bring live-saving treatments and help build pressure on national policies from the bottom up. To improve health services locally, practitioners must also have on-the-ground knowledge of communities and be able to identify local power players. In South Africa's KwaZulu-Natal Province, for example, where the HIV prevalence rate is an alarming 39.1 percent, the AIDS Healthcare Foundation supplied counseling, testing, lab monitoring, treatment, and care to community members through a clinic operated out of a local shopping center. Located in a popular setting, the clinic generated a high demand for treatment. Also critical to the program's success was the support of the Inkatha Freedom Party, a national minority opposition party that was in power locally. For the party, it was an opportunity to criticize President Mbeki.[112] The success of the program and support of the opposition put added pressure on the national government to change its policies. Such interventions will have little effect without a thorough understanding of the local culture, players, and power dynamics.

Disease control efforts should find ways to expand the health care workforce without depleting the state's essential human resources. Poor and weak states have major shortages in health workers trained to deal with HIV/AIDS. This reality is made harsher by the "brain drain" of health professionals from rural areas to cities and to more developed countries. In many of the PEPFAR focus countries, the supply of available workers is unable to meet patient demands as clinics overflow their capacity, patients wait to receive treatments, staffs are small and overburdened, and care does not extend to remote regions.[113] Funding from HIV/AIDS efforts should give workers incentives to operate in remote regions—such as performance bonuses, free lodging, and educational stipends for their children. More health workers must be trained and dispatched to fight HIV/AIDS, but international organizations and NGOs must be careful not to sap national systems of health workers assisting with other critical health programs. In the long term, funding should help train health workers in general practices as well as in AIDS-specific tasks. [114] But this training can take years. In the short term, task shifting of health responsibilities from highly specialized workers to less specialized workers is one approach that can make the most impact in resource-constrained environments.[115]

Donors should leverage core competencies of the private sector to scale up health programs and build sustainable health systems. The private sector already has economic incentives to halt the AIDS crisis, since the disease reduces consumption, lowers worker productivity, saps the labor pool of qualified and trained workers, and breeds insecurity risky for investment. By matching funds and in-kind contributions, PEPFAR has encouraged private sector donations to HIV/AIDS initiatives.[116] But the private sector can do more than serve as an ATM machine for AIDS programs. To achieve a lasting impact, donors should harness industry's unique skills and expertise in scaling up efforts, promoting efficiency in service delivery and supply chains, building capacity, and linking up with indigenous businesses. Recent public-private partnerships have succeeded in introducing creative solutions in poor countries. A PEPFAR partnership with Becton, Dickinson and Company sends staff to train laboratory technicians in focus countries, helping to increase laboratory capacity there by an estimated 15 to 20 percent.[117] Phones-for-Health, a $10 million public-private partnership with cell phone and technology companies, uses existing software technology and cell phone infrastructure to build national health information networks. The program allows health workers in even remote regions to immediately report outbreaks to health authorities and to refer patients to nearby clinics. This program works in the developing world, where Internet connections may be scarce but cell phones are used by 60 percent of the population—a figure expected to increase to 85 percent by 2010.[118] These partnerships are beneficial for communities and businesses alike and can help promote growth and sustainable health.

Outside groups play an essential role in responding to health emergencies in difficult environments, but policymakers should be reminded that outside groups can have long-term consequences for state capacity and sustainability. Preventing, surveying, and controlling HIV/AIDS depends on a strategic and sustainable response, which can only be achieved if the international community, donors, NGOs, local communities, and the private sector harmonize their efforts and focus on building state capacity over the long term.

BREAKING THE CYCLE: TACKLING HEALTH IN POOR AND WEAK STATES

No country will be safe from dangerous pathogens and pandemics until all countries have at least minimal health systems in place to prevent, survey, and control infectious diseases. Disease prevention is the first important step. Interventions must target malnutrition, lack of access to essential medicines, and basic sanitation—all factors that exacerbate poverty and make people sick. But prevention will not stop all diseases from emerging. When dangerous pathogens arise, it is essential to detect them early. Then, all states need to be able to rapidly contain them. These responses can only be sustained if state health systems are stronger and health services reach a majority of the population.[119] If the United States fails to help developing countries fight diseases that burden them in the present, it will be all the more difficult to gain their cooperation on diseases that threaten everyone in the future.

The central message of this is chapter is that communities, NGOs, businesses, governments, and the international community can strengthen U.S. national security by bolstering the capacity of poor and weak states to tackle infectious disease threats. The following recommendations illustrate ways this can be done.

Support Antipoverty Efforts That Improve Health

To combat the transnational threat of infectious diseases emerging from developing countries, solutions must address the conditions that launch families into a negative cycle of disease and poverty. This means improving living conditions through better water and sanitation, infrastructure projects, and nutrition programs—a great challenge if countries are unable to contribute to such efforts. What, then, can be done to this end?

Reduce the Costs of Health Services through Conditional Cash Transfer and Cash-for-Work Programs. The poor are less likely to pay for preventive health services like vaccines if the costs are prohibitively high. Donors should encourage national governments to provide preventive health care for poor families. Two methods have proved successful in low-capacity environments: conditional cash transfers and cash-for-work program.

1. *Conditional cash transfer programs tied to health goals.* These programs provide funds to poor families in exchange for certain behavior, such as attending school, obtaining nutritious food, and accepting basic immunizations. Conditional programs have improved health and the demand for health institutions in Latin America and Turkey by giving poor families incentives to use health resources that they would otherwise find too expensive. Such programs are said to have three major benefits: (1) they are cost-effective and flexible; (2) they help cultivate responsible relationships between governments and their citizens by enabling families to use national and local health institutions; and (3) they promote reinforcing benefits in health and education, for example, by providing immunizations in schools.[120]

2. *Cash-for-work programs that build infrastructure and health institutions.* In this case, poor workers receive essential income and at the same time are employed in projects that build community infrastructure. Such infrastructure could include health-related entities such as hospitals and clinics, roads that connect villages to health clinics, and water-sanitation systems that improve health and help reduce disease. Without investments in basic health infrastructure, poor families will be less able to halt the onslaught of disease and more likely to die from diseases that are preventable and treatable. The World Bank has found that states with low resources and political will are only able to build sustainable health institutions when the communities that stand to benefit pool their own resources to pay for its operation and maintenance.[121] Cash-for-work programs provide not only this local ownership but also the infrastructure critical to delivering health services and conducting disease surveillance in neglected regions.

Partner with Local Media and Schools to Educate Populations about the Importance of Health and Sanitation. Even countries with a solid health infrastructure can have trouble persuading populations to use it. In some cases, this means reversing centuries-old practices of sanitation or undoing harmful misinformation and conspiracies about immunizations. Particular attention should go to ensuring that mass media, teacher and peer training, and health education programs bring positive change to health behavior.[122] To be successful, these programs would have to reach marginalized and at-risk groups, including populations that do not go to school—or those, like pregnant young girls, that are barred from attending.[123]

Build a Health Care Workforce

In recent years, more than 4 million health workers have migrated to countries with higher-paying jobs and increasing demand because of the HIV/AIDS crisis.[124] Without these workers, children will not be vaccinated, emerging diseases will not be detected, and dangerous outbreaks will not be rapidly controlled at their source. The following recommendations seek to build a robust workforce that can reach neglected populations and detect outbreaks in remote settings, even in resource-poor countries with difficult governments.

Use "Task Shifting" to Fill Health Worker Deficits. Task shifting distributes the lighter responsibilities of skilled health care providers such as doctors and nurses to less skilled community health workers who can handle simple treatments and disease surveillance. Workers can be recruited from rural areas and assigned to their own communities, extending care to neglected regions. Task shifting is not a suitable replacement for a professional health workforce, and the workers still require basic training and continuing education to deliver health services properly.[125] It has, however, been used successfully for a wide range of health issues in resource-poor settings like Malawi, Tanzania, and Zambia, particularly in dealing with the HIV/AIDS crisis, for example, by increasing access to HIV treatment and expanding the reach of AIDS testing.[126] Task shifting taps into a pool of workers who can be trained quickly and cheaply to deliver essential services and conduct disease surveillance in remote regions while more skilled health workers are being recruited and trained.

Encourage Health Workers to Remain in Developing Countries and to Operate in Neglected Regions. Donors should help pay for competitive salaries and improve management, training, and morale.[127] Managers could draw up formal contracts that pay workers on the basis of performance and that mandate service to neglected groups in remote regions in exchange for perks such as specialized training or licensing.[128] Benefits could also extend to the worker's family, by providing housing and education. When offering these incentives through NGOs, donors must be careful not to outcompete governments and drain them of health professionals, who are sometimes lured away by nongovernmental groups with high budgets to target vertical diseases. Governments must be able to compete for professional talent, or they will find it difficult to build sustainable health systems.

Build and Link Professional Networks of Personnel Well Trained in Data Collection and Analysis and Regularly Evaluate Their Performance. For surveillance to operate effectively, laboratory workers must be trained to collect, analyze, and pass on surveillance data quickly and accurately. The international community could improve the quality of worker performance by establishing professional networks that regularly train and assess the capability of workers. Training programs should be expanded and funded. The CDC's Epidemiological Intelligence Service, which provides critical on-the-job training in epidemiology and whose graduates made important contributions to Ebola and Rift Valley fever outbreaks, is a successful model.[129] Laboratory performance should be evaluated regularly. Existing programs do so by distributing samples to national laboratories for analysis and scoring the quality of the assessment. But these programs do not reach many critical countries and the WHO does not fully fund them.[130] The international community could strengthen global surveillance by linking up laboratories staffed by a professional cadre of workers that mutually reinforce surveillance efforts.

Support Vertical Disease Programs and Horizontal Capacity Building

Threat assessments, public opinion, and political organization around specific diseases encourage American policymakers to focus on those diseases. Vertical programs may mitigate the threat of individual diseases, but cannot provide long-term solutions that build health systems capable of containing all potential disease threats. At times they lure funding and critical professionals away from the public health system. Yet vertical programs targeting spcific diseases garner much public attention, bipartisan congressional support, and huge levels of funding. A concerted effort on behalf of HIV/AIDS motivated Congress to devote the largest sum of money ever to fighting the disease, and the successful results compelled it to authorize another $45 billion in funding. Moreover, vertical disease programs may be desirable when state health systems are weak and disease outbreaks require a rapid response.[131] The challenge arises with diseases for which eradication is not on the horizon, and it then falls to donors to continue to support recurrent program costs that are consumed in current expenditures but never build an underlying health care capacity.

Congress and NGOs Should Continue to Support Vertical Programs, with Provisions for Building Sustainable Health Institutions. Practitioners must persuade Congress that vertical programs are unsustainable and U.S. security is at peril unless effort is put into building general health capacity. Yet they must also be clear about the long-term challenges of building capacity in weak states and recognize that results may not be immediately apparent. In the current congressional climate, vertical disease programs are popular and well funded. Admittedly, they have advantages in difficult environments. Rather than eschew vertical programs altogether, policymakers should see that they include provisions for basic health and surveillance capacity. Congressional bills should ensure that money is not allocated in a way that erodes broader health capacity.

Engage in a Multilateral Dialogue with the International Community to Address Global Health Threats. In the absence of major disease outbreaks, the international community is less willing to focus attention and funding on global health efforts. However, the international community must be prepared in advance for such events. Specifically, the United States and its multilateral partners must engage in vigorous diplomacy at a high level to gain agreement on issues of virus sharing that permits the exchange of genetic materials while addressing the legitimate commercial concerns of developing nations. One question for further exploration is to what extent globally managed and funded programs can effectively complement state and local operations. These programs could help mitigate the threat of global infectious disease and circumvent countries like Indonesia that refuse to share virus samples, while still providing enough vaccines and equitable resources to all populations.

Work through Non-State Actors and the Private Sector

When weak states are unable or unwilling to deliver on health, non-state actors may work around governments and decentralize operations. This approach has had mixed success. As experience with HIV/AIDS shows, circumventing governments can save lives in emergency situations. In the most challenging environments, NGOs may be the only ones welcomed from the outside to help improve health on the ground. Over the long term, however, this approach may be unsustainable and may further weaken a state's health capacity. By and large, the potential for the private sector to develop innovative products and collaborate with the public sector to bring sustainable solutions has been untapped.

NGOs Should Partner with Host Governments to Build Sustainable Health Policies and Programs. NGOs should circumvent governments only in the most intractable environments or during health emergencies. They must do so with a nuanced understanding of local conditions. When national governments fail to create policy that supports the building of a viable health care system, it is often possible to partner with subnational governments to achieve progress locally. Service delivery at the local level can help build pressure for national reform, especially when groups generate publicity by partnering with the media and opposition leaders.[132] Such pressure must be directed at the power players inside and outside government and must link them together for common cause.

Support Public-Private Partnerships Having the Comparative Advantages of the Private Sector. Since infectious diseases can knock out a large part of their workforce in developing countries, businesses have an incentive to address health crises in those countries, whether they operate or hope to expand there. Their innovative ideas, technology, and sound management practices could be a boon to health reform, yet too often the private sector is merely viewed as a source of funding. Of course, private sector support through matching funding has worked successfully with PEPFAR. But as the HIV/AIDS case illustrates, the sector can be tapped for more than money. Phone companies can use already existing software to track disease outbreaks and immediately connect an infected patient to a local clinic. Companies can lure talent by offering opportunities to serve in health programs abroad in critical countries. Donors should rally businesses not only to raise donations but also to draw on the sector's strategic talents.

CONCLUSION

Alleviating the threat of infectious disease is a national security priority for the United States. Poor and weak countries cannot be ignored. Since globalization means that a threat anywhere can be a threat everywhere, Americans cannot afford to remain idle while governments in the developing world fail to provide adequate health services to the world's poorest and sickest people for a lack of will, capacity, or both. Rather, the United States can and should help build an effective global public health system that enables all countries to prevent, survey, and control infectious diseases within their borders. Ultimately such efforts advance not only humanitarian imperatives, but also U.S. national security interests.

NOTES

1. Thomas H. Maugh II, "AIDS Virus May Date Back to WWII, Study Says," *Los Angeles Times,* February 4, 1998, p. 1.

2. World Bank, "World Developing Indicators," WDI Statistics for 1960 (earliest year available).

3. There is no consensus on population loss in the Congo during this period. A loss of 10 million has been estimated by Adam Hochschild, *King Leopold's Ghost* (New York: Houghton Mifflin, 1999). See also Susan Spano, "Belgium Confronts Its Colonial Past," *Los Angeles Times,* March 13, 2005.

4. Centers for Disease Control and Prevention, "HIV/AIDS Surveillance Report: Cases of HIV Infection and AIDS in the United States and Dependent Areas" (2007) (www.cdc.gov/hiv/topics/surveillance/resources/reports/2007report/pdf/2007SurveillanceReport.pdf), p. 20.

5. National Intelligence Council, "The Global Infectious Disease Threat and Its Implications for the United States," National Intelligence Estimate, NIE 99-17D (January 2000), p. 53.

6. Robert W. Pinner, Steven M. Teutsch, Lone Simonsen, and others, "Trends in Infectious Diseases Mortality in the United States," *Journal of the American Medical Association* 275, no. 3 (1996): 189–93; Gregory L. Armstrong, Laura A. Conn, and Robert W. Pinner, "Trends in Infectious Disease Mortality in the United States during the 20th Century," *Journal of the American Medical Association* 281, no. 1 (1999): 61–66.

7. This is in part due to changes in human behavior, disease mutation and adaptation, and advances in technology that detects diseases and the pathogens causing them. National Intelligence Council, "The Global Infectious Disease Threat," pp. 5, 20.

8. World Health Organization (WHO), "A Safer Future: Global Public Health Security in the 21st Century," *World Health Report 2007* (Geneva, 2007), p. x.

9 . In August 2003, for example, 225 U.S. Marines entered Liberia to provide security to the U.S. embassy and support the peacekeeping force in Monrovia. Marines were on the ground for twelve days and suffered no casualties from hostile fire; nonetheless, fifty-three—nearly one-quarter of those deployed—contracted malaria. The high rates of infection have been attributed to the fact that soldiers did not follow proper protocols for taking malaria prophylaxis. Donald McNeil Jr., "Officials Say Malarial Marines Didn't Take Medication Properly,"

New York Times, December 5, 2003, p. A30; Amir Attaran, "Malaria, the Terrorists' Friend," *New York Times,* September 25, 2003.

10. WHO, "Avian Influenza: Assessing the Pandemic Threat" (January 2005), p. 30.

11. Thomas Abraham, *Twenty-First Century Plague* (Johns Hopkins University Press, 2004), p. 3.

12. WHO, "A Safer Future"; Lisa Mastny, *Vital Signs 2005* (New York: W. W. Norton, 2005), p. 60.

13. World Tourism Organization, "Tourism Highlights: 2008" (United Nations, 2008), p. 1.

14. See, for example, Bureau of Transportation Statistics, "Freight Data and Statistics," Research and Innovative Technology Administration (n.d.) (www.bts.gov/programs/freight_transportation/ [December 3, 2008]).

15. WHO, "Avian Influenza," p. 23.

16. BBC, "Timeline: SARS Virus," BBC News, July 7, 2004; Abraham, *Twenty-First Century Plague,* p. 2.

17. Joshua M. Epstein and others, "Controlling Pandemic Flu: The Value of International Air Travel Restrictions" (Brookings Center on Social and Economic Dynamics, December 2006) (www.brookings.edu/reports/2006/12healthcare_epstein.aspx), p. 17.

18. Kate E. Jones, Nikkita G. Patel, Marc A. Levy, and others, "Global Trends in Emerging Infectious Diseases," *Nature* 451 (February 2008): 993.

19. Ibid., p. 992; Alexandra Beatty and others, *Achieving Sustainable Global Capacity for Surveillance and Response to Emerging Diseases of Zoonotic Origin* (Washington: National Academies Press, 2008), pp. 992–93.

20. Jones and others, "Global Trends in Emerging Infectious Diseases," p. 992.

21. Ibid., p. 990.

22. Hazem Adam Ghobarah, Paul Huth, and Bruce Russett, "Civil Wars Kill and Maim People—Long after the Shooting Stops," *American Political Science Review* 97 (May 2003): 189–202.

23. Intergovernmental Panel on Climate Change (IPCC), *Climate Change 2007: Working Group II Contribution to the Fourth Assessment Report of the Intergovernmental Panel on Climate Change* (Cambridge University Press, 2008), p. 393.

24. Ibid., pp. 393, 407, 412, 418.

25. This subset consists of lower respiratory infections such as pneumonia and influenza, HIV/AIDS, diarrheal diseases, tuberculosis, malaria, and measles. These diseases are responsible for nearly 90 percent of infectious disease–related deaths worldwide. WHO, "Removing Obstacles to Healthy Development" (1999) (www.who.int/infectious-disease-report/pages/textonly.html); Global

Health Council, "Infectious Diseases: Global Disparity" (Washington, 2000–08) (www.globalhealth.org/view_top.php3?id=228).

26. UNICEF/WHO, "Pneumonia: The Forgotten Killer of Children" (2006) (www.childinfo.org/files/Pneumonia_The_Forgotten_Killer_of_Children.pdf), p. 11.

27. Andrea Gerlin, "A Simple Solution," *Time,* October 16, 2006.

28. WHO, "Spending on Health: A Global Overview," Fact Sheet 319 (February 2007) (www.who.int/mediacentre/factsheets/fs319.pdf). Other estimates of the minimum per capita spending necessary for basic health interventions can be found in Jeffrey D. Sachs and others, "Macroeconomics and Health: Investing in Health for Economic Development," Report of the Commission on Macroeconomics and Health (Geneva: WHO, 2001), pp. 54–55.

29. Low-income countries have five physicians per 10,000 people compared with twenty-eight per 10,000 in high-income countries. There are ten hospital beds per 10,000 people in low-income countries compared with fifty-nine per 10,000 in high-income countries. WHO, "World Health Statistics 2008," pp. 82–83.

30. WHO, "Counterfeit Medicines," Fact Sheet 275, rev. (November 14, 2006) (www.who.int/mediacentre/factsheets/fs275/en/index.html).

31. Cost-benefit ratio calculated using a discount rate of 3 percent. Scott Barrett, "Eradication versus Control: The Economics of Global Infectious Disease Policies," *Bulletin of the World Health Organization* 82, no. 9 (2004): 684.

32. Jaime Sepulveda, Charles Carpenter, James Curran, and others, eds., *PEPFAR Implementation: Progress and Promise* (Washington: Institute of Medicine, 2007), p. 134.

33. WHO, "Global Consultation on Strengthening National Capacities for Surveillance and Control of Communicable Diseases," WHO/CDS/CSR/LYO/ 2005.18 (November 22–24, 2003); Stanley M. Lemon, *Global Infectious Disease Surveillance and Detection: Assessing the Challenges—Finding Solutions: Workshop Summary* (Washington: National Academies Press, 2007), p. 1.

34. For greater detail on the evolution of public health security, see WHO, "A Safer Future," pp. xiv–xv.

35. The six diseases were cholera, plague, yellow fever, smallpox, relapsing fever, and typhus. WHO, "International Health Regulations 1969," 3rd ann. ed. (1983).

36. WHO, "International Health Regulations," 2nd ed. (2005), p. 1.

37. Ibid., annex 1, pp. 40–41.

38. IHR, art. 3, requires the WHO to assist countries in meeting surveillance requirements, yet provides no funding for this. Michael G. Baker and David P. Fidler, "Global Public Health Surveillance under New International Health Regulations," *Emerging Infectious Diseases* 12 (July 2006): 1060.

39. Sachs and others, "Macroeconomics and Health," p. 73.

40. Alan Sipress, "Battling a Virus and Disbelief," *Washington Post,* August 30, 2006, p. A12.

41. WHO, "Avian Influenza—Situation in Indonesia—Update 12" (May 18, 2006) (www.who.int/csr/don/2006_05_18b/en/index.html).

42. Warwick McKibbin and Alexandra Sidorenko, "Global Macroeconomic Consequences of Pandemic Influenza" (Sydney, Australia: Lowy Institute for International Policy, February 2006); Michael T. Osterholm, "Preparing for the Next Pandemic," *Foreign Affairs,* July/August 2005, cited in Andrew Burns, Dominique van der Mensbrugghe, and Hans Timmer, "Evaluating the Economic Consequences of Avian Influenza," Site Resources Report (Washington: World Bank, September 2008; updated from June 2006) (http://siteresources. worldbank.org/EXTAVIANFLU/Resources/EvaluatingAHIeconomics_2008. pdf), p. 1.

43. Hitoshi Oshitani, Taro Kamigaki, and Akira Suzuki, "Major Issues and Challenges of Influenza Pandemic Preparedness in Developing Countries," *Emerging Infectious Diseases* 14 (June 2008): 877.

44. Ibid.

45. Ibid.

46. Last available figure from 1999. United Nations, "Population below National Poverty Line, Rural, Percentage," UN data, updated (December 17, 2008) (http://data.un.org).

47. Indonesia National Committee for Avian Influenza Control and Pandemic Influenza Preparedness, "Indonesia: Culling Compensation Policy and Practice" (Jakarta: Komnas FBPI, February 13, 2007) (http://siteresources.worldbank.org/ INTTOPAVIFLU/Resources/GDLNCompensationIndonesia.pdf); Seth Mydans, "Indonesian Chickens, and People, Hard Hit by Bird Flu," *New York Times,* February 1, 2008.

48. Ian Patrick and Tristan Jubb, "A Scoping Study Investigating Opportunities for Improving Biosecurity on Commercial Poultry Farms in Indonesia: Final Report" (Australian Centre for International Agricultural Research, April 2008), p. 4.

49. Indonesia National Committee, "Indonesia: Culling Compensation Policy and Practice; Karima Anjani, "Bird-Flu Festers in Indonesia as Deficit Hinders Disease Fight," Bloomberg News, October 4, 2006; Mydans, "Indonesian Chickens, and People, Hard Hit by Bird Flu."

50. World Bank, "Decentralization in Indonesia" (n.d.) (http://go.worldbank. org/P65PRQ0VV0 [January 30, 2009]).

51. Siwi Padmawati and Mark Nichter, "Community Response to Avian Flu in Central Java, Indonesia," *Anthropology and Medicine* 15 (April 2008): 44.

52. Steve Bjorge, WHO epidemiologist, in Jakarta in 2006, quoted in ibid., p. 44.

53. WHO, "WHO Country Cooperation Strategy 2007–2011: Indonesia" (Country Office for Indonesia, 2008), pp. 4–11 (www.ino.searo.who.int/LinkFiles/WHO_in_Indonesia_country_cooperation_strategy.pdf).

54. Transparency International, "2008 Corruption Perceptions Index" (Berlin, 2008) (www.transparency.org/news_room/in_focus/2008/cpi2008/cpi_2008_table).

55. Lisa Schnirring, "Indonesia Claims Wide Support for Virus-Sharing Stance" (University of Minnesota Center for Infectious Disease Research and Policy, May 27, 2008) (www.cidrap.umn.edu/cidrap/content/influenza/panflu/news/may2708sharing.html).

56. Thai delegate Suwit Wibulpolprasert, quoted in "Poor Countries Hold Out for Bird Vaccine," *New Scientist,* no. 2591, updated (February 16, 2007) (www.newscientist.com/article/mg19325914.600-poor-countries-hold-out-for-bird-vaccine.html).

57. WHO, "Production and Availability of Pandemic Influenza A (H1N1) Vaccines," WHO Global Alert and Response, updated (July 12, 2009) (www.who.int/csr/disease/swineflu/frequently_asked_questions/vaccine_preparedness/production_availability/en/index.html).

58. WHO, "Global Pandemic Influenza Action Plan to Increase Vaccine Supply" (2006) (www.who.int/vaccines-documents/), p. 4.

59. Ibid.

60. Burns and others, "Evaluating the Economic Consequences of Avian Influenza," p. 1.

61. Rebecca F. Grais, J. Hugh Ellis, and Gregory E. Glass, "Assessing the Impact of Airline Travel on the Geographic Spread of Pandemic Influenza," *European Journal of Epidemiology* 18 (November 2003): 1070.

62. Ambassador John E. Lange, U.S. Special Representative on Avian and Pandemic Influenza, remarks at "Threat of an Avian Influenza Pandemic: A Briefing on the Recent Sharm el-Sheikh Conference," Center for Strategic and International Studies, Washington, November 13, 2008.

63. Colin Russell, Terry Jones, and others, "The Global Circulation of Seasonal Influenza A (H3N2) Viruses," *Science* 320 (April 18, 2008): 340; Centers for Disease Control and Prevention, "Questions and Answers Regarding Estimating Deaths from Influenza in the United States," last modified March 12, 2009 (www.cdc.gov/flu/about/disease/us_flu-related_deaths.htm).

64. WHO, "Avian Influenza: Assessing the Pandemic Threat," p. 23.

65. Ibid.

66. John M. Barry, *The Great Influenza: The Epic Story of the Deadliest Plague in History* (New York: Viking, 2004), p. 452.

67. WHO, "Assessing the Severity of an Influenza Pandemic" (May 11, 2009) (www.who.int/csr/disease/swineflu/assess/disease_swineflu_assess_20090511/en/index.html); WHO, "What Is the New Influenza A(H1N1)?" updated (June 11,

2009) (www.who.int/csr/disease/swineflu/frequently_asked_questions/about_ disease/en/index.html).

68. McKibbin and Sidorenko, "Global Macroeconomic Consequences of Pandemic Influenza."

69. Burns and others, "Evaluating the Economic Consequences of Avian Influenza," p. 2.

70. Ibid.

71. Ibid., pp. 2–3.

72. Ibid., p. 3. For an interesting study of the advantages and disadvantages of restrictions on international air travel, see Epstein and others, "Controlling Pandemic Flu."

73. WHO, "Avian Influenza: Frequently Asked Questions," rev. (December 5, 2005) (www.who.int/csr/disease/avian_influenza/avian_faqs/en/).

74. McKibbin and Sidorenko, "Global Macroeconomic Consequences of Pandemic Influenza."

75. Ibid., p. 27.

76. David Nabarro, Senior UN System Coordinator for Avian and Human Influenza, remarks at "Threat of an Avian Influenza Pandemic: A Briefing on the Recent Sharm el-Sheikh Conference," Center for Strategic and International Studies, Washington, November 13, 2008.

77. Kevin Sack, "Local Health Agencies, Hurt by Cuts, Brace for Flu Risk," *New York Times,* April 30, 2009, p. A15.

78. "Budget of the United States Government: Fiscal Year 2010," updated (U.S. Government Printing Office [GPO], May 8, 2009) (www.gpoaccess.gov/USbudget/fy10/index.html).

79. George W. Bush, "Fact Sheet: Safeguarding America against Pandemic Influenza," Office of the Press Secretary, November 1, 2005 (http://georgewbush-whitehouse.archives.gov/news/releases/2005/11/20051101.html).

80. United Nations, "Responses to Avian Influenza and State of Pandemic Readiness," Fourth Global Progress Report of UN System Influenza Coordinator and the World Bank (October 2008), p. 19.

81. Ibid., pp. 8, 13.

82. Ibid.

83. Lange, remarks at "Threat of an Avian Influenza Pandemic" Conference.

84. Nabarro, remarks at "Threat of an Avian Influenza Pandemic" Conference.

85. UN Development Group (UNDG), "Avian Influenza Prevention and Control and Human Influenza Pandemic Preparedness in Africa," Assessment of Financial Needs and Gaps, Fourth International Conference on Avian Influenza, Bali, December 6–8, 2006 (www.undg.org/archive_docs/9050-Africa__Assessment_of_Financial_Needs_and_Gaps.pdf), p. 21.

86. UNAIDS/WHO, "South Africa Epidemiological Fact Sheet on HIV and AIDS: 2008 Update," UNAIDS/WHO Working Group on Global HIV/AIDS and

STI Surveillance (September 2008) (www.who.int/globalatlas/predefinedReports/EFS2008/full/EFS2008_ZA.pdf), p. 4.

87. P. Chigwedere and others, "Estimating the Lost Benefits of Antiretroviral Drug Use in South Africa," *Journal of Acquired Immune Deficiency Syndrome* 49 (December 1, 2008): 410, 414.

88. Ibid., p. 412.

89. Quoted in Celia W. Dugger, "Study Cites Toll of AIDS Policy in South Africa," *New York Times,* November 25, 2008.

90. WHO/UNAIDS, "Global Summary of the AIDS Epidemic" (December 2007) (www.who.int/hiv/data/2008_global_summary_AIDS_ep.png).

91. Quoted in Glenn Kessler and Rob Stein, "Powell Says U.S. Leading Efforts on AIDS," *Washington Post,* September 23, 2003, p. A24.

92. Sepulveda and others, *PEPFAR Implementation.*

93. Eran Bendavid and Jayanta Bhattacharya, "The President's Emergency Plan for AIDS Relief in Africa: An Evaluation of Outcomes," *Annals of Internal Medicine* 150 (May 19, 2009): 727–28.

94. Ibid.

95. An Institute of Medicine evaluation of PEPFAR calls this "the primary early accomplishment of the U.S. Global AIDS Initiative," particularly in treating HIV/AIDS. Sepulveda and others, *PEPFAR Implementation,* p. 5.

96. See, for example, Courtney Barnett, Catherine Connor, and Pamela J. Putney, "Contracting Non-governmental Organizations to Combat HIV/AIDS," Special Initiative Report 33 (Bethesda, Md.: Partnerships for Health Reform, February 2001). Bendavid and Bhattacharya point out that PEPFAR focus countries scored significantly higher in government effectiveness at the time of PEPFAR's start than did countries in the control group. Bendavid and Bhattacharya, "The President's Emergency Plan for AIDS Relief in Africa."

97. Chris Berry and others, "Approaches to Improving the Delivery of Social Services in Difficult Environments," PRDE Working Paper 3 (U.K. Department for International Development, October 2004), p. 20.

98. Henry Chang, Vice President of Impact Initiatives, Global Business Coalition on HIV/AIDS, Tuberculosis, and Malaria, personal communication, April 9, 2009. Grants from the Global Fund to fund efforts in China "have contributed to opening up the political space for NGO participation in the [Country Coordinating Mechanism] process and for services for marginalized populations," notes J. Kaufman, "The Role of NGOs in China's AIDS Response—Update, Challenges, and Possibilities," in *Serving the People: State-Society Negotiations and Welfare Provision in China,* edited by J. Schwartz and S. Shieh (New York: Routledge, forthcoming), cited in Dongbao Yu and others, "Investment in HIV/AIDS Programs: Does It Help Strengthen Health Systems in Developing Countries?" *Globalization and Health* 4 (September 16, 2008).

99. Yu and others, "Investment in HIV/AIDS Programs."

100. Job Ailuogwemhe and Jean-Louis Sankale, "Building Effective Infrastructures for HIV/AIDS Control," in *AIDS in Nigeria*, edited by Olusoji Adeyi and others (Harvard University Press, 2006), p. 288.

101. Sepulveda and others, *PEPFAR Implementation*, p. 1. See also World Bank, "Improving Effectiveness and Outcomes for the Poor in Health, Nutrition, and Population: An Evaluation of World Bank Group Support since 1997," Independent Evaluation Group (Washington, 2009).

102. Chang, personal communication, April 9, 2009.

103. Joyce Msuya, "Horizontal and Vertical Delivery of Health Systems: What Are the Trade-Offs?" (Washington: World Bank, 2003) (www-wds.world bank.org).

104. Yu and others, "Investment in HIV/AIDS Programs."

105. Office of the U.S. Global AIDS Coordinator (OGAC), "The Power of Partnerships: Fourth Annual Report to Congress on PEPFAR" (GPO, February 2008) (www.pepfar.gov/press/fourth_annual_report/).

106. Chang, personal communication, April 9, 2009.

107. The rest of the budget allocates 15 percent to palliative care and 10 percent to orphans and vulnerable children. "United States Leadership against HIV/AIDS, Tuberculosis, and Malaria Act of 2003," H.R. 1298, sec. 402 (GPO, 2003); Sepulveda and others, *PEPFAR Implementation*, p. 134.

108. Bendavid and Bhattacharya, "The President's Emergency Plan for AIDS Relief in Africa," p. 134.

109. Hoosen M. Coovadia and Jacqui Hadingham, "HIV/AIDS: Global Trends, Global Funds and Delivery Bottlenecks," *Globalization and Health* 1 (August 1, 2005).

110. Wafaa M. El-Sadr and David Hoos, "The President's Emergency Plan for AIDS Relief—Is the Emergency Over?" *New England Journal of Medicine* 259 (August 7, 2008): 554.

111. Bendavid and Bhattacharya, "The President's Emergency Plan for AIDS Relief in Africa."

112. Chang, personal communication, April 9, 2009; AIDS Healthcare Foundation, "AHF in South Africa" (Los Angeles, Calif.: March 2009) (www.aidshealth.org/assets/pdf/country-reports/south-africa-fact-sheet.pdf).

113. Sepulveda and others, *PEPFAR Implementation*, p. 51.

114. Ibid., p. 244.

115. OGAC, "The Power of Partnerships."

116. Chang, personal communication, April 9, 2009.

117. PEPFAR, "New Public-Private Partnership to Strengthen Laboratory Systems," U.S. President's Emergency Plan for AIDS Relief, updated (January 2009) (www.pepfar.gov/documents/organization/94561.pdf).

118. PEPFAR, "Connecting to a Healthy Future," U.S. President's Emergency Plan for AIDS Relief, updated (January 2009) (www.pepfar.gov/documents/organization/80489.pdf).

119. United Nations, "Public Investments to Empower Poor People," in *A Practical Plan to Achieve the Millennium Development Goals: Country-level Processes to Achieve the Millennium Development Goals*, UN Millennium Project (2005), chap. 5 (www.unmillenniumproject.org/documents/MainReportChapter5-lowres.pdf).

120. Laura B. Rawlings and Gloria M. Rubio, "Evaluating the Impact of Conditional Cash Transfer Programs," *World Bank Research Observer* 20 (Spring 2005): 29, 33.

121. World Bank, "Water: Water Supply and Sanitation" (n.d.) (http://go.worldbank.org/GJ7BOASPG0 [May 26, 2009]).

122. Kamran Siddiqi, James Newell, and Mike Robinson, "Getting Evidence into Practice: What Works in Developing Countries?" *International Journal for Quality in Health Care* 17, no. 5 (2005): 447–53.

123. OECD/WHO, "Poverty and Health," DAC Guidelines and Reference Series (2003), pp. 57–59 (http://whqlibdoc.who.int/publications/2003/9241562366.pdf).

124. Leading Edge, "Task Shifting May Prove Key to Tackling Infectious Diseases," *Lancet* 8 (February 2008): 81.

125. WHO, "Task Shifting: Rational Redistribution of Tasks among Health Workforce Teams: Global Recommendations and Guidelines" (2008), pp. 6–8.

126. R. Zachariah, N. Ford, M. Philips, and others, "Task Shifting in HIV/AIDS: Opportunities, Challenges and Proposed Actions for sub-Saharan Africa," *Transactions of the Royal Society of Tropical Medicine and Hygiene* 103, no. 5 (2009): 533–35.

127. Berry and others, "Approaches to Improving the Delivery of Social Services in Difficult Environments," pp. 18–19.

128. Charles Hongoro and Charles Normand, "Health Workers: Building and Motivating the Workforce," in *Disease Control Priorities in Developing Countries*, 2nd ed., edited by Dean T. Jamison, Joel G. Breman, and others (Oxford University Press, April 2006), pp. 1311, 1313–17.

129. U.S. General Accounting Office (GAO), "Global Health: Challenges in Improving Infectious Disease Surveillance Systems," Report to Congressional Requesters, GAO-01-722 (GPO, August 2001), pp. 37–38.

130. Michael G. Baker and David P. Fidler, "Global Public Health Surveillance under New International Health Regulations," *Emerging Infectious Diseases* 12 (July 2006): 1060, 1064; GAO, "Global Health," p. 34.

131. Rifat A. Atun, Sara Bennett, and Antonio Duran, "When Do Vertical (Stand-Alone) Programmes Have a Place in Health Systems?" (WHO, 2008) (www.euro.who.int/document/hsm/5_hsc08_epb_8.pdf), p. 4.

132. Berry and others, "Approaches to Improving the Delivery of Social Services in Difficult Environments," p. 11.

CHAPTER SEVEN

Conclusion and Policy Implications

CARLOS PASCUAL and CORINNE GRAFF

Fragile states are the toughest development challenge of our era.

—*Robert Zoellick,* September 12, 2008

This volume grapples with a broad spectrum of global challenges, ranging from civil conflicts and violent extremism to vulnerability to climate change and the spread of infectious diseases. Yet all the chapters converge on one point: poor states are often weak in critical areas of government responsibility, posing a risk not just to their own people, but also to regional and potentially American and global security. Poverty heightens the risk of civil war. Civil wars in turn have spillover effects, including serving as a conduit for transnational criminal enterprises, violent extremist ideologies, and deadly illnesses. Even when they are not in conflict, weak states may be vulnerable to violent extremist groups and may lack the capacity to implement effective, long-term counterterrorism strategies, or to prepare for or respond to the impacts of global climate change. Likewise, low income is in its own right an important factor in the prevalence of disease.

The linkages among poverty, weak states, and transnational threats are not just theoretical nightmares but real human tragedies. In the Democratic Republic of the Congo (DRC), these deadly and reinforcing ties have caused an estimated 5 million deaths and have kept a potentially rich nation simmering in conflict, even after the antagonists have made peace. In Sierra Leone, corruption, conflict, and the collapse of the state have allegedly been linked to financing for al Qaeda and possibly

Hezbollah. Whether environmental stress caused war in Darfur may be open to question, but there is little doubt that land and water issues, exacerbated by the stress of climate change, must be a central concern in any sustainable solution to that crisis. In Haiti, poverty is also linked to deforestation, but how can so weak a state invest in fixing this environmental disaster? Disease outbreaks compound all these problems. And, of course, the impact of terrorism in Yemen upon U.S. national security could hardly have been more direct than the attack on the U.S.S. *Cole*.

The examples of transnational threats to American security discussed in this volume—disease, conflict, terrorism, environmental tragedy—are a reminder of the perils of ignoring the links between them and with poverty and state weakness. Weak and failed states mired in poverty have ineffective government institutions, ultimately making the countries more vulnerable to global threats. When such states lack the capacity or willingness to provide for their citizens and maintain security over their territory, they pose a threat to the welfare and security of people across the planet, including those in the United States. The global financial crisis adds new urgency to the challenge of states that are both weak and poor, since the poorest countries are also the most vulnerable to the impact of the downturn.

The overarching policy recommendation emerging from this book is the need to alleviate poverty and build capacity in weak states in order to break the vicious cycle of poverty, state weakness, and transnational threats. Strategies designed to prevent or respond to specific global threats in poor countries have been discussed elsewhere and in other chapters of this book.[1] This chapter focuses on strategies to help break the relationship between poverty and state weakness. There is no simple way to unravel this relationship. But it is clear that tackling these threats without addressing poverty and weakness is unlikely to produce sustainable results. Furthermore, different types of states—whether their problems are associated with corruption, conflict, authoritarianism, ethnic intolerance, or exploitable natural resources—will require different solutions. In the following pages we offer a set of tools that can help achieve better results in diverse and challenging weak states.

The main challenge in such countries is that they lack the effective national policies and leadership needed to attract investment and ensure that external assistance is well used. In addition, weak states typically lack the manpower, administrative structures, know-how, and resources to absorb large volumes of aid. Nor do they have the the checks and balances to ensure that aid meets the needs of citizens and is not captured by special interests. Hence it is not surprising that donors, including the United States, tend to allocate most of their development funding to stronger states where aid works best.[2] For weak states ranging from the DRC to Somalia, official development assistance (ODA) generally comes in the form of humanitarian assistance, largely food aid. Although humanitarian aid and one-shot disease prevention campaigns can help save lives, they fail to address the longer-term need to build state capacity. Needless to say, the best solutions for such weak states are those that involve them in setting the agenda, even if outside assistance is needed to implement it.

Equally challenging, the downward cycle of poverty and weakness in developing countries has become more entrenched in the wake of the food crisis and current global economic downturn. Whatever gains emerging markets have achieved are being reversed as the earnings of commodity exporters—those hardest hit by the decline in global demand for their products—slide. Poor countries are among the world's most vulnerable to the impact of these crises. Policymakers should resist the temptation to see unfavorable budgetary conditions in the United States as a reason for complacency. Rather, as the new funding for development announced at the Group of Twenty (G-20) 2009 London Summit demonstrates, the current crisis is an opportunity to renew the commitments of rich and poor countries alike to achieving the Millennium Development Goals (MDGs). Should countries follow through on their commitments at the G-20, this would not only improve the plight of the world's poorest but would also be a worthy investment in the future security of people across the planet.

IMPROVE PERFORMANCE

During the cold war, aid was primarily utilized by donors to support client states in regions of strategic concern, rather than to promote development and alleviate poverty in poor states.[3] The results were for the most part predictable: the United States spent huge sums wooing partners such as Sudan, Zaire, Somalia, the Philippines, and Egypt, with little sustainable development impact. Today, the DRC, Sudan, and Somalia are the most acutely unstable areas in Africa. The lesson is clear: resources spent in bad policy environments without a clear development strategy are wasted and may further entrench elites and corrupt practices. Contrary to the approach of the superpowers during the cold war, focusing on capacity building and poverty alleviation in weak states can help the United States mitigate twenty-first-century threats such as civil war, terrorism, and disease.

In the 1990s ODA increasingly emphasized pro-poor growth, as donor governments and aid agencies became intent on improving aid's economic and development impact. The new attention to ODA and its effectiveness culminated in two landmark international agreements. The 2001 UN Millennium Development Goals recognized that donors must provide additional financing to assist impoverished countries and spelled out global and individual country targets to be reached by 2015 in eight areas of development. The 2002 International Conference on Financing for Development held in Monterrey, Mexico, provided an opportunity for donors to renew their commitment to the MDGs. It places particular emphasis on the fact that increased funding for development alone is not enough to reach the eight MDGs in the absence of mechanisms that will ensure aid funding is allocated and spent as effectively as possible.[4]

Spurred by the scholarly consensus that aid works best in better-performing states, aid donors and recipients have forged agreement on a number of foreign assistance best practices.[5] These are enshrined in the 2005 Paris Declaration on Aid Effectiveness, which provides guidance both to donors and recipient countries. Several new aid programs, including the Millennium Challenge Corporation in the United States, now reflect this growing consensus. Yet weak states pose a special challenge because these are precisely the states in which scholars have found that traditional aid instruments are least effective.

The challenge of development in weak states cannot be overemphasized. The historical record confirms that aid's impact on growth and poverty reduction has been less in weak states than in the average developing country.[6] Although gross domestic product (GDP) per capita in the developing world has tripled over the past fifty years, 1.4 billion people still live below the poverty line, and most reside in poor, weak states.[7] While donors tend to give greater attention to stronger states where aid works best, ignoring weak states is not a sustainable approach. Weak states are furthest away from achieving the MDGs and arguably have the greatest need for foreign assistance.[8]

Recognizing this dilemma, the international community has responded with a new set of guiding principles tailored specifically to weak states.

The 2007 Organization for Economic Cooperation and Development (OECD) agreement on Principles for Good International Engagement in Fragile States and Situations reflects the international community's effort to grapple with the challenge of development and capacity building in weak states. The document underscores the need for donors and recipient countries to work together more effectively. In recipient countries, the promotion of better governance and a greater commitment to democracy are key to helping them tap into global markets and achieve better results. On the donor side, both the *quantity* and the *quality* of aid are important.

Strategies for Recipient Countries

Governance is now widely considered one of the most important factors affecting development in the poorest countries.[9] Poor governance has been cited as the greatest obstacle to pulling the bottom billion poorest people—who reside mainly in weak states—out of poverty.[10] The MDGs will not be achieved unless governments can deliver services to their citizens, protect human rights, and spur economic development. Good governance is essential for creating the policies that address inequality and stabilize weak states. Sound governance is also necessary for managing shocks and external pressures that can interrupt economic growth and threaten stability, such as climate change and resource scarcity.

Nearly 30 percent of all people in extreme poverty live in fragile states. By 2015 extreme poverty in these countries is projected to increase by more than 50 percent (from 1990 levels). By definition, these states do not have the capacity for governance required to meet the needs of their people. Aid supplied in this context can be wasted. Yet withholding assistance from poor states until they govern effectively is a recipe for continued poverty. These states need help to change their performance. To sustain progress, external support must build local capability.

Studies of the impact of governance on development report a large "development dividend" for improvements in this sphere. A country that improves its governance from a relatively low to an average level can nearly triple per capita income in the long term and drastically reduce infant mortality and illiteracy.[11] Sub-Saharan Africa, which averaged zero annual per capita growth between 1970 and 2000, now grows at about 5 percent a year, driven by countries that have embraced good governance, instilled stronger macroeconomic management, and received significant debt relief.

Good governance along with accountability is a hallmark of democracies, and these attributes account in part for the strong relationship between democracy and development. Although some have suggested that authoritarian states such as China, Singapore, and now Vietnam may offer an alternative economic path for developing countries, democracies generally perform better than autocracies. Better governance helps in the fight against poverty and improves living standards. Research by the World Bank Group's Worldwide Governance Indicators Project over the past decade demonstrates that improved governance encourages development, not the other way around. When governance as measured by these indicators is improved by one standard deviation, infant mortality declines by two-thirds and income rises threefold. Good governance has also been found to enhance the overall effectiveness of development assistance.

From the opposite perspective, autocracies that govern well—particularly those that uphold the rule of law, enforce contracts, and allow markets to drive their economies—can sustain economic growth, but they are the exception rather than the rule. Freedom House ranks 60 percent of critically weak states (which are also the world's poorest countries) on the Index of State Weakness in the Developing World as "not free." As states move up the ladder toward greater state stability, more are democratic: 80 percent of developing and emerging economies in the top quintile of state stability are ranked as "free" and just 3 percent as "not free." Authoritarian regimes find the so-called China model attractive because of their desire to maintain political control. To follow the China model, however, they must liberalize their economies, increase competition, enforce the rule of law, and prosecute corruption. As the examples of China and Singapore show, over time considerable tensions may arise between liberal markets and authoritarian polities.

The central policy challenge for donors is to support the capacity of poor and weak states to improve leadership and the policy environment within their borders. The analysis of conflict in chapter 4 makes it especially clear how unrealistic it is to expect countries in the throes of war to fix decades-old problems of corruption and ineffectiveness. But the leaders of weak states with a legacy of decay and conflict can decide whether to turn their situation around. As a starting point, political will creates a platform for constructive work by recipients and donors. Consider the political will of Mozambique in the early 1990s compared with that of the DRC at the end of the same decade. Mozambique, despite more than ten years of civil war and limited control over parts of its territory, not to mention horrific poverty and weak state structures, emerged as one of the best performers in Africa over the next decade. Congo, by contrast, remains at the edge of conflict in 2009 despite a peace agreement in 2003 and the presence of a major UN mission. Regional factors certainly account in part for the performance gap between these two countries, but so does the difference between each country's commitment to reform.

The question is, how might other countries follow the example of Mozambique in improving governance? One approach is to strengthen regional pressures and incentives for good governance. The ideal example of a positive incentive structure is the European Union. The prospect of membership in the union, its success as a political and economic body, and the clear and rigid rules for membership have provided a strong incentive for countries throughout central and eastern Europe to reform internally, a prerequisite to membership. Hungary, Poland, the Czech Republic, and the Baltic states, to name a few, embarked on internal reform campaigns because they were committed to Europe and had only one path to get there.

Whether other regions can create similar incentives remains to be seen. The African Union has certainly progressed since the days of the Organization of African Unity, when there were no regional standards of governance. Countries tolerated the bad policies of their neighbors under the guise of respect for national sovereignty. Although gaps still remain in practice—working with a recalcitrant Zimbabwe, for example, is still a challenge——the African Union has adopted a policy of responsible sovereignty that holds nations accountable both for their treatment of citizens and for the spillover effects of their policies on neighbors.[12] Likewise, the Organization for American States (OAS) now subscribes to a commitment—the Santiago Commitment—to take action when democratic governance and accountability are threatened.

In Asia, sovereignty norms are evolving. During Thailand's 2006 military coup, members of the Association of Southeast Asian Nations (ASEAN) remained silent.[13] Nor has ASEAN contributed to regional peacekeeping or peace-building efforts, such as in Afghanistan and East Timor. Still, ASEAN members were allowed to observe the peace process in Aceh, Indonesia, in 2005–06. In summit discussions in 2007 regarding an ASEAN charter, members adopted the principle that decisions should be made by majority voting and that sanctions be taken against any member breaking the rules. Slowly, such changes in norms and practices will put pressure on the members of regional organizations to change domestic governance in order to benefit from regional bodies that can advance national stability.

A different form of incentive structure can be created through peer reviews. Thus far, such mechanisms have generally been lackluster, but the concept should not be abandoned. African countries moved in this direction in creating the New Partnership for Africa's Development (NEPAD) in 2001. The partnership's rationale was that African states had to create a foundation for good governance as a means to monitor and drive their commitments. To this end, the group launched the African peer review mechanism (APRM), which initiates periodic reviews of participating governments in the areas of democracy and political governance, economic governance and management, corporate governance, and socioeconomic development. Fellow African governments conduct the review, which is overseen by a panel of eminent African leaders. Most observers feel the review process is too slow and not sufficiently incisive—but it is a step toward accountability.

At the global level, one alternative could be to create peer review networks in common fields of expertise. Current and former officials, policymakers, and academics might be invited to participate. Standards and checklists could be established on the basis of lessons learned from other reviews. Individuals could make themselves available for confidential consultations with professional counterparts. Ministers of finance or justice could request such consultations to provide guidance on new plans or could assess performance on reform efforts as a means of learning from each other. Such a network could be housed at the United Nations Development Program (UNDP) and used as a learning tool that would give national officials positive incentives to seek advice, especially if positive reviews could reinforce better credit ratings, better loan rates on official credits, and grant financing under programs such as the Millennium Challenge Corporation (MCC).

As for stimulating economic growth, an essential step is to link into global markets. Countries with sound economic policies and aggressive export-led strategies have been better able to sustain economic growth and weather the impact of the global recession. Globalization has given these countries unprecedented access to capital, technology, and markets. Exports of goods and services accounted for 38 percent of China's GDP in 2006, double the share of a decade earlier.[14] In India, once largely closed to the global economy, trade in goods and services as a proportion of the GDP has risen from 16 percent in 1990 and 1991 to 49 percent in 2006 and 2007.[15] In contrast, exports of goods and services in oil-importing low-income African countries accounted for only 25 percent of GDP in 2006.[16]

To strengthen their economies, the world's poorest countries must participate in a global trading system. But that is much easier said than done. Despite political pledges to include the poor since the Doha Round was launched in November 2001, with added commitments from G20 leaders in November 2008 and April 2009, negotiations remained frozen as of the summer of 2009. The Doha Round put developing countries' priorities at the center of the agenda for the first time in World Trade Organization (WTO) negotiations. The fact that the Doha Round collapsed in part because India and China sought stronger protection for their farmers from trade surges—surges most likely to come from Brazil or other emerging economies—underscores the risk of new protectionist coalitions, even among those who have benefited most from an open global trade regime.[17] In the future, if Doha succeeds or if there is a successor agreement, the tensions that caused this round to collapse will only become more acute as poor countries enter into competitive niches dominated by China, India, and other emerging economies.

Strategies for Donor Countries

Countries that are too poor to tap into global markets will need further donor country leadership. Donor performance may not rise to the occasion, however, if financing falls short of the development needs of poor countries, is insufficient to promote development, and is not coordinated among donors. Perhaps most important, donor analysis of the conditions that either constrain or enhance the effectiveness of aid funding remains inadequate. Despite the central importance of linking into global markets, it will be difficult to combat poverty unless the approaches used reflect the realities facing the poor. To complicate matters, many of the world's poor reside in middle-income economies. Their plight reflects the unkind side of market-based growth: rising income inequality across and within states. Improved policies and responsive governance will be needed to narrow the gap between rich and poor.

In both quantity and quality, the international community is not keeping pace with its commitments. Much larger and sustained increases in aid will be needed to reach the MDGs. Under the Monterrey Consensus, sixteen of twenty-two OECD donor nations have achieved or are on track to achieve their commitment to allocate 0.7 percent of gross national product (GNP) for development aid. Six countries are not on track: Australia, Canada, Japan, New Zealand, Switzerland, and the United States. The United States—the largest missing element in financing the MDGs—accounts for almost half of the foreign assistance shortfall. If it spent about one-tenth of its defense budget on foreign aid, it would double its funding for the fight against poverty. The share of U.S. GNP devoted to helping the poor has declined for decades and is only a fraction of what the country has repeatedly promised. In addition, most ODA does not translate into funds available for projects and development programs. Aid flows are often used for special purposes such as debt relief, humanitarian and emergency spending, technical assistance costs (such as salaries for Western workers in developing countries), administrative costs, and food aid. As pointed out in chapter 6, even when international assistance helps support life-saving treatments, it does not necessarily contribute to systemic changes in health systems or policies needed to sustain progress once foreign aid flows diminish.

As for aid coordination, international mechanisms should be broadened to include emerging economy donors and to reflect the role of private capital flows. The international aid system must also take better advantage of private capital flows and nontraditional players in poverty alleviation. Bilateral development assistance from countries such as China, India, Thailand, Turkey, and Brazil is growing and promises to change the international aid landscape. Private flows from corporate partnerships to philanthropic activities now amount to more than twice the level of global ODA. While government funds continue to dwarf private flows in certain key areas—such as HIV/AIDS—there are equally impressive counterexamples, such as Warren Buffett's $37 billion donation in 2006 to the Bill and Melinda Gates Foundation, which enabled Gates to disburse more in grants than the U.S. Millennium Challenge Corporation disbursed in the same year.

With the proliferation of new public and private development actors, there has also been a growing fragmentation of aid. The amount of aid passing through new bilateral donors, NGOs, and new corporate philanthropists is now higher than aid through traditional official channels. Multilateral aid agencies, now totaling about 230, outnumber donors and recipients combined. Each of these providers focuses on its own areas of interest, goals, and constituencies, creating an enormous coordination burden for recipient countries. Furthermore, development agencies often hire away the best local personnel with an offer of high salaries, leaving governments to waste their valuable time and limited capacity in coordinating multiple donor requirements. The Paris Declaration on Aid Effectiveness sought to improve the harmonization of aid, but gains have been muted by an increasingly complex and crowded development landscape.

One way to deepen and operationalize the Paris Declaration guidelines would be to put them through field tests using the UNDP and World Bank as coordinating points. The two agencies could pick a cross-regional subset of fifteen countries and ask country missions to convene all official and nongovernmental donors, along with the host governments, to garner recommendations on implementing and refining the declaration on the basis of experience. Using the UNDP and the World Bank for this makes sense because both organizations have country missions around the world and together have created tools for jointly assessing country needs and strategic plans. The objective should be to ensure that external assistance supports national development strategies, reduces the pressure on host governments working with tens (if not hundreds) of official and nongovernmental donors, and ends the exodus of talented personnel from public and private jobs in developing countries leaving for jobs in donor agencies.

Donors can also help structure incentives so as to encourage recipient countries to put sound policy environments in place. To date, the leading mechanism for this has been the MCC in the United States. It invests in "compacts" with developing countries that achieve performance targets across independent and transparent policy indicators related to governance, such as ruling justly, investing in people, and encouraging economic freedom.[18] The prospect of major, multiyear funding commitments is intended to increase the incentive for countries to improve performance. The MCC's limitation is that it excludes developing countries with the weakest governance systems, which cannot meet the eligibility criteria.

In encouraging good performance, donors also need to adopt a balanced perspective that includes democracy and human rights. That was not the case in Iraq, where U.S. rhetoric and actions fused democracy promotion with violent and unilateral regime change. As a result, many countries believe that international interventions to promote democracy are a breach of national sovereignty. Others consider U.S. support for democracy disingenuous in light of U.S. violations of the Convention against Torture and Other Cruel, Inhuman or Degrading Treatment or Punishment (for example, at Guantánamo Bay and Abu Ghraib), or in selective U.S. support for election results (for example, in rejecting Hamas in the Palestinian territories), or inconsistent U.S. signals toward some democratic movements (for example, in Egypt). These critics deduce that for the United States, global efforts to combat international terrorism take precedence over democracy and human rights. In this climate, many Europeans and other donors avoid programs in support of democracy.

Donors need not be apologetic about advocating principles of democracy and human rights as part of an aid strategy. These are universal principles enshrined in the Universal Declaration of Human Rights. Still, donors need to appreciate that the concept of imposing democracy is an oxymoron—and a recipe for policy failure. Much still needs to be done in the post-Iraq era in order to find effective ways to incorporate universal principles like democracy and human rights into engagement with national governments.

The task would be easier if donors strengthened their capacity to engage governments, NGOs, and the private sector in poor and weak states. The importance of collecting data on local conditions in weak states and analyzing this information cannot be overemphasized. To obtain such information, donors need to increase their presence on the ground and, ideally, invest in personnel who know the country best. By ending all assistance in Zimbabwe and North Korea, for instance, donors—having withdrawn their staff—now lack substantial information on local developments, not to mention any leverage to influence government policy. Such action also creates an untenable situation in that reinstating field staff, even when it serves the donor's interests, may be seen as a "concession" to the recipient. Not only should development professionals maintain a presence, but adequate resources should also be provided to allow diplomats and local hires to collect adequate data.

Weak states are often complex environments about which the international community possesses limited knowledge. Thorough knowledge of local conditions is critical to developing policies that reflect the distribution of power among local actors without exacerbating underlying political tensions. Furthermore, if donors understand not just who the power players are but also who is disenfranchised or oppressed within a society, they can identify key stakeholders liable to help build support for policy reform in their communities. Because donors lack a clear understanding of what works in weak states, more data are urgently needed to help build better theories and practice of development in these environments.

All of these factors underscore the need for more foreign service personnel, greater local expertise, better-quality data, and the ability to track trends and progress. Together, they can increase the capacity of donors to engage more effectively in their diplomatic, development, and security endeavors. To put in perspective the imbalance in international deployment capacities, in his 2008 State of the Union address President George W. Bush called for and subsequently won support to add 90,000 troops to the U.S. military, whereas the combined number of foreign service officers at the State Department and U.S. Agency for International Development (USAID) remained under 10,000. Left with limited capacity in complex environments, civilian aid functions began migrating to the U.S. military.

Across the U.S. government, aid to developing countries, including weak states, lacks coordination and strategic coherence. More than fifty government entities in the executive branch share responsibility for aid delivery and are committed to countless development objectives ranging from preserving biodiversity to countering narcotics activities. Adding to this jumble of overlapping tasks are several new institutional projects, among them the President's Emergency Plan for AIDS Relief (PEPFAR) and the President's Malaria Initiative.

Bipartisan momentum is gathering, however, for a modernization of the U.S. foreign assistance architecture to meet the goals of the twenty-first century, a primary one being to strengthen weak states. A new bipartisan bill, the Foreign Assistance Revitalization and Accountability Act of 2009 (S.1524), is designed to start the process of aid reform. It seeks to restore planning capacity to USAID and to bolster development expertise. Yet because the USAID administrator is one of the last high-level officials to be appointed by the Obama administration, U.S development policy as of the summer of 2009 still lacks strategic leadership. U.S. development policy in weak states will continue to be ineffective as long as the U.S. aid architecture remains obsolete and incoherent.

SUPPORT THE RULE OF LAW

Whether poor states are in conflict, unstable, or in the grip of an authoritarian ruler, they all suffer from an absence or deficit of the rule of law.[19] Decisions tend to be made by "the few," guided by self-interest rather than legal precepts, and thus fuel distrust and instability. These conditions make it harder to achieve reconciliation or attract investment.

Although investments in the rule of law and security are not traditionally part of an agenda to fight poverty, they are essential to creating an environment in which government, the private sector, and civil society can function and devote themselves to economic, governance, social, and humanitarian goals and can break the link between poverty and state weakness.

As discussed in chapter 4, the literature on building an effective capacity for administering the rule of law is now extensive. Certain of its maxims seem obvious, particularly the need for a foundation of transparent laws, a judicial system to administer them in a transparent way, police to enforce the law and deter crime, and a penitentiary system that treats prisoners humanely. Despite this accepted wisdom, performance has lagged. There is no single repository of expertise for assistance in establishing the rule of law. Most nations do not have a national police force and thus do not have a common capacity for training and mentoring forces in other states. Nor do most nations have large numbers of police who can be deployed outside of day-to-day service, making it harder to recruit police for international missions. International capacity and experience should be augmented through investments in multilateral and regional bodies. The European Union, for one, has started down this road with the creation of an EU gendarme force and civilian crisis management capacity that includes national police.[20]

One common misconception in this regard is that building an indigenous police force is just a matter of training and deploying units. That was tried in Afghanistan and Iraq in the first phases of police training in those countries, with a zealous focus on numbers flowing through the pipeline. The results were disastrous. Trained police deployed in corrupt interior ministries merely produced corrupt policemen. Only when entire ministries were restructured, with new incentives and accountability mechanisms, did retraining begin to have a positive impact. Yet even by mid-2009, after billions of dollars in successive training efforts, Afghanis claimed the police were still part of the problem, not the solution.[21]

Another important consideration is that it takes time to rebuild police and judicial systems. In the United States, an individual with at least a high school education can emerge a police officer in eighteen months, from the time of entering training to deployment. The task of training judges is even more challenging. With large sums often at stake, corrupt elements in post-conflict societies typically resist reforms. Donors have to be willing to stick with the process. To some extent, international police can help in the short term, but few countries are willing to deploy them long enough to build indigenous capacity. If donors want sustainable solutions, they must create both the international capability and the political will to stick with the process of building state capacity over the long haul. That is true both in fragile states and in those recovering from conflict.

MAKE SECURITY A HIGH PRIORITY

In states emerging from conflict, security investments also require international peacekeeping and often the development of a depoliticized national armed force. In the mid-1990s, failures in Bosnia, Rwanda, and Somalia appeared to have discredited peacekeeping. But subsequent efforts to broker or enforce peace in a number of volatile regions (including the western Balkans, the West African littoral, the Great Lakes region of central Africa, and the broader Middle East) have spawned a new generation of peace operations.

UN and non-UN peace operations can play a significant role in bringing about short-term stability and in providing a framework for longer-term peace building and reconstruction in areas torn by conflict. One such area is Darfur—where the moral imperative for international action is very clear. But such operations would also benefit places that act as havens for terrorists (such as Afghanistan and Somalia), that serve as bases or conduits for international criminal activity (such as Haiti), or are located at the hub of regional conflicts central to U.S. regional policies (such as southern Lebanon).

Peacekeeping operations can make a twofold contribution to international security. Operationally, they bring direct security to troubled territories. Politically, they build frameworks for international cooperation in conflict management—whether through military alliances such as the North Atlantic Treaty Organization (NATO) or ad hoc coalitions such as the UN force in Lebanon. In addition, peacekeeping is a critical first step toward progress on development in weak states with a history of conflict. The United States thus has several incentives to build confidence in and through peacekeeping operations in weak states.

This plays out primarily in Africa, the main theater of UN operations, where upward of 75 percent of its Blue Helmet peacekeeping force is deployed, and in the greater Middle East, where the United Nations and NATO combined have deployed more than 70,000 peacekeepers. In both regions, the international community has been turning to "hybrid" peace operations, which entail the simultaneous or sequential deployment of missions by two or more international or multinational actors.

Peacekeeping's mounting success can be seen in current UN-led peace operations. A RAND study of eight current UN-led peace operations found that seven of these countries are still at peace.[22] In second missions to both Haiti and the DRC, the UN is making progress despite massive underfunding and huge political complications.

These are not the only kinds of persistent problems for these operations: it continues to be difficult to locate suitable troop contingents and mobilize early funding for recovery, especially in hard cases, typically the weakest states. Approximately 130,000 to 140,000 troops a year will have to be rotated to maintain the current level of UN military personnel in the field. Even though sufficient numbers of infantry have been found for current UN operations, more specialized assets— helicopters, light armor, and similar equipment necessary to mount credible operations in hostile environments such as the DRC and Darfur, Sudan—have been less easy to acquire. In addition, not enough long-range airlift is available to rapidly deploy new missions.

Pressed to carry out multidimensional mandates, the United Nations deploys peacekeepers not only to implement agreements after civil wars or in response to state collapses, but also at times to take on important governance, capacity building, rule-of-law, judicial, policing, and economic functions. In these multidimensional missions, the peacekeepers contribute not just to military stabilization, but—in theory—also to the broader stabilization and reconstruction effort. UN operations face substantial problems in implementing these mandates.

The surest way to avoid a new generation of wars is to invest adequately in securing and stabilizing the peace in weak states where conflict has ended, by building up effective peacekeeping and peace-building capacities. Security forces must be at adequate levels to uphold the peace and enforce law and order immediately after a conflict. In Bosnia and

Kosovo, the troop-to-population ratios were 19:1,000 and 20:1,000, respectively. In Iraq and Afghanistan, the ratios were 7.5:1,000 and 1.5:1,000, respectively, during at least the first three years of those missions.[23] The subsequent insurgencies in Iraq and Afghanistan should not be a surprise. Once a mission loses control over the use of force and criminal activity, it creates a space for insurgency.

Creating jobs and building infrastructure are essential to establishing a tangible sense of progress. But these objectives require enough security to permit large numbers of civilians to move and act freely. Without that underlying sense of peace and stability, it will be virtually impossible to sustain progress in post-conflict areas.

FOSTER NATIONAL DECENTRALIZATION

State building will not succeed unless local populations have a stake in supporting a national identity and vest in their government the legitimacy to govern. That is to say, people must see a benefit to better governance in their own lives. Security is usually the first priority. Jobs, food, education for their children, and access to medical care complete the equation. Decentralization takes on a special importance in this context. It can not only help populations buy into the idea of a new state but help foster development, an approach too often dismissed in development practice.

A common assumption about weak states is that their local governments are also weak, which may well be true. But when national governments are bankrupt, corrupt, or ineffective, then relying strictly on national-level intervention is a recipe for failure. At least at the local level, citizens may have a more direct stake in success. As World Bank president Robert Zoellick has pointed out, "Legitimacy in fragile situations is not just achieved through elections or agreements that share power among factions. . . . It needs to be earned by delivering basic services, especially visible ones. Clean up the garbage. Build institutional capacity by doing things."[24]

Perhaps the most emblematic national decentralization program in a weak state today is Afghanistan's National Solidarity Program (NSP), launched in 2003 in an effort to empower local communities through the establishment of local governance bodies—or Community Development Councils (CDCs). The entire program is overseen by the central government and financed by a consortium of international donors, but funding for individual projects requires a consensus on how to spend the funds at the community level. While the program is often held up as a desirable model and has achieved impressive results—most notably increased access to improved water and sanitation and school attendance—the challenges for the NSP and further development in Afghanistan are a vivid reminder that progress cannot be sustained without security.[25] Furthermore, if donor activities are not coordinated, national resources are not forthcoming, and donors are reluctant to invest resources through weak state channels, efforts at expansion and institutionalization are likely to falter.

Many donors prefer tackling similar types of projects through NGOs so as to achieve the same outcomes as national stabilization programs but with greater control. When best practiced, such community-driven development (CDD) follows a set of core principles, including local empowerment, participatory governance, administrative autonomy, and enhanced local capacity.[26] In post-conflict or conflict-prone countries, such programs allow donors to channel funds through NGOs to address urgent local community needs. Community programs can help repair relationships between contending groups and become a catalyst for stabilizing the situation on the ground. They can help restore peace and security in the immediate aftermath of conflict, while peace consolidation and emergency reconstruction are still under way. Over the longer term, the CDD approach facilitates the transition from emergency response to development and can support institution building, while also strengthening the practice of inclusive governance.[27] One possible drawback, however, is that NGOs may not build enough local capacity or may focus exclusively on delivering programs, especially when they feel donors are expecting rapid disbursement. Another large concern is whether the recurrent costs to such projects are built into national and local budgets.

Social funds allow donors to support a decentralized capacity for the delivery of social services. These mechanisms vary widely as to how far removed they are from central government agencies; funding may be disbursed through local governments, community groups, or third parties on behalf of a given community.[28] Social funds were first widely used in the 1980s to provide a short-term safety net in countries undergoing structural adjustment.[29] Today, these funds are used to provide local governments with a greater role in project decision, especially when central governments are not inclined or do not have the capacity to do so.[30] For instance, the Angola Social Action Fund and Cambodia

Social Fund have proved to be an excellent vehicle for donors to rapidly and effectively disburse significant funding in crisis situations. The risk, however, is that excessive reliance on social funds could detract from building trust in the government, undermine legitimacy, and thus further destabilize weak states.

FOCUS ON HUMANITARIAN ASSISTANCE

In countries that are still in conflict or just beginning to emerge from civil strife, humanitarian assistance can serve populations in acute need without appearing to support a failed, corrupt, or contested government.[31] Humanitarian assistance is the primary vehicle for engagement in places such as Somalia and Sudan, although ground conditions make it difficult for aid workers to reach the population. Humanitarian aid may also enable donors to gain leverage and promote policy reform in the context of poor human rights or political oppression.[32] In zones of long-standing conflict, humanitarian assistance often starts out as crisis relief supplying populations with basic welfare and social services.[33]

A growing concern in recent years, however, especially in a handful of high-profile countries, is that donors have come to rely on humanitarian assistance at the expense of development aid.[34] Humanitarian assistance has been climbing upward globally, by 33 percent since 2000 and by 175 percent in real terms since 1990.[35] The objection is that humanitarian aid does not lay the foundations for long-term development.[36] Pressure is building for a better-managed transition from humanitarian to development assistance in weak states marred by chronic instability.[37]

A related concern is that agencies and structures created at the national level to serve humanitarian functions are operating in parallel with government institutions. Although such structures are indeed vital to meeting urgent humanitarian needs and saving lives in weak states, they often prevent governments from developing adequate bureaucratic and governance systems. This only serves to perpetuate weakness and to create aid-dependent countries with a limited capacity to take charge of their own destinies or to generate growth and alleviate poverty.

AS A LAST RESORT, CIRCUMVENT THE STATE

While circumventing the state perpetuates aid dependence, there are two overriding rationales for doing so in some circumstances. The first is that human life may be at such great risk that obstructionist governments should not be allowed to block life-saving interventions. This is the thinking behind programs such as PEPFAR and the Global Fund to Fight AIDS, TB, and Malaria. The second is that specific threats have such urgent global implications that direct interventions may be necessary, even if their sustainability is in doubt. Vaccine programs to stop the spread of infectious disease or investments to stop deforestation fall in this category.

As the assessments in this book make clear, threat-specific interventions are important, but their limitations are not well understood. Interventions aimed at diseases like HIV and malaria are tangible and easy to justify, making them attractive to donors. These programs now account for a substantial share of assistance to developing countries—up to 40 percent or more of health funding in some weak states—and unfortunately they are crowding out longer-term health investments.[38] There are now signs that large, narrowly targeted expenditures on communicable diseases are reducing the overall capacity of national health systems, perhaps leaving weak states unable to provide adequate care in the longer term. That is not an argument against investments to eradicate diseases like HIV, malaria, and TB, but a reminder that it is equally important to invest in systemic capacity. Peer reviews to sustain attention on creating viable health systems could be one mechanism to ensure that disease-focused assistance does not crowd out investments in preventive and primary care.

Other examples in this book also help to illustrate the point. Emergency national vaccine programs are sound in principle to prevent global pandemics, for instance, but to implement them one needs virus samples, production capacity, and the ability to deliver and administer vaccines quickly and safely. The principle behind investments in rain forests is equally sound in that forests help curb a major source of greenhouse gases, but in states like the Congo one needs reliable evidence of the impact on forest preservation. The international community is willing to help poor countries adapt to climate change—for example, by erecting seawalls to control flooding—but any such assistance will be of little use if governments cannot manage their industrial development and sprawling slums.

Even if measures are taken to circumvent governments in delivering aid, they are merely stop gaps. They work best if they are one-time interventions (such as administering a vaccine) or create local or interest groups that build pressure to improve national policies (such as projects to combat AIDS). Yet investing in these areas does not in any way lessen the need for systemic policy reform.

Another form of investment that allows donors to circumvent national governments originates in the private sector, particularly investment in the development of small and microenterprises. Both can generate jobs and growth. Because of their close involvement with concerned populations and other local stakeholders, private sector entities are often in the best position to assess economic risk and opportunity. While the institutional and policy environment directly affects the growth and impact of the private sector, businesses themselves provide opportunities for the rural poor to diversify their incomes, create new sources of economic growth, and generate additional employment opportunities. If private enterprises are permitted to have an equity stake in projects, they have an interest in assessing the security and viability of their own investments. Firms can also become allies in advocating policies and infrastructure investments that foster business development and growth.

In poor and weak states, finance for micro-, small, and medium enterprises is perhaps the private sector's most effective tool for cultivating development and entrepreneurship at the local level. As experience demonstrates, even small loans, often on the order of $200 or less, can sustain businesses and keep banks viable. The most successful microfinance institutions provide business advice, counseling, and solidarity circles for peer support. Institutions receiving broad peer and community support benefit from a high rate of repayment on their loans. In some countries the majority of loans go to women, who are more likely to reinvest their earnings in their business and in their families.[39] If a woman falls ill and cannot run her business for several days, for example, her solidarity circle often helps with the business until the borrower is well again. Repayments multiply the impact of each dollar loaned.

Some microfinance institutions have issued bonds to create a sustainable base of capital and thereby reduce their dependence on donor support. This has occurred in all regions and cultures: with the Grameen Bank in South Asia, Accion in Latin America, and ProCredit Banks in Eastern Europe, Russia, and Eurasia. Such programs are now reaching out to Africa.

WHY NOW?

A central message of this book is that the development community simply cannot leave the poorest, weakest countries behind. The security risks are too numerous and too dangerous. Nor can it ignore the complexity of working with central governments that are bankrupt, unstable, ineffective, or corrupt. Although the members of this community are beginning to identify and agree upon a set of principles and tools that policymakers can rely on in weak states, much still needs to be done to find effective ways to help these states achieve sustained growth and enable their institutions to deliver services to their citizens.

The international community has already learned a great deal about strategies for breaking the cycle of poverty and weakness. A checklist of best practices for international policy is presented in table 7-1.

Timing is crucial. The global financial crisis and housing downturn in the United States are taking a heavy toll on the U.S. economy, which is expected to contract by as much as 2.6 percent in 2009 and to begin recovering in earnest only in 2010. To stem global warming, nations will have to achieve massive reductions in emissions that in the near term will cost additional jobs in carbon-intensive industries, such as automobiles and steel. Yet the financial crisis makes it imperative to prevent a dramatic deterioration in economic conditions and welfare in the developing world. In the United States, the wealthiest country on earth, massive fiscal and monetary stimulus packages were necessary to shield the economy and American jobs from the worst possible impacts of the crisis. The resources for a similar response in developing countries are simply not there. The World Bank is projecting that economic growth will fall to 1.2 percent in developing countries in 2009, from a high of 8.1 percent in 2007 and 5.9 percent in 2008.[40] When China and India are taken out of the picture, GDP in all the remaining developing countries will fall by 1.6 percent. Another 90 million more people could be trapped in poverty, on top of the 155 million already pushed into poverty in 2008, in the wake of soaring fuel and food prices. More than 1 billion could go chronically hungry in 2009 alone, reversing recent gains in fighting malnutrition.

As the contributors to this book have argued, the effects of deteriorating economic conditions in poor countries will not be limited to the developing world. Director of National Intelligence Dennis Blair warns that the global economic crisis represents "the primary near-term security concern of the United States," and that "economic crises increase the risk of regime-threatening instability if they persist over a one- to two-year period. Besides increased economic nationalism, the most likely political fallout for U.S. interests will involve allies and friends not being able to fully meet their defense and humanitarian obligations. Potential

TABLE 7-1. Confronting Poverty: Tools for Supporting Poor and Weak States

Mechanism	Purpose	Limitations	Guidelines
National performance			
Regional standards	Create incentives for national performance and mutual accountability.	Members must be willing to expel or sanction violators.	Develop regional and member institutional capacity, improve standards, create mechanisms to review and act.
Peer review	Encourage peer dialogue and exchange of lessons.	Peers may not share information honestly; reviews can be used for political purposes.	Invest in peer networks, standards, lessons learned.
Donor performance			
Aid levels	Counter impacts of recession; achieve MDGs.	Good recipient policies are critical to sustain impact.	Target aid to job creation, human and physical infrastructure. Assess recipient progress against both MDG and Monterrey guidelines.
Foreign Service, diplomatic and development personnel	Engage national stakeholders in creative and locally tailored solutions.	Congressional resistance to appropriating funds for personnel.	Recruit and deploy personnel with language and local expertise. Apply staff skills to building national capacity, not replacing it.
Donor coherence	Reduce drain on recipients; set common standards.	Provides tool for effectiveness, but few enforcement mechanisms.	Test at country level; draw in official donors and NGOs.
MCC	Create donor incentives for good recipient policies.	Alone cannot help weak states break out of negative cycles; inadequate political support.	Recognize toughest cases are often excluded.
Democracy and human rights	Incorporate universal principles into transitional strategies.	Authoritarians and human rights violators will resist.	Encourage local dialogue in shaping solutions that reflect democratic principles.
Rule of law and security			
Police and judicial reform	Strengthen indigenous capacity to administer rule of law.	Provokes confrontation with sources of power and corruption. Training operational units without changing institutions is unsustainable.	Change takes time, close monitoring, economic incentives, and sustained donor commitment. Must proceed from both top and bottom to reform institutions.
Peacekeeping and peace building	Sustain peace after war.	Outsiders can create an enabling environment but must phase out to local actors.	Institution building of local actors must start concurrently with international force deployments.

Mechanism	Purpose	Limitations	Guidelines
		Absence of international standby forces with common doctrine and training delays deployments.	Invest in international capacity to combine national and regional forces into interoperable units.
Decentralization			
National solidarity programs	Build local initiative in context of national strategies.	Difficult to secure recipient resources and personnel to fund and support local action. Donors deterred by gaps in local planning capacity, implementation, accountability.	Local proposals must reflect community consensus across interest groups. Activities must tie into building allegiance to nation-state, not separatism.
NGO community development	Build local initiative through NGO channels.	Pressures for rapid delivery and impact can short-shrift building state capacity.	Seek means to tie NGO programs to national strategies. Build local capacity to sustain, not just deliver projects.
Social funds	Direct donor resources to subnational projects and specific sectors	Creates risk that funding and capacity cannot be sustained without donors.	Use to build subnational capacity and pressure groups that can influence better national policies.
Provincial training	Strengthen local capacity to plan, implement, account for projects.	Inability to mobilize appropriate international skills in significant numbers.	Foster rather than impose vision. Mentor, build capacity.
Humanitarian assistance			
Food and other humanitarian aid	Avoid loss of human life.	Does not produce sustainable outcomes; can encourage dependence. Donor funding not easily transferable to development aid.	Provide when there is no alternative. Use to bridge to strategies for sustainability. Engage local populations in administering.
Circumventing the state			
NGO delivery programs	Avoid loss of human life. Stop diseases and crises that will spill over regionally or globally.	Results potentially unsustainable without donor funding. National capacity limitations can thwart or deter international efforts.	Consider if one-time interventions possible. Build local or interest group capacity to change state policy.
Private sector support	Increase private investment and job creation.	Confiscatory tax policy, corruption, or war can undermine incentives.	Require private equity participation to ensure private stake. Draw from local knowledge of security and practices.

refugee flows from the Caribbean could also impact Homeland security."[41] Now is the time to begin making the necessary investments to help stave off the security fallout from the crisis.

Some may question the need for action and additional support to developing countries at this juncture. Why not continue responding to crises as they emerge? This passive approach would be not only more dangerous than prevention—as recent crises in countries like Somalia, North Korea, Zimbabwe, and Pakistan demonstrate—but also more costly. The human costs in countries that are weak or in conflict are enormous: on average, people there die ten years earlier than those in other developing countries. Infant mortality is much steeper.[42] The financial costs of state failure to the international community are also extreme. Putting peacekeepers on the ground in postconflict countries and providing humanitarian assistance are exponentially more expensive than development assistance. Economists estimate that the total annual cost of each instance of state failure, including lost income to the countries experiencing conflict as well as to their neighbors, is as high as $270 billion.[43] In addition, there are numerous less tangible costs that are more difficult to measure, including the cost to societies of spikes in the drug trade and other spillover effects from conflict zones.

The global financial crisis, tragic as it is, offers a historic opportunity for the United States to reach out to other donor and developing countries and push for a renewed commitment on all sides to the MDGs and the Monterrey Consensus. The governments gathered in Monterrey in 2002 declared that "achieving the internationally agreed development goals, including those contained in the Millennium Declaration, demands a new partnership between developed and developing countries." At the time, soon after the terrorist attacks of September 11, there was a shared sense of urgency that countries must resolve to act together to face the challenges of development in the poorest countries.

Today, in the wake of the global financial crisis, a similar window of opportunity has opened. Leaders gathered in London for the 2009 Group of Twenty summit recognized this when they committed to providing a "substantial increase in lending of at least $100 billion by the Multilateral Development Banks (MDBs), including to low income countries."[44] The time to follow through on these promises is now. It is incumbent on the development community to seize this moment before it slips away.

NOTES

1. On development assistance as a means of addressing global security threats, see, for instance, United Nations, *A More Secure World: Our Shared Responsibility, Report of the High-Level Panel on Threats, Challenges and Change* (2004), p. viii; National Commission on Terrorist Attacks upon the United States, *9/11 Commission Report: Final Report of the National Commission on Terrorist Attacks upon the United States* (New York: W. W. Norton, 2004), p. 363; World Bank, "Improving Effectiveness and Outcomes for the Poor in Health, Nutrition and Population," Independent Evaluation Group Report (Washington, 2009), p. xvii; British Treasury, "Stern Review on the Economics of Climate Change" (London, 2006), chap. 20.

2. Victoria Levin and David Dollar, "The Forgotten States: Aid Volumes and Volatility in Difficult Partnership Countries (1992–2002)," DAC Learning and Advisory Process on Difficult Partnerships (Organization for Economic Cooperation and Development, 2005).

3. Parts of this section draw on Bruce Jones, Carlos Pascual, and Stephen Stedman, *Power and Responsibility: Building International Order in an Era of Transnational Threats* (Brookings, 2008), chap. 9.

4. United Nations, Monterrey Consensus on Financing for Development (Monterrey, Mexico, 2003) (www.un.org/esa/ffd/monterrey/MonterreyConsensus.pdf).

5. Craig Burnside and David Dollar, "Aid, Policies and Growth," *American Economic Review* 90, no. 4 (2000): 847–68; Paul Collier and David Dollar, "Development Effectiveness: What Have We Learnt?" *Economic Journal* 114, no. 496 (2004): 244–72.

6. World Bank, "Engaging with Fragile States," Independent Evaluation Group Report (Washington, 2006).

7. In 2008 the World Bank proposed a revised figure that categorizes poverty as living on less than $1.25 a day. See Shaohua Chen and Martin Ravallion, "The Developing World Is Poorer Than We Thought, but No Less Successful in the Fight against Poverty," Policy Research Working Paper 4703 (Washington: World Bank, 2008).

8. See Andrew Branchflower with Sarah Hennell, Sophie Pongracz, and Malcolm Smart, "How Important Are Difficult Environments to Achieving MDGs?" PRDE Working Paper 2 (United Kingdom: Department for International Development [DFID], September 2004); Levin and Dollar, "The Forgotten States"; World Bank, *Aid That Works: Successful Development in Fragile States* (Washington, 2006); DFID, "Why We Need to Work More Effectively in Fragile States," White Paper (United Kingdom, 2005).

9. Parts of this section draw on Jones and others, *Power and Responsibility*, chap. 9.

10. Paul Collier, *The Bottom Billion: Why the Poorest Countries Are Failing and What Can Be Done about It* (Oxford University Press, 2007).

11. Daniel Kaufmann, "10 myths about Governance and Corruption," *Finance and Development*, September 2005, available at www.imf.org/external/pubs/ft/fandd/2005/09/basics.htm.

12. See Jones and others, *Power and Responsibility,* pp. 10–11.

13. Amitav Acharya, "ASEAN at 40: Mid-Life Rejuvenation?" *Foreign Affairs,* August 15, 2007.

14. "World Risk: Alert—Global Downturn Will Test Asian Resilience," Country Briefing, Economist Intelligence Unit, The Economist Group, March 28, 2008.

15. Arvind Panagariya, "India's Growing Economy: Song of the Crossroads," *Hindustan Times*, February 18, 2008.

16. International Monetary Fund (IMF), "Regional Economic Outlook: Sub-Saharan Africa" (Washington, October 2007), p. 55.

17. "These days, industrialists in India mostly want protection against imports from China, not the United States. Perhaps the biggest loser from India's and China's resistance to lower farm tariffs was the agricultural powerhouse Brazil. The North-South frame of the Doha negotiations ignored these cleavages." See "The Next Step for World Trade," *New York Times,* August 2, 2008.

18. See www.mcc.gov.

19. This section draws on Jones and others, *Power and Responsibility,* chap. 7.

20. Information on the European Union's gendarme force is available at www.eurogendfor.eu/.

21. Carol Graham and Soumya Chattopadhyay, "Well-being and Public Attitudes in Afghanistan: Some Insights from the Economics of Happiness," Foreign Policy Working Paper 2 (Brookings, 2009).

22. James Dobbins and others, *The UN's Role in Nation-Building: From Congo to Iraq* (Santa Monica, Calif.: RAND Corporation, 2005).

23. Ibid.

24. Robert Zoellick, "Fragile States: Securing Development," *Survival* 50, no. 6 (December 2008–January 2009): 67–84.

25. Information on Afghanistan's National Solidarity Program is available at http://web.worldbank.org.

26. World Bank, "Community-Driven Development in the Context of Conflict-Affected Countries: Challenges and Opportunities," Social Development Department & Environmentally and Socially Sustainable Development Network (http://siteresources.worldbank.org/INTCDD/Resources/CDD_and_Conflictpdf?&resourceurlname=CDD_and_Conflict.pdf)

27. See also World Bank, *Aid That Works.*

28. More information on social funds is available at http://web.worldbank.org.

29. Julie Van Domelen, "Social Capital in the Operations and Impacts of

Social Investment Funds" in *The Search for Empowerment: Social Capital as Idea and Practice at the World Bank,* edited by Anthony J. Bebbington and others (Washington: World Bank, 2003) (http://siteresources.worldbank.org/INTSF/Resources/395669.1135699157512/VanDomelen_SocialCapitalinSFs_DRAFT.pdf).

30. See also World Bank, *Aid That Works.*

31. Joanna Macrae and others, "Aid to Poorly Performing Countries: A Critical Review of Debates and Issues" (London: Overseas Development Institute, 2004), p. 13.

32. Judith Randel, with Maya Cordeiro and Tasneem Mowjee, "Financing Countries in Protracted Humanitarian Crisis: An Overview of New Instruments and Existing Aid Flows," in *Beyond the Continuum: The Changing Role of Aid Policy in Protracted Crises,* edited by Adele Harmer and Joanna Macrae (London: Overseas Development Institute, Humanitarian Policy Group, 2004).

33. Macrae and others, "Aid to Poorly Performing Countries," p. 13.

34. Ibid.

35. Development Initiatives, "Global Humanitarian Assistance" (2009) (www.globalhumanitarianassistance.org).

36. DFID, "Why We Need to Work More Effectively in Fragile States," White Paper (United Kingdom, 2005).

37. Brookings, "When Displacement Ends: A Framework for Durable Solutions," Brookings-Bern Project on Internal Displacement (June 2007) (www.unhcr.org/refworld/docid/469f6bed2.html).

38. World Bank, "Improving Effectiveness and Outcomes for the Poor in Health," p. xvii.

39. World Bank, "Using Microcredit to Advance Women," PREM Notes 8 (Washington, 1998).

40. World Bank, "Financial Crisis" (www.worldbank.org/financialcrisis/ [August 2009]).

41. Denis Blair, Director of National Intelligence, "Annual Threat Assessment of the Intelligence Community for the Senate Select Committee on Intelligence," February 12, 2009.

42. Anke Hoeffler, "State Failure and Conflict Recurrence," in J. Joseph Hewitt, Jonathan Wilkenfield and Ted Robert Gurr, eds., *Peace and Conflict 2010,* Center for International Development and Conflict Management, University of Maryland, forthcoming February 2010.

43. Lisa Chauvet, Paul Collier, and Anke Hoeffler, "The Cost of Failing States and the Limits to Sovereignty," UN-WIDER working paper (2006).

44. G-8, "Global Plan for Recovery and Reform: the Communiqué from the London Summit" (www.londonsummit.gov.uk/en/summit-aims/summit-communique/ [August 2009]).

Contributors

JOSHUA BUSBY
LBJ School of Public Affairs, University of Texas–Austin

MIRIAM ESTRIN
U.S. Department of State

CORINNE GRAFF
Fellow in Foreign Policy and in Global Economy and Development, Brookings Institution

ANDREW LOOMIS
U.S. Department of State

CARL MALM
Georgetown University

CARLOS PASCUAL
Former Vice President and Director of Foreign Policy, Brookings Institution, and current U.S. Ambassador to Mexico

SUSAN E. RICE
Former Senior Fellow in Foreign Policy and in Global Economy and Development, Brookings Institution, and current U.S. Ambassador to the United Nations

Index

Accion, 222
Acholi people of Uganda, 2
Adaptation Trust Fund, 155–56
Aedes mosquito, 13
Afghanistan: al Qaeda in, 54, 92, 95; drug
  trafficking in, 95; National Solidarity Program (NSP), 79, 113, 218–19;
  police force training in, 215; poverty
  in, 25; security, lowest ranking for,
  29; security forces in, 218; Soviet war
  and origin of al Qaeda in, 54; terrorist
  assistance and acts in, 48, 57, 60; U.S.
  military deployment to, 34, 78, 93,
  114; as weak state, 28
Africa: causes of civil war in, 96; critically
  weak states in, 34; decline in number
  of conflicts in, 129; and infectious
  disease spread, 170; instability in, 204;
  peacekeeping operations in, 35, 216,
  217; peer review mechanism (APRM),
  209; poverty in, 25; terrorist recruiting
  in, 47; vulnerability to climate change
  in, 134. *See also specific countries and
  regions*
African Union, 34, 113, 208
African Union Mission to Somalia
  (AMISOM), 76
Agent Orange, 145
Ahmed, Sharif, 71
Aid reform: best practices, list of, 224–25;
  and climate change, 127; coordination
  of assistance, 115, 211–12; decentral-

ized delivery to overcome effects of
  conflict, 113–14; and disease control
  and prevention, 190–93; and NGOs,
  219; performance improvements in
  development and poverty reduction
  as goals for, 204–16; social funds,
  219–20; strategies for donors, 36–38,
  97, 114–15, 206, 210–14, 224; strategies for recipients, 206–10; tailoring
  assistance to individual weak states,
  38–39, 203
AIDS. *See* HIV/AIDS
AIDS Healthcare Foundation, 185
Air travel and spread of disease, 169–70
Albright, Madeleine, 1
Algeria: conflict in, 35; as weak state, 35
Allied Democratic Forces (ADF, Uganda), 3
Al Qaeda: Afghan link of, 54, 92, 95; cells
  in U.S. and Europe, 62; civil conflict
  as opportunity for, 53; exploitation of
  poverty by, 47; Mali link to, 9; Pakistan
  link to, 62; pervasiveness internationally, 8; presence in poor weak states, 6;
  profile of members of, 52; recruiting by,
  53, 54; Saudi link to, 43, 67–68; Sierra
  Leone link to, 202–3; Somalia link to,
  8, 72, 73, 75, 95; unemployment, link
  to, 68–69; U.S. embassy attacks in
  Africa by, 3, 8, 72–73, 105; U.S. strikes
  against leaders of, 78; Yemen link to,
  42–43. *See also* Terrorism and violent
  extremism

Al Shabaab movement (Somalia), 8
American Political Science Association's
   Task Force on Difference, Inequality,
   and Developing Societies, 96
Amman, Jordan, attack (2005), 57
Angola: as critically weak state, 34; Social
   Action Fund, 219
Animal transmission of disease to humans,
   170
Annals of Internal Medicine 2009 article
   on effectiveness of PEPFAR, 183
Annual Threat Assessment (2009), 25
Antiretroviral drugs, 181, 185
AQIM (Islamic Maghreb), 9
Aristide, Jean-Bertrand, 149, 150
Asia: vulnerability to climate change in,
   134. *See also specific countries and
   regions*
Assistance. *See* Aid reform; Humanitarian
   assistance
Association of Southeast Asian Nations
   (ASEAN), 208–09
Authoritarian or autocratic regimes, 36,
   37, 38, 207
Avian and Human Influenza Facility, 180
Avian influenza. *See* H5N1 avian influenza

Bali car bombing (2002), 46, 57
Bamba, Morifère, 90
Bangladesh: and climate change, 14, 138;
   health care in, 12
Ban Ki-moon, 125
Becker, Gary, 52
Becton, Dickinson and Company, 186
Belgian Congo and origins of HIV, 167–68
Bergen, Peter, 45
Bill and Melinda Gates Foundation, 211
Bin Laden, Osama, 42, 47, 54
Blair, Dennis, 223
Blue Helmet peacekeeping force, 217
Bombers. *See* Terrorism and violent
   extremism
Bosnia: peacekeeping operation in, 217–
   18; terrorist assistance in, 48
Botswana: as capable state, 37; economy
   in, 29
Brazil: bilateral development assistance
   from, 211; as capable state, 37; dengue
   fever in, 13
Breaking the cycle in poor and weak states,
   187–93; best practices, list of, 223,
   224–25

British Department for International
   Development, 28, 70, 79
Buffett, Warren, 211
Burma: climate change's effect on, 13; as
   critically weak state, 34; governance
   in, 36
Burundi: civil conflict in, 92; as critically
   weak state, 34
Busby, Joshua, ix, 125
Bush, George W.: pandemic preparedness,
   180; State of the Union (2008) request
   for troops, 214; war on terrorism, 78
Business development, investment for,
   222–23
Byman, Daniel, 47

Cambodia: civil conflict in, 146; lack of
   sanitation in, 24
Cambodia Social Fund, 219–20
Cameroon: as critically weak state, 34;
   governance in, 35
Capable states, 36, 37
Capacity building, 114–15; and disease
   prevention, 184; and governance, 36–38;
   prioritizing, 203; and rule of law, 215
Cap-and-trade legislation (U.S.), 131, 156
Cash-for-work programs and health
   improvements, 188
Castro, Fidel, 150
CDD (community-driven development),
   219
Center for International Earth Science
   Information Network (CIESIN), 133
Centers for Disease Control and Preven-
   tion (CDC): on dengue fever, 12–13;
   on Ebola, 174; Epidemiological Intelligence Service, 190
Central Africa: civil conflict in, 92, 110;
   poverty in, 109. *See also specific
   countries*
Central Asia: poverty in, 25; weak states
   in, 29. *See also specific countries*
Chad: as likely location and source for terrorism, 54; peacekeeping mission in, 93
Child mortality, 10, 24, 72, 171, 226
Chile as capable state, 37
China: authoritarian regime model in, 207;
   bilateral development assistance from,
   211; infectious disease spread in, 170;
   poverty in, 25; protectionist approach
   to Doha Round, 210; vulnerability to
   climate change in, 134

Cholera, 173

Circumventing weak states: best practices, list of, 225; HIV/AIDS and international response, 184–87; reasons for, 220–22

Civil conflict, 17, 90–116; capacity-building strategies to reduce likelihood of, 114–15; decentralized aid to overcome effects of, 113–14; and disease, 92, 170–71; economic causes of, 6–8, 99; education as preventive strategy for, 111; environmental effects of, 145–47; GDP's effect on, 6–7, 96–97; geographical clustering of, 94, 129, 130; and governance, 96; integration of former combatants into society after, 115–16; peace enforcement and peacekeeping, 112–13; peer reviews as preventive strategy for, 111; persistence of, 73–77, 92, 100; policy recommendations, 37, 110–16; and poverty, 91, 95–98; prevalence of, 91; prevention of, 111–12; recruitment in, 99–100; recurrence of, 100–01; spark initiating, 98–101; spillover effect of, viii, 1, 2–3, 7–8; terrorism's opportunity during, 54; transparency and accountability, effect on, 112; and U.S. national security, 92, 93–95; in weak states, 29, 36. *See also* Peace enforcement and peacekeeping; Refugees; *specific countries and regions*

Civil Liberties Index, 51

Climate change, viii, 17, 125–66; adaptive needs, 155–57; assistance for poor states to manage, 221; death rates and number of people affected by natural disasters, 142–43, 149; and Democratic Republic of the Congo, 151–54; and disease spread, 171; evidence of connection with conflict, 132–35; and Haiti, 147–51; need for immediate action, 223; policy implications of, 154–57; and poverty, 13–15; and refugees, 139–40; as security issue, 127–47, 155; as "threat multiplier," 135–41; in Uganda, 3–4; U.S. public and partisan debate over, 129–32, 156; vulnerability to disasters, 133–35, 140, 144–45, 155; and weak states, 141–45

Clinton, Bill, 42, 151

Cocaine production and trafficking, 95

Coffee, 3–4

Cold war, 4, 204; effect of end of, 95–96

Cole. See U.S.S. *Cole*

Collier, Paul, 24, 92, 98

Colombia: cocaine production and trafficking in, 95; integration of former or potential combatants into society, 116; security and stability in, 35; as weak state, 35

Columbia University's Center for International Earth Science Information Network (CIESIN), 133

Combating Terrorism Center (West Point), 9

Communicable diseases. *See* Infectious diseases

Community-driven development (CDD), 218

Community programs, importance of, 79–80, 218–19

Comoros, poor economic performance of, 35

Conditional cash transfer programs and health improvements, 188

Conflict: countries in, 36; international threat, vii, 101; policy approaches for, 37; types of (1946–2006), 128, 129. *See also* Civil conflict; National security

"Conflict trap," 7, 92

Congo, Democratic Republic of the. *See* Democratic Republic of the Congo

Congo, Republic of. *See* Republic of the Congo

Convention against Torture, U.S. violations of, 213

Corruption, 91, 114

Corruption Perceptions Index (Transparency International), 176

Côte d'Ivoire: conflict in, 91; economic status of, 90–91; military deployment to, 35; peacekeeping mission in, 93

Council on Foreign Relations report (2002), 67

Country Reports on Terrorism 2006 (State Department), 72

Critically weak states, 29, 34–35; map of, 32–33

Cross-country statistical analysis on terrorism, 51–52

Cyclone Nargis. *See* Nargis cyclone (2008)

Darfur: cause of conflict in, 125–26, 137, 203; droughts in, 125, 138; peacekeeping mission in, 93, 216, 217

Decentralization as goal, 218–20, 225

Deforestation, 108–09, 151–54, 203, 221

Democracy: fragile democracies, 36; policy approaches for, 37; promotion of, 207, 212–15

Democratic Republic of the Congo (DRC): civil conflict in, 36, 101, 106–10, 208; as critically weak state, 34, 204; deaths and continuing conflict in, 202; as disease source, 11–12, 109; environmental degradation in, 108, 151–54; forest preservation in, 221; military deployment to, 35; peacekeeping mission in, 93, 151, 208, 217; poverty in, 106, 107, 109; refugees from, 94; resource richness of, 106, 107–08; spillover of Ugandan conflict in, 1, 3; terrorism likely to result from, 54; as weak state, 28

Dengue fever, 12–13

Destabilization of areas. See Spillover effects

Developing countries: diseases in, 24, 170–74, 179; financial crisis, effect on, 204; as source of terrorist threat to U.S., 61–62; unemployment in, 24; violent extremism in, 44, 56–63. See also specific countries

Development in Fragile States: The Toughest Cases (Brookings workshop, 2009), ix

De Waal, Alex, 135, 136

Diamond trade. See Gem and gold trade

Diarrheal disease, 171

Disaster preparedness, 142; and pandemic, 180–81

Diseases. See Infectious diseases

Djibouti, economic performance of, 35

Doha Round, 210

Dominican Republic, comparison to Haiti, 147–48

Donors. See Aid reform

DRC. See Democratic Republic of the Congo

Droughts, 14–15, 125–26

Drug production and trafficking, 8, 92, 95

Dysentery, 4

Earthquakes, 141

East Africa as terrorist source, 62, 73. See also specific countries

East Asia and pandemic effects, 179

Eastern European states: internal reform to become EU member, 208; microfinance in, 222

East Timor: ASEAN peace-building efforts in, 208; economic performance of, 35; security and stability in, 7

Ebola virus, 4, 11–12, 109, 174, 190

Economic Community of West African States (ECOWAS), 105

Economic performance: al Qaeda and terrorist attacks aimed to weaken, 62; in countries with civil war, 96, 99, 102; cross-country statistical analyses, 51; and disease spread, 179; globalization as stimulant for, 209–10; investment to improve, 222–23; in sub-Saharan Africa, 25; of weak countries, 35. See also specific countries

Education: of local populations about health and sanitation, 189; as preventive strategy for civil conflict, 111; as preventive strategy for infectious diseases, 186; in Yemen, 67

Egypt: poverty's relationship to terrorism in, 50, 53; U.S. assistance to, 79, 204

Embassies, U.S., attacks on, 3, 8, 43, 72–73, 105

Environment: harm from conflicts, 145–47. See also Climate change

Environmental Performance Index (2008), 146, 147

Environmental Protection Agency, U.S., 156

Equatorial Guinea: as critically weak state, 34; distribution of wealth in, 29

Eritrea as critically weak state, 34

Estrin, Miriam, ix, 167

Ethiopia: as critically weak state, 34; intervention in Somalia, 8, 92; vulnerability to climate change in, 133

European Union: gendarme force and civilian crisis management capacity, 215; as incentive structure for improved governance, 208; military deployment to failed or critically weak states, 35; Muslim radical threat in, 46; as terrorist source, 62

Extractive Industries Transparency Initiative (EITI), 112

Extradition of terrorists, 45

Failed states, 35, 217, 226. See also Critically weak states

Failed States Index (Fund for Peace), 54

Fatah al Islam, 46

Federal Reserve, 62

Financial aid. *See* Aid reform
Financial crisis, effect of, 24, 25, 203, 204, 223, 226
Floods, 14. *See also* Sea level, rise of
Food and Agriculture Organization, 13, 108
Food prices and shortages, 24, 63, 76, 204, 223
Foreign aid. *See* Aid reform
Foreign Assistance Revitalization and Accountability Act of 2009, 214
Forest fires, 142
Forests. *See* Deforestation
Former Soviet states, poverty in, 25
Fragile democracies, 36
France, military deployment to failed or critically weak states, 35
Freedom House, 51, 207
Fundamentalism. *See* Islamic extremists
Fund for Peace, 28; Failed States Index, 54

The Gambia as weak state, 35
GDP of poor countries, 6–7; aid's impact on, 205; global trade in goods and services as way to improve, 209–10; relationship to civil conflict, 96–97; 2009 levels, 223
Gem and gold trade, 3, 104, 105, 108, 112
Genocides, 92, 106
Georgia, civil service program in, 114
Gettleman, Jeffrey, 71
Ginting, Puji, 175
Global Emerging Infections Surveillance and Response System (GEIS), 173
Global Environment Facility (World Bank): funds administered by, 155–56; U.S. as contributor, 131, 156
Global Facility for Disaster Reduction and Recovery (GFDRR), 156
Global Fund to Fight AIDS, Tuberculosis, and Malaria, 182, 221
Globalization, effect of, 5; and disease spread, 178–79
Global Outbreak Alert and Response Network (GOARN), 173
Global Peace Index (2008), 146
Global warming. *See* Climate change
Governance: and civil war, 96, 101; incentives to improve, 208; peer review networks, recommendation to establish, 209; strategies for aid recipients, 206–10; in weak states, 16, 35
Graff, Corinne, viii, 42, 202

Grameen Bank, 222
"Greed" model and motivation for rebellion, 98
"Green blackmail," 153
Gross domestic product. *See* GDP of poor countries
Group for Preaching and Combat (GSPC, Algeria), 9
Group of Twenty (G-20), 204, 226
Guantanamo Bay: detainees' motivations for joining radical groups, 48; Haitian and Cuban refugees housed at, 151
Guinea-Bissau as critically weak state, 34

Haiti: as critically weak state, 34; and environmental challenges, 13–14, 134, 143, 147–51, 203; peacekeeping mission in, 93, 149, 217; refugees from, to U.S., 150–51; U.S. military deployment to, 34, 143; as weak state, 28
Hamas, 213
Hamdan, Salim, 68–69
Health initiatives: antipoverty actions that improve, 187–89; and cash-for-work programs, 188; and conditional cash transfer programs, 188; education of local populations about, 189; health care workers, dealing with shortage of, 185–86, 189–90; NGOs, role in, 183, 186, 187, 190, 191–92; scaling up to build sustainable health systems, 186–87, 191–92; targeted expenditures on specific diseases, effect on national health systems, 221; training of health workers, 186; in Yemen, 66–67. *See also* Infectious diseases
Hepatitis C, 10
Hezbollah, 105, 203
H5N1 avian influenza, 10, 11, 170, 175–76, 178, 179
Hirsch, John, 104
HIV/AIDS: antiretroviral treatment for, 181, 185; and civil conflict, 92; data on, 183; health workers, dealing with shortage of, 190; interim data on, 182–84; international response to, 172, 181–87; lessons of circumventing weak states, 184–87; origins of, 10, 167–68; and sub-Saharan Africa, 29; U.S. deaths from, 169; U.S. funding for, 190–91. *See also* President's Emergency Plan for AIDS Relief (PEPFAR)

Hoeffler, Anke, 98
Homer-Dixon, Thomas, 135, 136
H1N1 swine flu, 170, 179, 180
Human Development Index (UNDP), 102
Humanitarian assistance: best practices, list of, 225; in countries at risk for conflict, 110; in natural disasters, 141–45; official development assistance (ODA) as, 204, 205, 211; pros and cons of, 220; role of, 38; in Somalia, 71, 76; in Yemen, 67
Human rights, 212
Huntington, Samuel, 96, 116
Hurricane frequency, 149–50
Hurricane Jeanne, 14
Hurricane Katrina, 133, 140, 142
Hurricane Mitch, 143
Hutus vs. Tutsis, 3, 92, 94, 107

Ikombi, Grace, 90
Index of State Weakness, 28, 30–31, 34, 38, 133, 134, 144, 147, 151
Index of State Weakness in the Developing World (Rice & Patrick), viii, 28, 207
India: bilateral development assistance from, 211; poverty in, 25; protectionist approach to Doha Round, 210; terrorist attacks in, 57; vulnerability to climate change in, 134, 138
Indigenous support for disease prevention and treatment, 185
Indonesia: and ASEAN, 208; and disease outbreaks, 175–76; refusal to share virus samples, 175–76, 177, 178; as terrorist source, 62; vulnerability to climate change in, 134
Infectious diseases, viii, 10–13, 17, 167–201; Belgian Congo as source of HIV, 167–68; breaking cycle in poor and weak states, 187–93; corruption and risk, 176–81; in DRC, 109; global approach to address, 178–79, 191; global surveillance, 172–74; health care workers, shortage of, 189–90; indigenous support for prevention and treatment, 185; and national security, 168–70; new diseases, 169; NGOs, role in health initiatives, 183, 190, 191–92; originating in developing world, 10, 24, 170–74; prevention of, 171–72, 185; targeted expenditures, effect on national health systems, 221;

threat assessments, usefulness of, 184; in Uganda, 4; U.S. and international policy, 168, 180–81; vertical disease programs and horizontal capacity building, 184, 190–91; virus sharing, 175–76, 177–78. *See also* Health initiatives; *specific diseases*
Influenza, 10, 178–79. *See also* H5N1 avian influenza; H1N1 swine flu; Pandemic influenza
Inkatha Freedom Party (South Africa), 185
Institute of Medicine, 182
Insurgencies, 218. *See also* Civil conflict
Integration of former or potential combatants into society after civil wars, 115–16
Intergovernmental Panel on Climate Change (IPCC), 13; Fourth Assessment (2007), 149
International Conference on Financing for Development (Monterrey 2002), 205, 211, 226
International Crisis Group, 149
International Health Regulations (IHR), 173
International Sanitary Conference of Paris (1851), 173
Iraq: as critically weak state, 34; democracy promotion in, 212; integration of former combatants into society in, 116; police force training in, 215; security forces in, 218; terrorist attacks and fatalities in, 56, 57, 60; as terrorist source, 62; U.S. military deployment to, 34, 93
Islah Charity Society, 67
Islamic charities, 48, 67, 79
Islamic Courts Union (ICU), 72, 74, 75
Islamic extremists: link to poverty, 53–55; in Muslim world, 44, 45–46, 47, 60; in Somalia, 8; in Uganda, 3
Islamic Maghreb (AQIM), 9

Jemaah Islamiyah, 46
Jones, Bruce, 111
Judicial system, construction of, 216

Kabila, Laurent, 106
Kashmir conflict, 46
Kenya, elections and violence in, 28
Kidnapping, 9, 57
Kimberley Process, 112

Kosovo: Mercy Corps' role in, 114; security forces in, 218
Krueger, Alan, 45, 51
Kyrgyzstan: governance in, 29; Mercy Corps' role in, 114; poverty in, 25

Laos, governance in, 35
Lashkar-e-Taiba, 46
Lassa hemorrhagic fever, 12
Latin America and the Caribbean: cocaine production and trafficking in, 95; conditional cash transfer programs and health improvements in, 188; dengue fever in, 12–13; microfinance in, 222; poverty in, 25. See also specific countries
Least Developed Country Fund (LDCF), 155
Lebanon: poverty's relationship to terrorism in, 50; terrorist recruiting in, 46; UN force in, 216
Lesotho, economic performance of, 35
Levy, Marc, 137
Liberation Army/Movement (Sudan), 2
Liberia: as critically weak state, 34; peacekeeping mission in, 93; U.S. military deployment to, 35
Life expectancy, 10
Lindh, John Walker, 68
Lome Agreement (1999), 105
London underground attack (2005), 57
Loomis, Andrew, ix, 90
Lord's Resistance Army (LRA, Uganda), 1–3
Low-income countries. See Developing countries

Madrassas, 53–54
Madrid bombing (2004), 57
Maersk Alabama, 73
Malaria, 4, 171, 221
Malawi: health workers, dealing with shortage of, 189; security and stability in, 35; as weak state, 35
Mali: governance in, 36; security and stability in, 35; terrorist presence in, 9, 53
Malm, Carl, ix, 167
The Management of Savagery: The Most Critical Stage through Which the Umma Will Pass (Naji), 9
Map of weak states, 32–33
Marburg virus, 12, 109

Maritime insurance, 63
Marshall-Fratani, Ruth, 90
Mauritius: as capable state, 37; economy in, 29
Mbeki, Thabo, 181, 185
MCC. See Millennium Challenge Corporation
MDGs. See Millennium Development Goals
Media partnering to educate local populations about health and disease, 186–87, 188–89
Menkhaus, Ken, 72, 76
Mercy Corps, 114
Mexico, drug trafficking and violence in, 95
Microfinance, 222
Middle East: peacekeeping operations in, 217. See also specific countries
Military mobilization for disaster relief, 140, 142–44
Millennium Challenge Corporation (MCC), 110, 209, 211, 212
Millennium Development Goals (MDGs), 24, 101, 204, 205, 206, 211, 226
Mineral wealth of DRC, 106, 107–08. See also Gem and gold trade
Mobutu Sese Seko, 106, 107, 108, 151
Monterrey Consensus, 205, 211, 226
Moroccan Islamic Combatant Group (GICM), 46
Morocco: terrorist recruiting in, 46; vulnerability to climate change in, 134
Moynihan, Daniel Patrick, 96
Mozambique: civil conflict in, 146; security and stability in, 7, 35, 38, 207–08; vulnerability to climate change in, 133
Multilateral aid agencies, 212
Multilateral Development Banks (MDBs), 226
Mumbai attacks (2008), 46, 57
Museveni, Yoweri, 2
Muslim Aga Khan Development Network, 16
Muslim Brotherhood, 53
Muslim extremists. See Islamic extremists
Myanmar, disaster relief to, 143

Naji, Abu Bakr, 9–10
Nargis cyclone (2008), 13, 143
National Commission for War-Affected Children (Sierra Leone), 111

National Counterterrorism Center, 56, 70–71

National Oceanic and Atmospheric Administration (NOAA), 14

National security: changed paradigm of, 4–5; civil conflict in other countries, effect on U.S., 92, 93–95; and climate change, 127–47, 155; and infectious diseases, 168–70; poverty as threat to, vii, 5–15, 39; prioritizing of, 216–18; transnational threats to, vii, 5, 101

National Solidarity Program (Afghanistan), 79, 113, 218–19

NATO. See North Atlantic Treaty Organization

Natural disasters. See Climate change; specific type of disaster

Nepal: as critically weak state, 34; security, lowest ranking for, 29

New Partnership for Africa's Development (NEPAD), 111, 209

NGOs. See Nongovernmental organizations

Nigeria: as critically weak state, 34; vulnerability to climate change in, 133; weaknesses in, 34

"Night commuters," 1

9/11 Commission, 44, 53

Nipah virus, 12

Nongovernmental organizations (NGOs): aid to weak states from, 16, 38, 115, 225; and community-driven development, 218–19; on Ebola, 174; health and education initiatives in Yemen, 67; health assistance from, 183, 186, 187, 190, 191–92; in Somalia, 75

North Atlantic Treaty Organization (NATO), 93, 216

Northern Ireland, poverty's relationship to terrorism in, 50

North Korea: as critically weak state, 34; governance in, 35, 36; termination of assistance to, 213

Nuclear reactor in Congo, 108

OAS (Organization for American States), 208

Obama, Barack: Afghanistan and Pakistan policy of, 78; pandemic preparedness, 180; USAID administrator, appointment of, 214

OECD countries: agreement on Principles for Good International Engagement in

Fragile States and Situations (2007), 206; commitment to fund development aid, 211; terrorist attacks in, 58, 59

Official development assistance (ODA). See Humanitarian assistance

Oil, 3, 63–64

Open Society Institute, 114

Operation Restore Hope (1992), 143

Opium production and trade in Afghanistan, 95

Organization for American States (OAS), 208

Organization for Economic Cooperation and Development. See OECD countries

Othrop, Ali Mohammed, 68

Pakistan: conflict in, 35; Federally Administered Tribal Areas, 53, 62; security, lowest ranking for, 29; security and stability in, 35; terrorist presence in, 46, 48, 53–54, 61, 62; U.S. assistance to, 78–79, 143; violence in, 57, 93; as weak state, 35

Palestine, poverty's relationship to terrorism in, 50, 53

Pandemic influenza, 11, 109, 169, 170, 177, 178–79, 180–81

Pandemic Influenza Act (2006), 180

Paris Declaration on Aid Effectiveness (2005), 205, 212

Pascual, Carlos, viii–ix, 111, 202

Patrick, Stewart, 28

Peace enforcement and peacekeeping: ASEAN participation in, 208–09; in conflict and postconflict countries, 93; in DRC, 151; in failed or weak states, 35, 217; "hybrid" operations, 217; important role of, 76, 217; multilateral and regional capacity for, 112–13; prioritizing, in terms of security investments, 216–18; in Sierra Leone, 105

Peer review networks, recommendation to establish, 209, 221, 224

People's Defense Forces (Uganda), 1

PEPFAR. See President's Emergency Plan for AIDS Relief

Pew Center poll on global warming, 130

Pharmaceuticals, 171–72, 177; antiretroviral drugs, 181, 185. See also Vaccination

Philippines: as terrorist source, 53, 62; U.S. assistance to, 204; vulnerability to climate change in, 134

Phones-for-Health, 186
Pilot projects to coordinate assistance, 115
Piracy, 8, 73, 75–76
Plague, 109
Pneumonia, 10, 171
Poland: as capable state, 37; internal reform to become EU member, 208
Police force, construction of, 215–16
Policy approaches to build capacity of weak states, 36–39. *See also* Aid reform; Capacity building
Polio, 12, 109
Political performance. *See* Governance
Political Rights Index (Freedom House), 51
Polity IV Project's Polity Index, 51
Population growth, 10, 13, 63, 142, 170
Poultry sector, 176
Poverty, 16, 23–41; and civil war, 91, 95–98; conflict as consequence of, 6–8; and critically weak states, 34–35; criticism of theory that poverty is linked with terrorist threat, 15–16; and disease, 10–13, 171; donor country leadership needed for poor countries, 210; prevalence of, 23–27; and recruitment of rebels, 99–100; threat of, vii, 5–15, 39; and violent extremism, 8–10, 43–44, 45–55; and weak states, 16, 28–34, 203. *See also specific countries*
Powell, Colin, 182
Power and Responsibility: Building International Order in an Era of Transnational Threats (Jones, Pascual, & Stedman), 111
President's Emergency Plan for AIDS Relief (PEPFAR), 182, 184–86, 192, 214, 221
President's Malaria Initiative, 214
Prevention of civil wars, 111–12
ProCredit Banks, 222
Public-private partnerships to deal with infectious diseases, 192

Rainfall, 138–39
Rain forests. *See* Deforestation
RAND study of UN peace operations, 217
Recruitment in civil wars, 99–100
Recurrence of civil wars, 100–01
Reduced emissions from deforestation and forest degradation (REDD), 151, 153, 154
Refugees: camps as terrorist breeding grounds, 53, 94; from countries in conflict, 94; from Haiti, 150–51; from Somalia, 71; as trigger for conflict, 139–40
Regional organizations advancing democracy and stability, 208–09
Religious groups' aid to weak states, 16. *See also* Islamic charities
Republic of the Congo, 34
Research: on climate change as cause of conflict, 137–41; country studies on terrorism, 48–50; cross-country statistical analysis on terrorism, 51–52; on infectious disease programs' effectiveness, 183–84; limited qualitative case studies on causes of conflict, 136–37
Resources for the Future, 152
Revolutionary United Front (RUF, Sierra Leone), 102–04, 105
Rice, Susan E., viii–ix, 1, 23, 28
Rift Valley fever, 12, 190
Romania, as capable state, 37
Rule of law, support for, 115, 215–16; best practices, list of, 224–25
Rumsfeld, Donald, 43
Rural areas and spread of disease, 170, 171
Rwanda: civil conflict in, 92, 94, 106, 146; as critically weak state, 34; environmental harm from conflict in, 145; governance in, 36; invasion of DRC by, 3, 106; peacekeeping failure in, 216

Sachs, Jeffrey, 137–38
Sada al-Jihad on Africa's vulnerability to Islamic extremists, 10
Sageman, Marc, 52
Saleh, Ali Abdullah, 64, 69
Sankoh, Foday, 103
Santiago Commitment (OAS), 208
SARS, 10, 169, 170
Saudi Arabia: aid to Yemen and other low-income Muslim countries, 67; al Qaeda link, 43, 67–68; and terrorism, 62
Sea level, rise of, 14–15, 139
Security. *See* National security
September 11, 2001, terrorist attacks, 62. *See also* 9/11 Commission
Al Shabaab (Somalia), 72, 74, 75
Sierra Leone: al Qaeda link to, 202–03; child mortality in, 24; civil conflict in, 101, 102–06; as critically weak state, 34; economic collapse of, 102; governance in, 36; National Commission for

War-Affected Children, 111; poverty in, 25; Truth and Reconciliation Commission, 112; UK military deployment to, 35, 105; UNAMSIL in, 105
Singapore's authoritarian regime, 207
Smallpox, 172
Smuggling, 8, 9, 64
Social funds, 219–20, 225
Social welfare as factor in weak states, 35, 38
Solomon Islands, economic performance of, 35
Somalia, 70–77; absence of rule of law in, 71, 73; al Qaeda link to, 8, 72, 73, 75, 95; anti-American sentiment in, 73, 75; conflict, persistence in, 36, 73–77, 92; as critically weak state, 34, 71; humanitarian assistance to, 220; lack of public services and jobs, 73–77; as likely location and source for terrorism, 8, 54, 62, 72, 73; peacekeeping failure in, 216; and piracy, 73, 75–76; poverty in, 71; terrorist attacks in, 57, 70–71; U.S. assistance to, 63, 75–76, 204; U.S. military deployment to, 35, 73, 75, 142; vulnerability to violent extremism in, 73, 74; as weak state, 28
Sons of Iraq Program, 116
South Africa and HIV/AIDS programs, 181–82, 185
South Asia: and infectious disease spread, 170; microfinance in, 222; vulnerability to climate change in, 133; weak states in, 29. See also specific countries
Soviet Union, 4
Special Climate Change Fund (SCCF), 155
Spillover effects, viii, 1, 2–3, 5, 7–8
Sri Lanka: conflict in, 35; security, lowest ranking for, 29
Stanford University, 182
State Department's Country Reports on Terrorism 2006, 72
State Failure Task Force (now Political Instability Task Force), 136
Stedman, Steve, 111
Sub-Saharan Africa: critically weak states in, 34; economic growth in, 25; governance, effect of improvements in, 206; poverty in, 23, 25; U.S. aid to, 110; vulnerability to climate change in, 133; weak states in, 29. See also specific countries

Sudan: and Darfur conflict, 125; humanitarian assistance to, 220; as likely location and source for terrorism, 54; peacekeeping mission in, 93; and Ugandan conflict, 2–3; U.S. development efforts in, 204; vulnerability to climate change in, 134
Suicide attacks, 42, 47, 72
Supari, Siti Fadilah, 177
Surveillance of infectious diseases, 172–74
Swaziland as weak state, 35
Swine flu. See H1N1 swine flu

Tajikistan: governance in, 29; Mercy Corps' role in, 114; poverty in, 25
Taliban, 48, 53, 93, 138
Tanzania: governance in, 36; health workers, dealing with shortage of, 189; poverty in, 25; security and stability in, 35; as weak state, 28, 35
Task shifting to fill health worker deficits, 189
Taylor, Charles, 104
Terrorism and violent extremism, viii, 17, 42–89; civil conflict as opportunity for, 54; country case studies on, 50–51; criticism of theory that poverty is linked with, 15–16; cross-country statistical analysis of, 51–52; definition of terrorism, 52; in developing world, 44, 56–63; extradition of terrorists, 45; global fatalities from, 57; peacekeeping missions in countries offering havens to, 216; and poverty, 43–44, 45–55; successful bombers and attacks, 57; types of studies of, 48–50; unsuccessful bombers and attacks, 52, 57; U.S. counterterrorism strategy, 44–45, 77–80; in weak poor states, 6–7, 8–10, 43. See also Al Qaeda; specific countries and attacks
Thailand: bilateral development assistance from, 211; military coup (2006), 208
Threat assessments, usefulness of, 184
Tilly, Charles, 48, 52
Timor Leste, governance in, 36
Tobias, Randall L., 182
Transitional Federal Government (Somalia), 71, 76
Transition to stability and capability: countries in, 36; as goal for weak states, 36–37; policy approaches for, 37–38

Transparency and accountability, effect on civil wars, 112
Transparency International's Corruption Perceptions Index, 176
Truth and Reconciliation Commission (Sierra Leone), 112
Tsunami (Asia 2004), 143
Tuareg rebellion in Mali, 9
Tuberculosis. *See* Global Fund to Fight AIDS, Tuberculosis, and Malaria
Turkey: bilateral development assistance from, 211; conditional cash transfer programs and health improvements in, 188
Turkmenistan: governance in, 35; as weak state, 35
Tutsis vs. Hutus, 3, 92, 94, 107

Uganda: aid to and economic status of, 2; climate change effects in, 3–4; conflict's effects in, 1–2, 96; disease and health risks in, 4; spillover of conflict from, 1, 2–3; terrorism in, 3
Unemployment levels: and financial crisis, 24; in Somalia, 75; in Yemen, 68–69
United Kingdom: Department for International Development, 28, 70, 79; foreign aid to Yemen, 65; military deployment to Sierra Leone, 35, 105; Muslim radical threat in, 46; on WMDs and terrorism, 60
United Nations: African Union Mission to Somalia (AMISOM), 76; Food and Agriculture Organization, 13, 108; Global Compact, 112; health assistance from, 183; International Strategy for Disaster Reduction (ISDR), 156; intervention in critically weak or failed states, 34; Joint Program on HIV/AIDS (UNAIDS), 182; Mission in Sierra Leone (UNAMSIL), 105; Peace Building Commission, 113; Responsibilities of Transnational Corporations and Other Business Enterprises with Regard to Human Rights, 112; Security Council report on Saudi funding of Islamic extremists (2002), 68. *See also* Peace enforcement and peacekeeping
United Nations Children's Fund (UNICEF), 24
United Nations Development Program (UNDP): as coordinating agency, 212; Georgian civil service program, 114; Human Development Index, 51, 102; Human Development Report (2007/2008), 155; on natural disasters in Haiti and Dominican Republic, 148; peer review networks, recommendation to establish, 209
United States: climate change, public and partisan debate over, 129–32, 156; democracy promotion by, 213–14; disaster response, military used in, 140, 142–43; extremist groups within, 62; foreign assistance to fight poverty from, 211. *See other countries for U.S. foreign relations*
Universal Declaration of Human Rights, 213
Uranium in Congo, 108
Urbanization, 170
Uribe, Alvaro, 116
U.S. Agency for International Development (USAID): and aid to fragile states, 79; definition of weak state, 28; distribution of aid from, 113; international environmental adaptation, fund administration for, 156; lack of leadership and limited manpower for, 214
U.S. embassy attacks by al Qaeda: in Africa, 3, 8, 57, 72–73, 105; in Yemen, 43
U.S.S. *Cole*, 42, 63, 203
Uzbekistan: governance in, 29, 35; Mercy Corps' role in, 114; poverty in, 25

Vaccination, 172, 177–78, 221
Victor, David, 135
Vietnam and environmental harm from conflict, 145
Vietnam's authoritarian regime, 207
Violent extremism. *See* Terrorism and violent extremism
Virus sharing and global health, 175–76, 177–78
Vulnerability and environmental factors, 133–35, 140, 144–45, 155
Vulnerability Fund (World Bank), 111–12

Wahhabists, 9
War. *See* Civil conflict
War on terrorism, 56, 78
Water scarcity, 137–38. *See also* Droughts
Weak states: aid sources for, 16; characterization and types of, 36, 203; and

climate change, 141–45; critically weak states, 29, 34–35; defined, 28; lack of governance, 16, 35; map of, 32–33; peacekeeping operations in, 35, 216–18; policy approaches to build capacity of, 36–38; terrorist activity linked to, 54–55, 77–78; threat posed by, vii, 36–38, 43, 78; transition to stability and capability as goal for, 36–37; U.S. interest in, 36–38; and WMDs, 60–61. *See also* Poverty

Weapons of mass destruction (WMDs), 60

West Africa, critically weak states in, 34. *See also specific states*

West Nile virus, 10, 12

Woods Hole Research Center, 152

World Bank: and aid to fragile states, 79, 80; on cash-for-work programs, 188; on child mortality, 24; in conflict zones, 38; as coordinating agency, 212; definition of weak states, 28; on deforestation prevention, 151–52; on DRC's eligibility for REDD projects, 153; Global Environment Facility, 131, 155–56; Global Facility for Disaster Reduction and Recovery (GFDRR), 156; Social Fund for Development, 69–70; on sustainable health institutions, 188; on 2009 economic growth, 223; on Uganda's economic status, 2; U.S. failure to contribute to trust for disaster reduction, 131; Vulnerability Fund, 111–12; Worldwide Governance Indicators Project, 207

World Health Organization (WHO): on child mortality, 10; on Ebola virus, 11, 174; on expenditures needed for basic health services, 171; Global Outbreak Alert and Response Network (GOARN), 173; International Health Regulations (IHR), 173; on Uganda and disease increase, 4; on vaccination development, 177

World Trade Organization (WTO) Doha Round, 210

World Vision, 16

Yemen, 63–70; absence of local government capacity in, 64, 65–68; civil conflict in, 69–70; education in, 67; food shortage in, 63, 76; lack of employment opportunities in, 68–69; national security of, 64; poverty in, 43, 45, 50, 63; as terrorist source, 42–43, 53, 57, 62; U.S. assistance to, 44–45, 63, 64–65, 69–70, 76–77; U.S.S. *Cole,* attack on, 42, 63, 203; vulnerability to violent extremism in, 65, 66; water shortage in, 64; as weak state, 38

Zaire: civil conflict in, 92, 106; environmental degradation in, 151. *See now* Democratic Republic of the Congo (DRC)

Zambia: health workers shortage, 189; security and stability in, 35

Zimbabwe: governance in, 35, 36, 208; as likely location and source for terrorism, 54; termination of assistance to, 213; U.S. development efforts in, 204

Zinni, Anthony, 64

Zoellick, Robert, 111, 202, 218